ADVANCE PRAISE

"Imagine climbing through an extensive trauma web, unsure of where to turn or how to get to firm ground. Through this transformative workbook, Sarah Peyton provides a clear map to help navigate this labyrinth with exercises allowing the reader to rest, pause, and go deeper if desired."

—**Benjamin Burton, DPT**, Physical Therapy and Rehabilitation; Environmentalist; Entrepreneur; Educator in Interpersonal Neurobiology (IPNB) and Non-violent Communication

"The title of the first chapter of this wonderful book asks, 'Are you willing to like yourself?' If we are willing to make use of it, we can transform self-loathing into deep compassion. Sarah Peyton has gifted her resources to us in language that is clear, loving, accessible, warm, and resonant. Let's respond to her generosity by making full use of this book—until it's indelibly written in our souls."

—**Clare Crombie, UKCP**, Gestalt Psychotherapist and Supervisor

"Sarah Peyton's brilliance is in her ability to convey that healing is about being with the pain, getting curious about the pain, and sitting next to the pain; empathizing with and listening to the pain with wholeheartedness. We can become our own guide towards self-connection as we embark on a journey to experience accompaniment, often for the very first time. Sarah takes us there in the most expeditious, while simultaneously gentle, path: through love, warmth, and resonance."

—**Rajkumari Neogy**, Executive Coach, epigenetics and neurobiology, Founder of iRestart

"Brilliant, engaging, deeply nourishing, and often liberating, *Your Resonant Self Workbook* is a powerful and comprehensive resource for people wanting to increase the flow of life and love in their lives. The warm, engaged relationship that Sarah Peyton creates with her readers—through illustrations, stories, exercises, self-assessment tools, and gentle teaching—offers ways to see and shift mental and emotional patterns of anxiety, addiction, shame, and depression, and to find the ways that we have made vows that can be identified and released, to open ourselves more fully to the flow of life, love, and well-being. This book is for people interested in living a life with more freedom, connection, and less inner stress."

—**Bruce Nayowith, MD**, retired in Emergency Medicine, Fairview Hospital

Your
Resonant Self
WORKBOOK

Your Resonant Self

WORKBOOK

From Self-sabotage to Self-care

Sarah Peyton

W. W. NORTON & COMPANY
Independent Publishers Since 1923

Note to Readers: Standards of clinical practice and protocol change over time, and no technique or recommendation is guaranteed to be safe or effective in all circumstances. This volume is intended as a general information resource for professionals practicing in the field of psychotherapy and mental health; it is not a substitute for appropriate training, peer review, and/or clinical supervision. Neither the publisher nor the author(s) can guarantee the complete accuracy, efficacy, or appropriateness of any particular recommendation in every respect. As of press time, the URLs displayed in this book link or refer to existing sites. The publisher and author are not responsible for any content that appears on third-party websites.

This book is constructed around a series of recorded dialogues that took place in workshops with real people. All of the people in the dialogues consented to be in the book in service of others' learning and chose their own pseudonyms. Together, we all hope that their work will contribute to your learning and growth.

Illustrations by Travis Kotzebue

For information about permission to reproduce selections from this book, write to
Permissions, W. W. Norton & Company, Inc., 500 Fifth Avenue, New York, NY 10110

For information about special discounts for bulk purchases, please contact
W. W. Norton Special Sales at specialsales@wwnorton.com or 800-233-4830

Manufacturing by Sheridan Books
Book design by Carole Desnoes
Production manager: Katelyn MacKenzie

ISBN: 978-0-393-71464-7 (pbk.)

W. W. Norton & Company, Inc., 500 Fifth Avenue, New York, N.Y. 10110
www.wwnorton.com

W. W. Norton & Company Ltd., 15 Carlisle Street, London W1D 3BS

1 2 3 4 5 6 7 8 9 0

I dedicate this book to Matt Wood,
for decades of love, support, and delight.

CONTENTS

ACKNOWLEDGMENTS

The writing of this book could not have taken place without the commitment of the group of people who shared their personal processes and stories to create the explorations that you will read here, allowing me to create the transcripts that teach this approach to working with unconscious contracts. Thank you to each of you.

Additionally, and astoundingly, I was supported by warm community from beginning to end. I have been stunned by the care, responsiveness, help, and enthusiasm that has flowed for this book, from Rachel Lewett advocating for its creation, to Deborah Malmud's positive reception at Norton, to my family's trust and faith, to the inspiration of Tamyra Freeman, to the illustrations by Travis Kotzebue, to Michael Smyth who kept my home going, and to all the editors, readers, and proofreaders who contributed throughout the effort: Cristina Olsen, Natalie Soriano, Jean McElhaney, Benjamin Burton, Terry Cookson, Robert Sinkus, Mercedes Tune, Kristin Masters, John Porter, Sharran Zeleke, Nathaniel Kirby, Peggy Smith, Samantha White, Lalli Dana, Sandy Lin, Joe Rappaport, and Kristina Gaddy.

When I was young, I never imagined that I would live in a warm world. This journey toward resonance and making our brains good places to live has taken me into such good company. Thank you to Matt Wood, Nickolas Wood, Penny Walden, Kathryn Krogstad, Clare Crombie, James Peyton, Jennifer Jones, Elena Peyton Jones, Carol Ferris, Gloria Lybecker, Olga Ngyuen, Bev Parsons, Mika Maniwa, Susan Fusillo, Evie Rolston, Elena Veselago, Stein Hjelmerud, Sarah Hjelmerud, Dan Miller, Katherine Revoir, Jaya Manske, Miki Kashtan, Rajkumari Neogy, Tryg Steen, Lia Stuart, Elizabeth Wood, Jim and Jori Manske, Tamara Laporte, Bonnie Badenoch, Claudia Ellsberg, Jonine Lee Gabay, M'lyss Fruhling, Sam Qanat, Finn Beckett Ludlow, Bruce Nayowith, Eric Bowers, Laura Ricksecker, Turiya Gearhardt, Kamia Anderson-Harris, Carolyn Blum, Frith Maier, Carmen Votaw, Chuck Blevins, JJ Jackson, Vanessa Allen, Jo Pitcairn, Annie Harkey-Power, and Bobby Allen, with such gratitude to all of you for nourishing my heart.

And thank you to those of you in the world cocreating this work who I have not yet mentioned, for everything that you contribute: Pernille Plantener, Joanna

Berendt, Gail Donohue, Mali Parke, Kangs Trevens, Ann Malabre, Angela Watrous, forest chaffee, Shannon Casey, Tony Scruggs, Satori Harrington, Rosemary Renstad, Lucy Ascham, Celeste Kersey, Kellita Maloof, Amanda Blaine, Josh Blaine, Ocean Love Lauzon, Leah Boyd, Pavla Haluskova, Ken Anno, Shigeko Suzuki, and Sylvie Hoerning.

INTRODUCTION
Dissolving Blocks to Resonance: Unconscious Contract Work

The stakes are so high.

Self-warmth makes everything better: our health, our immune system, our life decisions, our sense of meaning, our capacity for engagement, our effectiveness, and our intimate connections with others.[1]

But we may have agreements with ourselves—agreements we don't even know about—to NOT be warm with ourselves. We may have contracts to not like ourselves, to be indifferent, even to hate and be cruel to ourselves (and others). Without knowing it, we make these self-agreements in order to leverage our nervous systems to take care of the people around us. For example, we may make sure we are never sad so that things are easier for our families. The long-term results for our bodies, minds, and nervous systems can be tragic, even though we originally wanted to do the best thing for everyone.

These contracts are often made before we can talk. The only thing a baby has to contribute to balancing a family is that baby's own nervous system.

"When my mother is sad, I will be happy in order to cheer her up."

"When my father is depressed, I will be angry in order to bring him to life."

"When my siblings are fighting, I will get sick in order to change the violence."

"I will hate myself in order to atone for being a burden on my mother."

When people have these contracts, it doesn't matter how much they practice liking themselves or do meditations to increase self-warmth. These contracts are the ground on which everything else is built, and so they create persistent stories about the self: *I am not worthy of love. I am an angry person. I am never sad. I cannot say no. I always get sick. My needs don't matter.* When these contracts and stories are present, they turn to stone inside a person, preventing the emergence of the organic, growing self that is supposed to be the heart of everyone's life journey.

After I finished writing my first book, *Your Resonant Self: Guided Meditations and Exercises to Engage Your Brain's Capacity for Healing,* I began to travel all over the world to teach people resonant language. Resonant language is a way we can talk with ourselves and others that creates connection, supports the emergence of a sweet sense of self, lets what's true be named, and heals emotional trauma. I discovered that, even when the material made sense to people, there were certain times that they were just unable to turn toward themselves with kindness and warm curiosity. Why was this happening?

As we learn about relational neuroscience, we discover that the brain is always trying to take care of us, usually based on lived, historical evidence. We are discovering that addictions, suicidality, incarceration, and diseases connected with a lack of self-care are the result of the brain doing its best to try to take care of us around trauma rather than a result of weakness or bad genes, as previous generations believed. Once I had this understanding of the brain, I wondered how the resistance to self-warmth could also be the brain's best attempt to take care of us.

Although I had an instinct that there was a very good reason for this resistance, I had no idea what it was. So I started looking at myself. What were my own blocks to self-warmth? (And believe me, even though I wrote the book *Your Resonant Self*, I still have plenty of these blocks.) I started to look at one puzzling way that I was sabotaging myself—I found it extremely difficult to take a room's attention when I was with women older than myself. If I had a good reason to collapse, what might it be? How could I discover it? It felt like this pattern of sabotaging myself was an iron-clad contract, and so I thought the right language might help me understand what was happening.

First of all, since it was gender specific, I had a guess that it was about my mother. I gave it a try: "I, Sarah, promise myself that I will not take up space when I am with my mother . . ." I stopped and felt deep into my own body, almost asking my belly about this way of being, and my belly answered me: ". . . in order to make sure that my mother receives enough attention to survive."

"Oh, dear," I thought. "What a loving but absurd vow." I was reminded of being a small child, seeing with such tenderness my mother's awkwardness in the world and wanting so much for her to have a sense of her absolute belonging. Here I was, a helpless child, leveraging the only thing I had, my own nervous system, to create the world I wanted to live in.

I decided to follow along with this process that was creating itself. What was the next logical step in working with the contract? Somehow the way that I had begun the wording, it sounded so legal and contingent, and the ritual unbinding of contracts came into my head. Since every contract has at least two parties, I imagined myself to be two different selves, the very best part of me, which I decided to call my "essential self," and the part of me who might originally have made this contract.

I started a dialogue between them to see if both parties still wanted to keep this ancient agreement:

"Sarah's essential self, did you hear the vow that Sarah made to you?"

"Yes, I did."

"Do you still want this contract?"

"No, this is a silly contract. Sarah, I release you from this contract and I revoke this vow."

To my surprise, I took a full breath and felt my whole body relax. I revisited my idea of not taking up space. Though before I began this piece of work, I had been utterly convinced that I could not take up space, the idea now seemed immaterial. It had nothing to do with me. I started to have an easier time co-facilitating with women who were older than me.

And I started thinking. If I had had such a contract, which had been structuring the way I defined myself, maybe other people also had these contracts, these old agreements made even before they had language, which gave them very good reasons for self-sabotaging behaviors like self-hate, rabid self-criticism, procrastination, an inability to try, lack of trust in self and others, and so on.

The next thing to do was to take this work into the world and find out if other people really did have these agreements with themselves. In this book, you will journey along with me in this discovery process, and as the people I meet do their work on these pages, you will be invited to follow along with them and enjoy the way this work can often help people turn toward themselves with an ease and warmth that are astounding.

Although unconscious contracts may take many shapes and have a wide range of impacts, the basic need underlying them is for our infant life energy and emotions to be welcomed by the people taking care of us. When we have to try to take care of others rather than getting to grow into our own selves, we can carry these limitations with us out of childhood, with lifelong implications for our health and well-being.

We also make these contracts in moments of trauma; they are knots we tie using ourselves as ends of the rope when something difficult happens (shame, overwhelm, horror, terror, rage, abandonment, emptiness) and we are unaccompanied by resonance. Surprisingly, these knots often have love or deep care at their core. In traumatic moments, our whole brain-body system tries to figure out what we can do to keep this difficult thing from ever happening again. We make all kinds of unconscious agreements with ourselves: *I will never open my heart again. I will not risk. I will never trust again. I will never complete anything. I will always give more than I have.*

No matter where we are, and what we've lived through, this book will address our shared human tendency to make unconscious contracts. The contracts can come from inherited family agreements ("I will work without ceasing"), and they can come from the invisible agreements made within societies ("If I am male, I will not show my tears in public").

To understand how this happens, we need to understand two things. First, we are made for relationship, not aloneness. Second, the amygdala glues everything that touches a trauma into one tangle of memory.

First, we'll touch on relationship. Many people in the world, including most descendants of ancestors from the United Kingdom and Northern Europe, are told that it is important to be independent and to be able to take care of themselves. But human neurobiology is created differently. Our nervous systems, our circulatory systems, and our immune systems all work at their best when we are in safe, warm relationships where we know that we matter. Our infant bodies don't actually know that we are separate beings at all. An infant only exists in relationship. It is natural for infants to try to give the only thing they have—their own nervous systems—to try to balance and care for their parents. This longing for the other's well-being can become an unconscious contract to always try to make things better for the people we love, no matter the cost to ourselves.

The second player in unconscious contracts is the amygdala. The amygdalae are tissues deep in the center of the brain, and they remember everything that is connected with any difficult moment. The amygdala doesn't differentiate, timestamp, or sort memories; it just tangles together everything it remembers, which can make knots of trauma.

This means that one trauma cue leads to the whole trauma memory. The sound of a car backfiring makes a person who has survived gunshots freeze, hide, or collapse. This is because the amygdala has no sense of time.[2] Everything is now. Past memories that are processed by the amygdala feel like the present, and this is why flashbacks and intrusive memories happen. For example, when we remember a moment of being shamed by a teacher when we were in the first years of school, we may still feel the prickling of heat in our cheeks and the desire to disappear. In that moment we might have told ourselves, "I will never speak in a class again," and the amygdala might have written that into the brain as an ongoing behavioral prohibition: *I will not do this ever again.* Because the amygdala has no sense of time, this prohibition doesn't fade into the past, but instead remains an active pattern that we use to guide our behavior. Although this may seem like a life sentence, it is not! Holding these knots and patterns in present time means that they are available even now to be dissolved with warmth and resonance.

When we're able to name the contract using the warmth of self-understanding, we can experience the surprise of giving voice to something that's never had words before. Then we can ask if this contract is something we really want. By bringing the unconscious agreement out of the body and into words, we create the space to wonder, "Do I really still want to keep this agreement? Is it still a good thing for me?" If this a contract we made to survive or to love beyond our limits when we were babies ("Mother, I will give you everything . . ."), it might be important to notice that things may have changed since then. When we release the contracts, our bodies can relax, and we can move into a larger, more compassionate sense of self.

I dream of a world where each human being can be received by self and others with expansiveness and the relaxation that comes with the release of contracts. Instead, it is as if we mostly live bound within a web of unconscious agreements. When I work with the contracts, I find that people become more willing to let the binding dissolve and to step into new places. The work with unconscious contracts is not a magic bullet and won't solve everything, but knowledge of the concept itself and a familiarity with the process are powerful tools in healing.

As I worked with this material, I wondered how these unconscious contracts, these invisible and strange strategies for self-care, would tie in with the journey through neuroscience described in my first book, *Your Resonant Self: Guided Meditations and Exercises to Engage Your Brain's Capacity for Healing.* This workbook explores those connections and can be used on its own or in conjunction with *Your Resonant Self.*

This workbook will take us on a journey through the world of relational neuroscience, looking at the ways our brains respond to other brains, our nervous systems respond to other nervous systems, and our bodies respond to other bodies, looking through the lens of unconscious contracts.

Each chapter gives you, the reader, stories of other people's experiences with this work and invitations for you to experience it for yourself through resonant language and contract practice, questionnaires, meditations, and writing. If you would like to access the guided meditations online for free, please go to www.yourresonantself. com to download them.

Additionally, we will spend time in each chapter learning and practicing the language skills that let us give ourselves understanding and warm curiosity, in other words, how to be resonant with ourselves. Here is a general overview of what we will be covering.

OVERVIEW OF THE CHAPTERS

CHAPTER 1 Are You Willing to Like Yourself?
Clearing Blocks to Self-Warmth

This chapter investigates the blocks to self-kindness that arise from unconscious contracts and their effect on the automatic and often critical voice of the brain. We spend some time with resonant language and introduce the resonating self-witness. We look at how unconscious contract work can reveal roots of self-criticism, and we clear some blocks to looking at ourselves with affection.

CHAPTER 2 It's Not Truth, It's Trauma: Resolving the Past

In this chapter, we bring our learning about the contract tool into relationship with the resonance skill of time travel empathy. We continue our exploration of the importance of resonant language to loosen the brain's hold on memory, with a comparison of resonance and reassurance, and we learn about our conscious and unconscious knowing.

CHAPTER 3 From Self-Sabotage to Self-Care in Everyday Life

This chapter provides simple ways to address unconscious contracts that negatively affect our daily lives. We begin to understand that we have a get-things-done brain and a resonating brain and that they are often entirely different brain systems that aren't communicating with each other. This chapter's resonance skills focus on body sensations.

CHAPTER 4 Healing Shame by Identifying Broken Contracts

This chapter introduces the relational roots of shame, which will help us understand the nervous system drop that results when we inadvertently break a contract. It also acquaints us with the brain circuits that carry our emotions and motivations. We learn about some of the most common contracts humans make with themselves to prevent shame and disappointment and how to discover broken contracts. We further our resonance practice with metaphors.

CHAPTER 5 Revoking the Five Contracts of Anxiety

We take a look at the contracts connected with anxiety, specifically those that concern fear and alarmed aloneness. Additionally, there is research that shows that anxiety can arise from:

- being torn between two authorities
- health imbalances
- carrying family burdens

We will look at resonance remedies for these types of anxiety. We also work with the resonance skill of impossible dream guesses, which can support the movement out of anxiety and into calm.

CHAPTER 6 Claiming Anger's Life-Giving Force

We trace the development of contracts, which can be made during moments of trauma, to never to be angry or to punish ourselves or others for getting angry. We learn how to release them. We also learn how rage can arise when the actions of others cause us to break our own contracts. We look at the reactions of our nervous systems and practice resonant language skills to support self-connection during difficult moments.

CHAPTER 7 Coming Back From Dissociation

In this chapter we continue to work with the contract tool to uncover and transform patterns of dissociation, including contracts that keep us from fully entering or inhabiting the body. We look at contracts we make to not feel anything. We bring our resonance skills to support exquisite gentleness in the face of immobilization and discover how this brings the gift of the return of our life energy.

CHAPTER 8 Healing Into Warmth and Safety in Relationship—Secure Attachment

Through the lens of our new understanding about the early contracts we made to maximize well-being, we gain a deeper understanding of how our nervous systems tried to care for us in the relationships we had with our parents—our attachment relationships. We look at avoidant patterns and contracts, ambivalent patterns and contracts, and we enjoy the signs of the movement into secure attachment.

We learn how we may have used self-hate, disgust, and contempt to take care of ourselves and how this makes sense if we've had to grow up in alarmed aloneness. We discover the role predatory aggression plays and how to begin to work with it. When we dissolve trauma-based contracts, we can reduce violence and recurrent fights in partnership and parenting. The work we have done to this point supports us in looking at these knots of trauma and untangling them so that we can move toward well-being.

Contracts that limit our life energy can lead to hopelessness and depression. When they are combined with negative self-talk, they can be toxic. The contracts of depression are often impossible to uphold, for example, a contract to carry the pain of self and of the entire world. The release of these contracts supports the reclamation of movement and agency. We also take a look at the attachment contracts that create the life-long loneliness that can be a contributing factor in depression, and we learn how to release them.

We discover that our brains take care of themselves with our addictions. Just as our brains make contracts with us to keep us safe, our brains can be said to make contracts with us on behalf of our addictions. We learn how to release these contracts. Resonance skills will be practiced to support self-compassion during this process.

No matter the level of our sexual interest or activity, the SEXUALITY circuit is important for well-being. The contracts that diminish this circuit diminish our life energy and our sense of potential contribution. We will work with these contracts and practice supportive resonance skills that help with personal issues as well as oppression internalized from the way that society judges and ranks our bodies in terms of mattering.

In this final chapter, we will learn how avoidantly attached parents diminish joy in their children. We will learn how contracts that block trust and connection also stop joy from happening. We will dissolve these contracts and celebrate and practice the resonance skills that support the feeling and expression of joy. This chapter includes a look at false Bodhisattva vows. (These are contracts made when children first perceive that there is pain in the world and commit their whole beings to a better world, no matter the cost.) Commitment and contribution are very important and life-serving when they do not cost us everything.

APPENDIX

- Daily practice log
  - The daily practice of remembering to be warm with ourselves is important for changing our brains, so this book also includes a sample daily log chart. You can use it to track the effort you are putting in and what the results are.
- Glossary

Your
Resonant Self
WORKBOOK

CHAPTER 1

Are You Willing to Like Yourself? Clearing Blocks to Self-Warmth

Do you like yourself?

Welcome, to those of you who are new to the *Your Resonant Self* journey, and welcome back, to those of you who have already begun this study and this practice of self-understanding and self-warmth.

━━━━━━━━━━━━━━ THE MAIN QUESTION FOR THIS CHAPTER ━━━━━━━━━━━━━━

Do you like yourself?

One of the most personally and socially transformative actions is our ability to be warm with ourselves.

However, it is dependent on:

- whether anyone we know has ever modelled self-warmth (this rarely happens);
- whether we have had the opportunity to make our own choices, or if others have always made our decisions for us;
- the socio-economic pressure chamber we have lived within (including poverty, racism, body shape/health/age/ability/religious prejudices, oppression from inside and outside ourselves, the safety and warmth of our childhood neighborhoods, etc.);
- whether we've lived through traumas that have turned the automatic voice of the brain, the default mode network, into a self-annihilating system of destruction;
- whether we have unconscious contracts with ourselves that forbid self-warmth; and
- how much healing we have done.

Why am I including social and economic influences in this list? So often, bodies and souls are reduced to a dollar value, based on transactions about how much they can make or sell or based on how many people want to look at them. In this atmosphere, we can be stripped of personal power and a sense of mattering. Internalized messages about making enough money, being too old or unattractive, having the wrong skin color, wearing the wrong clothes, thinking the wrong thoughts, coming from or having ancestors from the wrong countries, all create pressure to believe we are not of interest, not of value, and that we have no say. It is as if our very right to exist is being pulled out from under our feet. When socially pressured misconceptions about value and mattering are entangled with our unconscious contracts, we are stripped of the power to make and experience our world as a welcoming place for all its inhabitants—every person and every living species, including insects and soil microbes.

At this point in history we need everyone's full conviction of their worth and everyone's full understanding of the worth of all living beings. We no longer have time for unconscious contracts that rob us of our traction or stop us from moving into solidarity. By discovering and releasing these self-limiting contracts, we are taking another step toward working together to save as much of this gorgeous, beloved planet as we can.

RELATIONAL NEUROSCIENCE CONCEPT: THE DEFAULT MODE NETWORK, OR HOW THE BRAIN THINKS ABOUT THE SELF

We all have an automatic brain voice that lets us know how we feel about ourselves, and when it is free to work well, it can be a force for good. Its role is to make sense of the world, connect us with others, help us remember things, fuel our creativity, and create wholes from parts. This voice is called the *default mode network*, and it starts running whenever our brains relax. This happens when we aren't using our brains to solve problems, anytime we are not thinking intentionally, or when there are no distractions, such as video games, Netflix, or social media.[1] Although the default mode network is deeply shaped by the unconscious contracts we carry, the good news is that when it is working well, it easily learns self-warmth, even if the concept is new to us.

When we are stressed, our default mode network, our problem solver, is stressed. We start to worry all the time, and whatever anxiety we usually have to begin with becomes even noisier. The default mode network starts to become intrusive, and it becomes harder and harder to enjoy ourselves.

If the default mode network believes that the problem is *us*, and it often does

FIGURE 1.1 The Unstressed Default Mode Network (DMN)

FIGURE 1.2 The Stressed DMN

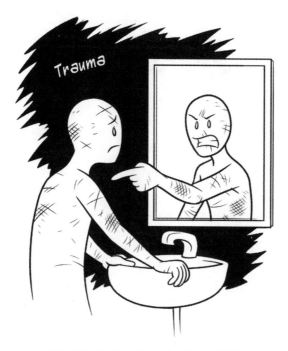

FIGURE 1.3 The Traumatized DMN

when we have survived trauma, the default mode network can become very critical and make the inside of our brain a difficult place to live. It will examine all our actions and memories for signs that we've done something wrong, and if it perceives a threat to our belonging, it will start ringing loud alarm bells and ruminating endlessly about better possible outcomes.

In both the stressed and traumatized situations, the default mode network can be very intrusive, so focusing on or enjoying life is impossible. Many of us are familiar with it as what wakes us from deep sleep and keeps us awake for hours on a mental hamster wheel.

In the worst-case scenario, those who are living with unresolved past or present trauma may experience waking and sleeping nightmares of self-criticism, self-denigration, and self-hate, all at the mercy of the traumatized default mode network.

This chapter demonstrates that releasing unconscious contracts can help self-warmth and resonance to begin to grow a permaculture garden of neurons that can hold us safely in our brains. Let's begin by taking a look at how your default mode network treats you.

QUESTIONNAIRE **Self-Warmth**

Circle 0 for "I can't even imagine liking myself," and 5 for "I like myself very much."

1. I like and enjoy my body as it is, with all its beauty, grace, awkwardness, and its signs of having helped me through this life journey, including "extra" weight by western standards, wrinkles, scars, gray hair, and any deviations from "health norms" or the "social norm," or any surgery I've had which takes me toward a "health norm" or a "social norm."

    0   1   2   3   4   5

2. I like and enjoy my mind as it is, with its speed or slowness, its clarity or confusion, its musings, its dreaming and creativity, its signs of trauma, its flexibility or rigidity.

    0   1   2   3   4   5

3. When I remember my day yesterday, the memory is accompanied by affection and understanding for myself.

    0   1   2   3   4   5

4. When I ask myself to be creative, I enjoy full self-confidence and flow.

    0   1   2   3   4   5

5. When I anticipate going to a social event where I don't know many people, I feel gentle anticipation of the possibility of meeting someone I will like.

    0   1   2   3   4   5

6. When I anticipate going to a social event where I don't know many people, I feel a certainty that others will like me.

    0   1   2   3   4   5

7. When I think about what my work is in the world and the way that I do it, I feel affection and appreciation toward myself.

    0   1   2   3   4   5

8. I can use the words "delight," "enjoyment," and "self" in the same sentence without experiencing shame, dismissal, or disgust.

    0   1   2   3   4   5

9. When I think of the most recent problem I have solved, I celebrate my solution.

    0   1   2   3   4   5

10. When I sink into my felt sense of being, my wordless sense of who I am, I feel a rush of affection and warmth for myself.

    0   1   2   3   4   5

Add up your points from the questionnaire.

0–20   **Hooray!** You have found this book! It is a very good resource for you. Pay particular attention to the next chapter on trauma's effects on self-warmth.

21–30   **Welcome!** You're on your journey. The work with unconscious contracts will move you further along in the direction of health and well-being.

31–40   **Wonderful!** You have a solid foundation with a little room for more delight and satisfaction.

41–50   **Celebrate!** You have been well-supported, and you have worked hard. This book will help you make contributions to others' well-being and self-warmth.

SELF-WARMTH: HOW THE BRAIN LEARNS TO HOLD ITSELF

Our brain has a lifelong capacity to grow the neurons that allow us to turn toward the self with affection and understanding. No matter how far-fetched it may sound at this moment, self-warmth can be easy, because these particular neurons love to grow in the human brain throughout our lifespan.[2] Once we have cleared away the contracts that keep us from caring about ourselves, we immediately start to catch glimpses of what warmth feels like. A couple of years of practice may be needed before we can hold ourselves when we are very angry, scared, sad, lonely, or ashamed. It's like building muscle to lift heavier weights.

Before we have built enough strength to hold our own emotions, it can be help-ful to identify warm "others" who can hold things with us. These people may be therapists or friends, or sometimes they will be resonance buddies or books like this one. We learn to turn toward the self with warmth as we experience being accom-panied, being and feeling understood, and discovering that others have had similar experiences. In these moments we are growing new neural connections that reach from the front of the brain, the prefrontal cortex (PFC), to deep inside, to our friend the amygdala.

When it is hard to imagine having warmth for ourselves, it can be helpful to personalize the parts of the brain that are capable of self-warmth and self-regulation. We can call these parts our "resonating self-witness." The PFC has the capacity to differentiate itself from the emotional part of the brain (centered in the amygdala) and can hold our emotions with understanding, linking into the warmth and reso-nance circuitry that we already have, but which is usually directed outward.

As infants, we are born to cry, to laugh, to communicate. But we aren't born to take care of ourselves. This is what we learn when a mothering person is able to let us know that we make sense rather than leaving us alone to "cry it out." Our reso-nating self-witness is born when the neurons from the middle part of the PFC—just behind the forehead—begin to reach back to the amygdala with affectionate and precise understanding.

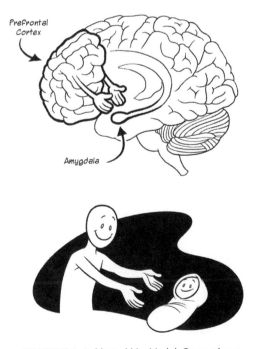

FIGURE 1.4 How We Hold Ourselves

I keep coming back to the quote from noted researcher Moshe Szyf, "Every cell in your prefrontal cortex (PFC) carries the signature of the presence or absence of your mother."[3] The human brain is composed of 86 billion cells. The PFC takes up approximately one-third of the brain, which means that we may have about 29 billion cells that carry the presence or absence of our mother. That is a lot of cells. That is one huge juggernaut of influence!

If nobody ever took care of the people who took the most care of us, the people who took care of us may never have learned the nurturing skills they needed to be able to take care of us with warmth. The mother inside every cell of our prefrontal cortex may be bewildered about how to bring nurturing to our emotional selves. This means we may have 29 billion bewildered cells saying, "What? Warmth for me?" There may be a fundamental, cellular bewilderment. And yet this disorientation can change when we have experiences with resonance, or when we even just experience a moment of grace when somebody makes a resonant facial expression. Last week, I was complaining about something, and my friend responded with just a facial expression, without any words, and I thought, "Wow, I have been utterly and completely understood." My whole body relaxed. It was exactly the right facial expression; it had all the nuance I needed to feel heard. People don't even have to use words to accompany us.

As we start to get used to being accompanied, we notice that throughout life we can cultivate, grow, graft, and weave our beloved people, animals, Earth, water, moon, spirits, stars, and trees into our prefrontal cortex. With this depth of resourcing, we discover a new integration of our resonant self-witness. It becomes our newly resonant self-mother inside our own brain.

Let's explore the word *resonant*. When I bring my attention to you with the intention of understanding, I'm attuning to you. You don't have to respond. I can be empathetic, sympathetic, or compassionate with you, and it still may not land for you. All of this may be going on in one person without the other knowing anything about it. For resonance to be resonance, a minimum of two people need to be participating. When I offer you an idea, verbally or nonverbally, and you say, "Yes, that's it!", then we have found resonance together. Throughout this chapter we have been finding out how we can be resonant with ourselves so that it is as if we are two people in one. We know when we have self-resonance because our bodies relax. This is important because it just so happens that the relaxation that accompanies resonance lights up the relational brain—the part of the brain that loves new learning and where change happens easily. (The good news I mentioned earlier!)

Here is an illustrated list of nine forms of resonant language, each of which has

FIGURE 1.5 Types of Resonant Language

been shown by research to be received by the right hemisphere and each of which we will practice in this book.

When someone accompanies us, verbally with resonant language or nonverbally, it's as if they're letting us know that they also feel and understand what's happening for us. We can imagine two cello bodies, side by side, and one relaxed cello body is vibrating along with the song life is playing through the other cello body, which in turn deepens the resonance for the cello being played by life. It knows it's being accompanied.

As we experience being received with a sense of "of course" (*Of course we are angry! Of course we're shocked! Of course we're torn! Of course we love so very, very much!*), we grow new neural fibers. Rather than adding to the neural fibers that let the amygdala run the brain with alarm, we grow new fibers and neural connections that let the prefrontal cortex hold the amygdala and say, "Of course you're angry! You need to know that you matter!" In response, the amygdala responds, "Ah, my message has been received. The body can relax."

JOURNALING PROMPT FOR
Noticing Your Critical Inner Voice

Take 10 minutes to think about a mistake or an error you believe you have made or the last time someone misjudged you or spoke harshly to or about you. Write down everything you are telling yourself as you think about the error. Take notes of the patterns of the way your brain addresses you: Is it kind? Is it cruel? Does it care about your difficulties or not? Does it have mercy and forgiveness for you, or is it unforgiving? Does your brain like you? By doing this, you will be tracking your brain's default network, and you will be learning a little about how your default mode network sounds when you are under stress. If you notice that this exercise is unbearable and unleashes the inner hounds of hell on you, this simply means that you are carrying unresolved trauma. Let yourself skip this section and move to Chapter 2 before trying this exercise and meditation again.

Example: *Yesterday at the airport, I was supposed to be meeting two different parties. They texted where they were and that they had found each other. I wasn't far away, but I wanted just a few moments of alone time, so I texted back that I would be there in a moment. I sat and breathed and looked at my email and drank a few sips of hot chocolate. At that moment, they arrived in a group and found me. I felt embarrassed to have been caught not serving the group and regretted having tried to take some moments for myself. I told myself that I no longer belonged, that I was selfish, that now they wouldn't trust me. I told myself that I had traded relationship and predictability for mistrust and lack of relaxation by taking some moments for self-care. My default mode network was telling me that I was wrong, that I didn't have the right to hold things up, that I was not the central party here, and that I hurt the others. My brain was masquerading as the authority, and it believed its own take on things. It was contemptuous and judgmental of me, and it has had a lot of experience trying to manage the consequences of Sarah trying to carve out time for herself. It was unforgiving, and it didn't like me. It would have liked to be able to distance itself from me. My body felt unsettled, anxious, and vigilant, waiting for my friends' anger.*

As I worked with this, I discovered that I had an unconscious contract against taking time for myself when I might be discovered in order to save myself from my mother's scorn and icy rage, no matter the cost to myself. I asked myself, "Do I want this contract?" "No more. Sarah, I release you from this contract and I revoke this vow, and instead I give you my blessing to say to Sarah, 'Of course you need a moment to breathe.'"

Even with this little bit of exposure, you may start to discover your own unconscious contracts as you do your journaling. If you find one, save it to work on in the contract section of this chapter.

Now you try it, and follow the prompts in this worksheet:

Timeframe and what happened:

_____

_____

_____

_____

I'm telling myself:

_____

_____

_____

_____

My brain is trying to help me by:

_____

_____

_____

_____

Reread what you have written. How does your body respond to the voice of your default mode network? Is there tension? Does this voice bring shame or a collapse to your body? How does your stomach feel? Does your body feel calm and even cozy with the default mode network's voice, whether it is scornful or warm? Or does this voice make your body want to get up and move, to shake it off, to switch the focus?

My body feels:

_____

_____

_____

_____

THE IMPORTANCE OF SELF-WARMTH

Research has shown that the more self-compassion and self-warmth we have, the less prone we are to post-traumatic stress disorder (PTSD). We've known for some time that when soldiers go into war, they are more likely to get PTSD if their early relationships were difficult.[4] An additional piece of research was done recently with soldiers with differing levels of self-compassion. Some of them had more self-compassion, some of them had less. The more self-compassion the soldiers had, the less likely they were to have PTSD, and if they did develop a PTSD response, they were more likely to heal from it.[5] The more self-compassion we have, whether from supportive early relationships or from our own healing work (or both), the better off we are in life, even when faced with potentially traumatic events.

The following meditation lays some groundwork for self-warmth.

GUIDED MEDITATION
Warmth for the Default Mode Network

To prepare for this meditation, review your previous journal entry, so that you remember how your default mode network treats you when you make a mistake.

Now, with this information in mind, here is the guided meditation to support the well-being of your brain by bringing warmth to the default mode network.

Begin this meditation by breathing . . . Notice yourself as a breathing being . . . Invite your attention to rest on the sensation of breath, wherever you feel it . . . See if you can invite your upper belly, around the bottom of your ribs, to move out when you inhale . . . and bring yourself back to breathing however your body breathes on its own, just allowing yourself to notice your breath . . . Where do you feel the sensation of breathing? . . . Is it in the rise and fall of your belly? . . . Is it in the small movements of your ribs and shoulders? . . . Is it the passage of air, a slight coolness, through your nose, sinuses, mouth, or throat? . . . Breathe for a moment . . . and allow yourself to notice the thoughts and worries that break over you like waves on a shore . . . taking you away from the sensation of breath . . . Let yourself remember what your brain was trying to do for you during your journaling . . . Do you find any of those thoughts in these waves?

Hello, automatic voice of the brain . . . Do you need time and space to unspool your worries and anxieties so that you will have confidence that everything you need to get done has been done? . . . Are you tracking everything that needs to happen and all the broken promises and all the unfinished tasks? . . . And would you like acknowledgment that, while we are alive, it isn't possible to do everything? . . . And that this might be a little hard on you? . . . Are you tired and cranky from working so hard all the time with so little result? . . . Would you like to protect your person from every possible bad thing that could happen? . . . Would you like to make sure that your person is always seen accurately, in the best light, and for their best intentions? . . . Do you sometimes worry that your person doesn't have any best intentions? . . . Would you like some acknowledgment that you carry the unresolved judgments you have heard said about your person, especially the words that have been said by people with more power than you, like your parents or teachers? . . . that you don't know what to do with these judgments but carry them and worry about them and try to find out how they are true so that you can always stay in relationship with those important people? . . . Do you long to live in a world where everyone is seen with true generosity of spirit? . . . Would you love to drop all judgments of self and others and live simply and safely and fluidly?

Automatic voice of the brain, are you noticing the body's disquiet, even without your person knowing what is happening? . . . Does the body's discomfort worry you, and are you always trying to figure out what to do to take care of it? . . . Are you always searching for a solution? . . . Would you like a little acknowledgment that nothing ever helps in the long-term? . . . And that you just seem to keep trying the same thing over and over again, with mixed hope and despair? . . . Do you long to live in a world where things can change, where brains can heal, where the inside of our skulls can become a sweet and cozy place to be, a place where we are loved and are able to have warmth and affection for ourselves?

Now, in this moment, see if you can connect to something larger than your own brain, something at the very center of your being that can hold your brain with affection and gratitude for the journey you both have been on, for what it has felt like to be you . . . Is it possible? . . . If it is, celebrate . . . If it isn't possible yet, let your brain know that you will be back to like it later in your journey . . .

You may be experiencing relief at learning that your critical voice is not you . . . that it is just a brain system, trying to help you . . . a wishfully helpful ally rather than a curse . . . that at the core of your being, you may not be as critical of yourself as you thought . . . If this is true for you, let yourself experience the surprise and relief . . . and celebrate a new world of possibilities for a different . . . and kind . . . and collaborative relationship with this voice . . .

Take a moment to reconnect with your breathing . . . Allow yourself once again to notice that you are a breathing being . . . that you are here . . . that you exist . . . and that you can bring your attention back to your external life . . . to this book . . . to the dishes . . . to your work . . . to whatever distractions or outer relationships support you . . .

Welcome back from your inner world!

Let's take a look at the way I was talking with the critical default mode network. As I was creating this meditation, I was imagining my own and your critical inner voice, and I was wondering what words I could use to help this voice feel that I understood it. I was looking for resonant language that would help our connection. I ended up using feelings and needs guesses from my Nonviolent Communication (NVC) practice. NVC is a way of thinking about communicating that was developed by Marshall Rosenberg and is now studied all over the world. Many of the resonance skills we'll work with in this book are rooted in the work he and other NVC trainers have done with this way of thinking about language.

These feelings and needs guesses are our first form of resonant language from the illustrated list shown a few pages ago.

RESONANT LANGUAGE PRACTICE
The Feelings and Needs of the Critical Inner Voice

Being able to find the deep needs beneath criticism is a resonant language tool that is specific to Nonviolent Communication. Using the feelings and needs pages following this worksheet, we can translate the following common statements of the dissatisfied inner voice.

Example:
Voice of critical default mode network: *"You did it again! Another social ball dropped! You completely forgot to thank George!"*

   Body sensations: *Tension in shoulders and stomach*
   Feeling(s): *Exasperated*
   Need(s): *Inclusion, gratitude, fluidity*

Question from prefrontal cortex to amygdala: *"Are you exasperated, and do you love inclusion, gratitude, and fluidity?"*

    Amygdala's answer: *"Yes, and worried that you'll never get it right and that you are constitutionally incapable of the attention it takes to be socially responsible!"*

    Body sensations: *Pain at temples*

    Feeling(s): *Worried, hopeless*

    Need(s): *Hope, trust, mercy from the universe*

Question from prefrontal cortex to amygdala: *"Are you worried and hopeless, and do you long for hope, trust, and mercy from the universe?"*

    Amygdala's answer: *"Yes!"*

    Body sensations: *Relief, relaxation*

(When you get a clear yes and relief and relaxation, you stop. There may be more to look at later, but we're just practicing at this point.)

Voice of critical default mode network: *Everyone will laugh at you.*

    Body sensations:

    Feeling(s):

    Need(s):

Question from prefrontal cortex to amygdala:

    Amygdala's answer:

    Body sensations:

    Feeling(s):

    Need(s):

Question from prefrontal cortex to amygdala:

    Amygdala's answer:

    Body sensations:

Voice of critical default mode network: *"I can't do anything right."*

    Body sensations:

    Feeling(s):

    Need(s):

Question from prefrontal cortex to amygdala:

    Amygdala's answer:

    Body sensations:

    Feeling(s):

    Need(s):

Question from prefrontal cortex to amygdala:
    Amygdala's answer:
    Body sensation:

Voice of critical default mode network (fill in your own criticism):
    Body sensations:
    Feeling(s):
    Need(s):
Question from prefrontal cortex to amygdala:
    Amygdala's answer:
    Body sensations:
    Feeling(s):
    Need(s):
Question from prefrontal cortex to amygdala:
    Amygdala's answer:
    Body sensations:
    Feeling(s):
    Need(s):

TABLE 1.1 Feelings List

CARE	Affectionate, calm, compassionate, composed, contented, empathic, friendly, grateful, loving, mellow, moved, open, peaceful, secure, serene, sympathetic, tender, thankful, touched, tranquil, trusting, warm
PANIC/GRIEF	Alarmed, anguished, anxious, ashamed, blue, bewildered, brokenhearted, chagrined, contrite, dejected, despondent, disappointed, disheartened, dismayed, distressed, downhearted, forlorn, grief-stricken, guilty, gloomy, heartbroken, hurt, insecure, lonely, melancholic, mystified, pained, panicky, remorse, sad, sensitive, shocked
FEAR	Afraid, alarmed, anxious, apprehensive, cautious, dread, edgy, fearful, frightened, hesitant, horrified, jittery, nervous, scared, shaky, shocked, startled, terrified, timid, trepidation, uneasy, unnerved, unsteady, worried

RAGE	Aggravated, agitated, angry, annoyed, bitter, cranky, edgy, enraged, exasperated, frustrated, furious, grouchy, grumpy, hate, infuriated, irate, irked, irritated, mad, miffed, peeved, resentful, sullen, surly, ticked off
LUST/SEXUALITY	Absorbed, alive, aroused, astonished, blissful, breathless, dazzled, desiring, ecstatic, effervescent, electrified, enlivened, exhilarated, expansive, expectant, exuberant, glorious, glowing, gratified, inspired, intense, invigorated, jealous, longing, moved, radiant, rapturous, stimulated, yearning
SEEKING	Antsy, apathetic, appreciative, blah, bored, confident, cross, depressed, despairing, despondent, detached, discouraged, disinterested, dull, eager, engrossed, enthusiastic, envious, excited, exhausted, expectant, fatigued, fulfilled, gratified, helpful, helpless, hopeful, hopeless, impatient, indifferent, inert, involved, jittery, lethargic, listless, longing, numb, overwhelmed, perplexed, pleased, pressured, proud, optimistic, overexcited, puzzled, refreshed, relieved, restless, reluctant, satisfied, skeptical, sour, stimulated, surprised, sulky, tepid, thrilled, tired, uptight, vexed, yearning
PLAY	Adventurous, amazed, amused, alive, animated, buoyant, carefree, cheerful, comfortable, confused, curious, delighted, ecstatic, elated, encouraged, energetic, enthusiastic, exalted, expansive, exuberant, fascinated, giddy, gleeful, good-humored, inquisitive, interested, intrigued, joyful, joyous, jubilant, merry, mirthful, overjoyed, secure, stimulated, surprised
DISGUST	Appalled, disgusted, disturbed, horror, repulsed, revolted
SEEKING (PREDATORY AGGRESSION)	Antagonistic, contemptuous, cruel, embittered, hateful, hostile, rancorous, suspicious, vengeful

TABLE 1.2 Needs List	
AUTONOMY	Choice, freedom, independence, power, agency, self-responsibility, ease
INTEGRITY	Authenticity, individuality, wholeness, healing, purpose/meaning
APPRECIATION	Acknowledgment, acceptance, self-acceptance, consideration
SELF-EXPRESSION	Creativity, growth, purpose, passion, work, spontaneity, to matter, to be seen, to be heard, to be known, to be understood
INTERDEPENDENCE	Contribution, community, consideration, cooperation, friendship, harmony, peace, mutuality, balance, preservation of life, respect, seeing others as whole, support, help, trust, honesty, connection, belonging, inclusion, communication, companionship, participation, partnership, relationship, shared values, shared history, shared reality
NURTURING/ NOURISHMENT	Affection, resonance, care, self-care, comfort, empathy, kindness, tenderness, intimacy, closeness, friendship, love, to be loved, to be welcome, warmth, the well-being of those we love
SURVIVAL (STREAMS OF NOURISHMENT)	Abundance, air, water, food, shelter, touch, movement, health, well-being, rest, sleep, safety, sexuality, sustainability, death, mourning
CELEBRATION	Aliveness, delight, fun, play, humor, joy, passion, flow
SECURITY	Consistency, reliability, stability, order, structure, predictability, protection, trust, dignity, dependability
MENTAL	Understanding, clarity, information, learning, stimulation
SPIRITUAL	Beauty, connection with life, faith, hope, harmony, inspiration, tranquility, serenity, presence

Now that you've looked at the feelings and needs behind self-criticism, you may be wondering why people are still self-critical if it is so easy to just understand what is going on. The decoding of criticism is incredibly helpful in our efforts to nurture self-warmth, but it only takes us so far if we have contracts that prevent us from holding ourselves with affection. Let's look at a piece of contract work that a real reader did with this process.

ONE-ON-ONE WORK
Unconscious Contract Work With a Reader

SARAH: *How are you with self-warmth?*

JENNIFER: *Not good. I can't like myself. Here I am, 67 years old, and I've never been able to like myself. I'm useless, no good to anyone. I'm just a burden.*

SARAH: *Do you have a lifelong contract? "I, Jennifer, solemnly swear to my essential self not to like myself in order to . . ." What happens when you say the words?*

JENNIFER: *"I, Jennifer, solemnly swear not to like myself in order to" . . . I don't know. I was my mother's eighth child. We were very poor. She didn't have enough resources to take care of all of us.*

SARAH: *"I, Jennifer, swear to my essential self not to like myself in order to make up for being a burden?"*

JENNIFER: *"I, Jennifer, solemnly swear to my essential self that I will not like myself in order to make up to my mother for being born, no matter the cost to myself." Yes, that's true. That makes me cry.*

SARAH: *Jennifer's essential self, do you like this contract?*

JENNIFER, speaking for her essential self: *No. my mother is long dead. "Jennifer, I release you from this contract and I revoke this vow."*

SARAH: *And instead, I give you my blessing to . . .*

JENNIFER: *"And instead, I give you my blessing to like yourself and to enjoy your life." It's about time! Sixty-seven years is too long to spend atoning for being born. Now a wave of mourning is hitting me. What a way to spend a life.*

SARAH (after a quiet moment in acknowledgment of the sadness): *How is your body doing now, after the release?*

JENNIFER: *It's strange, but even though there is grief, I feel lighter. Lighter than I have ever felt in my life.*

One year later, Jennifer writes:

It has been a strange and good year, to live without the sense that I should not like myself. There are many other things, many other worries, that have arisen in the wake of this process, but everything is lighter.

Jennifer's process may already be hinting to you that some of the blocks you might have to self-warmth, that you may have always thought were permanent, are not set in stone. The following section will show you the moving parts of the unconscious contract, and then you can follow the template to see what your own unconscious contract might be that would prevent you from having self-warmth or from liking yourself.

THE MOVING PARTS OF UNCONSCIOUS CONTRACTS

Take a look at the moving parts of the unconscious contracts, and circle the phrases that feel like they might be yours.

Common contracts involving the default mode network and everyday life:

I will not make mistakes . . .
I will get everything done . . .
I will know everything before I speak or write . . .
I will anticipate every bad thing that could happen . . .
I won't forget anyone/anything . . .
I will track everything for everyone . . .
I will make sure everyone is included . . .
I will believe I am a fraud . . .
I will believe I don't know enough . . .
I will believe I'm not good enough/not capable . . .
I will believe I am too much . . .
I will be forever vigilant . . .
I will say yes to everything asked of me . . .

Common contracts involving the default mode network and self-warmth*:

I will not like myself . . .
I will not forgive myself . . .
I will not include myself . . .
I will not believe that my needs matter . . .
I will not be warm or affectionate with myself . . .
I will believe I don't belong . . .
I will believe I am worthless . . .

IN ORDER TO . . .

The words "in order to" follow the initial promise in the unconscious contracts, inviting us to explore the possibility that we've made these agreements with ourselves for a reason. Our reason is usually very good: survival and love are two of the most common reasons. Here are some possible in-order-to's to try out if any of the above agreements seem familiar to you:

In order to (survive) . . .

. . . make sure I'm never humiliated or ridiculed again.
. . . keep from being beaten or kicked out.
. . . make sure I have a place.
. . . keep everyone safe.
. . . keep from being disappointed that others don't like/want me.
. . . punish myself so that I never do that again.
. . . keep myself from expecting anything good and being disappointed.
. . . belong in my family, where people don't like themselves.

In order to (love) . . .

. . . accompany my mother and never leave her.
. . . keep my father from being alone.
. . . maintain the balance of affection in my home.
. . . not compete with my parent/sibling.

---

* self-hate comes later, in Chapter 9

EXAMPLES OF CONTRACTS CONNECTED WITH THE CRITICAL INNER VOICE:

I, [*your name here*], solemnly swear . . .

> that I will believe that I am ugly and unattractive and that no one could ever love me in order to make sense of my parents' verbal abuse . . .
>
> that I will believe I am not likeable in order to make sense of my lifelong loneliness . . .
>
> that I will believe that I'm too much in order to try to understand my parents' dissociation . . .
>
> that I will believe that I do not deserve to live in order to atone for the burden of my birth/life on my mother . . .

EXAMPLES OF CONTRACTS TO NOT LOVE THE SELF OR TO NOT HAVE SELF-COMPASSION:

I, [*your name here*], solemnly swear:

> to you, my mother, that I will not love myself in order to protect you from loneliness . . .
>
> to you, my essential self, that I will treat myself harshly in order to protect you from the excruciating disappointment of dashed hopes for love . . .
>
> to you, my father, that I will dislike myself in order to protect you from ever being wrong . . .
>
> to you, the world, that I will not love myself in order to honor you for the harm that humans do to you . . .
>
> to you, my mother, that I will experience self-loathing in order to punish myself for breathing and save all the oxygen in the world for you . . .
>
> to you, my essential self, that I will not love myself as an act of integrity to protest for all the people in this world who are not loved . . .

> . . . no matter the cost to myself (or the people I love).

This last point, "no matter the cost," lets us take a realistic look at the price we are paying to continue on with this unconscious contract. The cost can be health, freedom, connection, satisfaction, or deep self-love. The price might be one that we pay personally, or it may be one that our children or loved ones pay.

Unconscious Contract Process Template

This process can be done between the person doing the contract work and their support people, or one can be one's own support person and simply switch between roles. It can be done verbally out loud, silently in one's own head, or in writing in a journaling format.

STEP 1. Work out the words of your original contract:

I, [your name here], solemnly swear to you, [choose one: essential self, parent, sibling, family line, God, universe], that I will [self-defeating behavior] in order to [survive, love, honor, accompany, create the world I want to live in], no matter the cost to myself or those I love.

I _____ *, solemnly swear to you,*

that I will

_____

_____

in order to

_____

_____

no matter the cost to myself or those I love.

STEP 2. Find out if the party with whom the contract was made heard it:

This is the step where you get to stop being yourself and become the person you made the contract with [your essential self, your parent, your sense of God, etc.].

Physically move so that you are standing or sitting in a different place, and step into the role of the party with whom you made the contract.

Ask, *"[Essential self, parent, sibling, family line, God, universe], did you hear the contract that [your name here] made to you?"*

Yes _____

No _____

If the answer is no, then repeat the contract so that it is heard. Once the answer is yes, then proceed.

STEP 3. Find out if the party with whom the contract was made still wants it:

Ask this party, *"[Essential self, parent, sibling, family line, God, universe],*
Is that a contract you want the person who made the contract to keep?"
      Yes _____
      No _____
      If the answer is no, then proceed with the process.
      If the answer is "Yes, the contract should be kept," then more needs to be
      named. Keep reading to find out the options for what to do when the answer
      is yes. For now, let's assume that the answer is "No, this is not a contract I
      want [*your name here*] to keep."

STEP 4. The release:

Have the party with whom the contract was made say, *"[Your name here], I*
release you from this contract, and I revoke this vow."

STEP 5. The blessing:

Create a blessing that encourages you to live in a new way: *"And instead of this*
contract, I give you my blessing to [love yourself, follow your dreams, marry who-
ever you'd like, enjoy your work, find work that you enjoy, etc.]."

Your blessing:

_____
_____
_____

Now you have a basic outline of the Unconscious Contract Process, and you've had a chance to try it out for yourself. You will discover that there are some twists and turns that the process can take. We will explore them and bring out ways to address resistances and discomforts. The most important part is the process of discovering the agreements we've made with ourselves. When we reach down deep into our bellies to discover the huge love, the disabling shock, or the drive for survival that lives there, we find the very good reasons that motivate us to make and keep these agreements.

The most common mistake that people make in trying to do this work on their own is to play too small and believe that their manipulative, egoic, social self has made these agreements. That is never the case. These are nervous system, cellular-level contracts that we make far below the level of manipulation, in the deepest levels of self and infancy. We often aren't used to seeing ourselves with such generosity, but in order to fully take advantage of the healing that is possible from recognizing and working with this phenomenon, we need to move in this direction. When we find a good "in order to . . ." there are often tears—at the very least, the body makes itself known with a change in sensation at the experience of self-recognition. These body sensations can be either in the direction of more tension or more relaxation.

Once the vow is released, we most often experience relaxation, but there can also be a little bewilderment or a little voice wondering, "Now what?" The blessing helps with this, offering a new direction, a new intention, or a new North Star that gives us something to orient toward.

As we come to the end of this first chapter, here is a journaling prompt to support you to record your journey along this path. The release of vows is often so complete that we are left without a memory of what it was like to live within their thrall. The journaling can give you a sense of the path you have travelled, and this can bring joy, self-knowledge, and a sense of satisfaction.

JOURNALING PROMPT FOR
Inviting Self-Warmth

Where were you on your self-warmth journey when you picked up this book? What has happened to you as you have made your way through this chapter? If you had no sense at all of self-warmth, how warm are you with yourself now? Do you have any discoveries, insights, protests, or doubts that you would like to register for yourself? Are there any questions peeking through that would like to be seen? Suspicions about other unconscious contracts you might have that you would like to bookmark for later?

In the beginning of the book, I mentioned that this journey is one of both personal healing and of global transformation. When we have a self-critical default mode network, we will have trouble with cortisol, energy levels, anxiety, depression, a compromised immune system, panic, dissociation, confusion, and PTSD.[6] When we have a self-critical default mode network, we won't know how to find solidarity with other beings on the planet. The compromised immune system happens on a personal level and at a global, systemic level. All of these things are part of the picture of what it's like to live with trauma while holding ourselves responsible for that trauma. Chapter 2 will take us into the nuts and bolts of healing from trauma and how that healing connects us with new levels of unconscious contracts.

CHAPTER 2

It's Not Truth, It's Trauma: Resolving the Past

INTRUSIVE MEMORIES

One day I asked a group of friends to track their intrusive memories—the memories that arise spontaneously, without being summoned, and which we don't really want to remember—and share them as they came up. When we heard that it was going to rain, one man changed his whole outfit to match his raincoat. "My older brother used to shame me for not matching my colors," he said. We were hurrying to meet up with another group, and a woman said, "My mother would tell me that if I was late again, she was going to beat me with my play mop." As we approached the group, another man shared that he was remembering trick-or-treating when he was five and that one house had made their stairs into what looked like a haunted house entry and that when he went up the stairs to go into the haunted house, they laughed at him because the stairway was the only place they had decorated, not the inside of the house. "I still remember the humiliation," he said. We started to cross the street when a bus loomed around the corner, and I grabbed another friend's arm to keep her from crossing. My heart was beating out of my chest because when I was in my twenties, I was in a head-on car accident with a bus that looked similar.

These are the kinds of memories that people live with every day, as our brains try to take care of us and keep us safe by watching for situations and cues that have signaled danger in the past. They are also the kinds of memories that make the brain difficult and prickly to live with. Fortunately, we can shift these memories with resonance, as we will learn in this chapter.

JOURNALING PROMPT FOR
Noticing Your Intrusive Memories

Over the next 24 hours, jot down all the intrusive memories that arise for you. In doing this, you will be tracking the effects that past traumas have on your present time:

RELATIONAL NEUROSCIENCE CONCEPT: UNDERSTANDING TRAUMA

As discussed in the introduction, our trauma memories, our intrusive memories, have no sense of time. They exist in an ever-available present. This is because the part of the brain that holds difficult or painful memories, the amygdala, can't link any chronological sense of the passage of time without the help of its memory partner, the hippocampus.[1] This lets the amygdala stay on guard at all times to save us from anything that has been dangerous in the past. If the amygdala doesn't know that the past is the past, it isn't slowed down by wondering, "Am I making a mistake here?" It just gets us out of the danger zone as quickly as possible.

During traumatic, unaccompanied moments, the amygdala brings the concepts, perceptions, and sensory cues of the original traumatic moment together with the power of superglue, creating distinct neural networks for each different trauma. The more numerous the difficult experiences we have had, the more our brains are fragmented by knots of memory that can hijack us. Another way of thinking about this is that the amygdala joins together whatever memory is consciously available with our unconscious memories and our sense of self. These tangles of traumatic memory live on in us until resonance and a sense of being understood dissolve the glue that binds these networks together, frees up our sense of self as someone separate from the trauma, and changes the way our brains hold the traumatic memory.

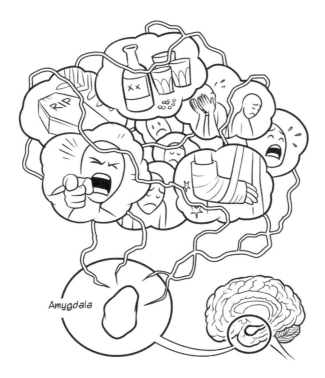

FIGURE 2.1 The Amygdala Creates Memory Tangles

It is important for us to understand that an event is not, in and of itself, traumatic and that people can have different reactions to the same events. For one person, their mother dying is not a trauma. It may feel like the right time for her death, or the person may feel warmly held and supported by their loved ones during this transition. But for others who go unaccompanied in the experience of their mother's death, no matter how old they are, this loss can be absolutely devastating.

With this understanding in mind, the working definition of trauma that I am offering is (different from classic definitions of trauma): the experience of something difficult, during or after which we are not accompanied by warm and precise understanding, either from ourselves or from others.

Most, but not all, traumatic memories are partially conscious. Every traumatic memory carries a seed of what is unknown. This seed might be an emotion that hasn't been named, a complexity that hasn't been considered, a feeling of being torn that hasn't been acknowledged, an actual lost memory, or a missing understanding. In some way, we have not been accompanied, and so we don't know everything that the body wants to tell us about the trauma. The unconscious contract work as well as the time travel resonance we will learn about a little later in

Ship of Our Explicit Awareness

Sea of Implicit

Serpents of Trauma

FIGURE 2.2 The Sea Serpents of Traumatic Memory

the book are both processes of accompaniment that help us discover the parts of our memories we aren't aware of and make them conscious. To familiarize yourself with this process further, you may want to refer to Chapter 6 of my first book, *Your Resonant Self*.

It is like we are small boats in an ocean of all the things that are happening around us and have happened to us throughout our lives—our explicit memories, or what we know that we know. The things we know about make up the boat of awareness, and we don't know much about the ocean. The ocean is our implicit awareness—what we don't know we know. In this ocean swim the sea serpents of unresolved trauma which we can run into without notice, and suddenly we have to find a way to live with the unresolved moments of the past, times when we were not accompanied. These are our intrusive memories and thoughts, and when we do our healing work, the serpents of trauma are transformed into life energy that helps to power our ship of consciousness.

With this perspective in mind, we arrive at:

THE MAIN QUESTION FOR THIS CHAPTER

When have you been too alone?

What memories seem like they are still happening in the present rather than in the past? If trauma comes from how alone we were during a difficult event rather than from the event itself, we can tell what was traumatic for us by noticing what sticks in our brains. Any conversation that we run over and over, often wishing we could have changed it, is a conversation in which we were too alone. And any memory that circles back around to stab us with shame or fear is also a moment in our lives when we were too alone.

A NOTE OF CARE WHEN WORKING WITH TRAUMATIC MEMORIES

Sometimes a person has survived their childhood and their past by NOT thinking about them, by not remembering. It is important to honor and respect the body's wisdom in coping this way. I invite you to use gentle discernment about turning your attention to these memories. For some people, doing so even with new warmth and understanding may be destabilizing. For others, it may be healing. You may want to consider things like whether you have adequate support, coping skills, and enough stability in your life to move into this territory. If you have any sense that you need to be protected from your memories, rather than explore them, please stop here. You can work for quite a long time with the first few chapters of my first book, Your Resonant Self, *and develop self-warmth without looking into the past. Another possibility is to work with this material with your counselor or therapist so that you always have warm accompaniment for the material. Whatever you choose, the most important thing is your well-being.*

CHARTING YOUR SELF-LOVE

To help us think about this, you can use this worksheet to graph the movement of your own self-love (warm, affectionate understanding for yourself) throughout your lifetime. When filling in this chart, keep in mind the difficult things that happened to both you and your parents during your lifetime.

By charting the ebb and flow of self-love throughout our lives, we are able to see where we might still carry unresolved, intrusive memories. With this awareness, we use our tools to dissolve the memories and reconnect with the life energy they carry.

The places where self-warmth dips indicate that some sort of difficult event or series of events happened in the period immediately before the dip. These events may include bullying; frightening teachers; abuse of any kind; the death of one or

FIGURE 2.3 The Ebb and Flow of Self-Love

both parents, of siblings, or of grandparents; war; moving house; natural disasters; the death/disappearance of beloved pets; illnesses or hospitalizations of any family member; divorce; economic difficulties; house fire; parental income loss; and many other possible challenging events.

As we work with these intrusive memories, we start to see that trauma is actually an unrealized resource. It's as if our life energy gets wrapped into and trapped in the trauma tangle of memory, making this life energy unavailable to us. As we resolve the traumatic memories, and reintegrate the trapped life energy, we get to live bigger, more comfortable, and more effective lives.

REASSURANCE VERSUS RESONANCE

Reassurance is when we say that everything is going to be okay. Resonance is when we attend to what is happening with the intention of attuning (using all our capacity for sensing another person) and then ask the other person (whether an actual other person or another part of ourselves) if we are understanding them. Making the distinction between reassurance and resonance is important because the dismissal

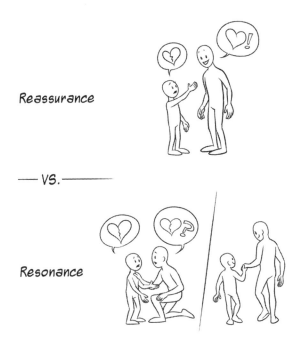

FIGURE 2.4 Reassurance Versus Resonance

inherent in reassurance is less likely to shift traumatic memories, whereas resonance is more likely to resolve difficult and intrusive memories. Reassurance glosses over the traumatic event, whereas resonance brings it back to life so that we can actually begin to heal the trauma through our full presence with it so it can be named, understood, and accompanied.

RESONANT LANGUAGE PRACTICE: REASSURANCE VERSUS RESONANCE

Begin by choosing a minor memory of trauma, such as a moment of social aloneness—it's best to begin our experiment with a smaller trauma instead of something connected with abuse. See if the past self who lived this moment is willing to connect with you in a new way, and then time travel to meet them in this difficult moment. Freeze the environment and the people in it so that the harm is stopped. You may need to cover the other people's faces and heads so that you don't have to look at their faces.

See the younger you in your imagination.

Notice how your past self responds to reassurance by choosing one or more of these statements and saying them to your past self.

Reassurance

> *It's going to be okay.*
> *You're going to be okay.*
> *Everything's going to be okay.*
> *It's not that bad.*
> *You will survive this.*

What happens with the body of your former self? You may be able to tell what is happening either by a change in your visual image of your former self or through your body if that former body is still available for you to feel.

_____

_____

_____

_____

_____

Now see what happens when your past self is met with resonance. Choose one or more of the following questions to ask your past self:

Resonance

> *Do you need acknowledgment of how hard this was?*
> *Would it be sweet if there were someone here who fully and completely understood what was happening for you?*
> *Are you frozen? Have you stopped breathing?*
> *Are you afraid nothing will ever be okay again?*
> *Are you needing understanding, protection, and advocacy?*

What does your past self answer? What do you notice in the body of your past self?

_____

_____

_____

_____

_____

What is the difference between reassurance and resonance for your past self?

_____

_____

Now we'll take a look at how a process unfolds when we are responding with resonance rather than reassurance, and we'll begin our exploration of always/never contracts, which usually have trauma at their root.

ONE-ON-ONE WORK
Old Trauma

GWEN: *I'm going to dive into the deep end of the pool. It's something that I've been working with for quite some time and I'm feeling really ready to deal with the situation. When I was six, I was molested by a great uncle. He gave me a quarter. My mother found the quarter and proceeded to accuse me of stealing it from her purse. When I explained what had happened, she accused me of lying to her. And in the house that I grew up in, if you lied, you had your mouth washed out with soap. I remember fighting her and I remember hitting my head on the sink and her just leaving me.*

SARAH: *Are you feeling the shock of this, of the entire experience, and especially the shock of being left?*

GWEN: *There have always been things between us. I do not trust her. Even up to that point, I had not trusted her completely, but that was the final break for me. I can recall the things that she would say, and I would just think, "You're lying to me." She's still alive. I have as little to do with her as possible.*

SARAH: *If we were to travel through time and space to this little one, where would we end up? What's the first moment that calls you in the memory?*

GWEN: *When I was trying to tell her how the quarter wound up in my pocket.*

SARAH: *Then we'll step through time and space and be with you right at that moment. And we'll freeze your mother. It may not be enough to lay her down and cover her with a cloth, so we may need to airlift her out of the house.*

GWEN: *Yes.*

SARAH: *We've taken her away. And as we come to you, as we come to the little Gwen . . .*

GWEN: *She's crouched in the corner.*

SARAH: *First of all, is it okay with her that we are here? Does she know who we are?*

GWEN: *Oh yes. Yes, this is what we've been preparing for.*

SARAH: *And maybe we would sit down beside her on the ground. Would that be okay with her?*

GWEN: *Yes.*

SARAH: *Then maybe we would make a first resonant language guess for her. What's the most intense thing that's going on for her right now that we need to acknowledge?*

GWEN: *Shame.*

SARAH: *Ah, we will say to her, "Little Gwen, do you need acknowledgment for the hugeness of the shame? Is there a complete nervous system body collapse in the face of one's own mother not being able to track truth?"*

GWEN: *I'm on fire. My whole body is on fire with bewilderment and terror.*

SARAH: *Is there terror that somebody we loved and depended on would tell us we were lying? Does this little one's body want to leave?*

GWEN: *Yes, take me away.*

SARAH: *We'll just bring her through time and space to this place, to this time, to this warm grown-up body that welcomes her and knows she's telling the truth and says, "Of course you're telling the truth."*

GWEN: *She needs to be believed.*

SARAH: *Yes. 100%, without question. To be believed and to matter.*

GWEN: *To be believed, to matter. It's just been so lonely.*

SARAH: *Yes, of course it's been lonely. I really want to know, how's the little one? Is she still experiencing shame?*

GWEN: *Puzzlement. Just confusion. So, so much confusion.*

SARAH: *Is it almost like her cells are confused?*

GWEN: *Yes. What holds this body together? What keeps it from flying apart into a bazillion pieces? The pieces aren't wanting to be here, but they want to experience life without this not-wanting-to-be-here.*

SARAH: *Wouldn't it be sweet to not have to hold the essential ambivalence? Does this little one need, and do you as a big one need, Acknowledgment that we're biologically made for our mothers to be our organizing principle? And that when we lose our mother's connection to reality, it's like we lose gravity?*

GWEN: *Yes.*

SARAH: *Yes . . . What's happening now with your body? What's happening with this sense of the bazillion pieces falling apart?*

GWEN: *It's quaky. It's very quaky. I feel like I want to just scream . . . What makes somebody do that? Why, why?*

SARAH: *And now we're touching the incredulity and the anger?*

GWEN: *How could a six-year-old make up something like that? There's no life experience to draw from as a six-year-old. Why, how? It feels just so completely—there's just no—I have no words . . . I don't know if there's another word beyond rage.*

SARAH: *Fury? Outrage?*

GWEN: *Outrage. Outrage is a beautiful word. Rage outside of self. Everything outside of self, because where does self exist in all this, and who is self?*

SARAH: *How does your body do with us acknowledging this?*

GWEN: *Some calmness. Some settling in the stomach. The stomach tension isn't there at all. And then in my throat, it's just tight right now. There are words trapped.*

SARAH: *Are there words like, "I will never trust you again?"*

GWEN: *Yes. I will never trust you. You get none of me. Although, at the same time I don't get any of me either. Thank you very much, mother.*

SARAH: *This is where we may be touching a contract. Is it okay to ask about one?*

GWEN: *Sure.*

SARAH: *"I, Gwen, solemnly swear to my essential self that I will shut everything down . . ." Is that the area that we're in?*

GWEN: *Shut down, shut out, rely only on myself. I will be independent of anybody. I don't need people.*

SARAH: *Is it, "I, Gwen, solemnly swear to my essential self that I will be independent of everybody and that I don't need people and that I will shut down everything to everyone, including myself"?*

GWEN: *In order to survive, no matter the cost to myself or anyone else.*

SARAH: *Essential self of Gwen, would you like to release this vow?*

GWEN: *Gwen, I release you from this vow, and I revoke this contract, and you have my blessing to go forth and thrive.*

SARAH: *How is your body doing?*

GWEN: *My throat is unstuck. My shoulders don't feel as tense. My stomach feels settled.*

SARAH: *How's the little one?*

GWEN: *The little one is just jumping up and down. It's interesting. Play has never been a priority for her. So that jumping up and down thing is pretty huge. I think we're going to go buy a purple hat. We've become somewhat consumer-oriented, which is confusing to me, but I'm going for it.*

SARAH: *Being with her jumping up and down really brings me delight.*

GWEN: *Yes. She's so delighted. Somebody listened. Somebody believes. I believe. I'm so grateful.*

SARAH: *I'm very happy, Gwen. It's a great honor to be trusted to hold something so big and important. Thank you.*

One year later, Gwen writes:

The changes I have noticed after doing this process are:
    a.   *I've released my self-blame for this incident.*
    b.   *I've reexamined my life choices without the self-blame, and I've experienced many "aha" moments.*
    c.   *All of this change led me to have a conversation with my father.*
    d.   *I've gotten clearer around boundaries when I'm interacting with my mother.*

As you can see from Gwen's process, and will see from the rest of the book, the unconscious contracts that we make are often entangled with our experiences of trauma. They are a part of what we try to do to make ourselves and others safe.

In Chapter 1, we started to discover the many different ways to use language and nonverbal connection to see if we are really understanding the other person. In the following time travel meditation for intrusive memories, we are going to practice identifying our feelings and needs, to support resonance rather than reassurance, while dialoguing with the past self.

GUIDED MEDITATION FOR
Intrusive Memories

Begin by focusing on your intrusive memory. How old are you in the memory? Where does it take place?

Let yourself experience what it feels like to exist as a breathing being . . . Where can you feel your breath? . . . Is it in your belly, rising and falling? . . . Is it in your ribs? . . . Is it a coolness inside your throat or your upper sinuses? . . . In your mouth if your nose is stuffed up? . . . Is it in your nostrils as the air moves? . . . As you bring your attention to your breath, hold your attention with affection. It may wander, as attention tends to do when it is watchful for what is happening in the environment and in the body. If it wanders, see what it's like to say, "Thank you, attention, for trying to take care of me."

Now allow yourself to fill all the cells of your being with a sense of the most patient, warm, understanding you—your resonating self-witness, your own natural ally . . . How does it feel, in this moment, to step into the aspect of yourself that witnesses your own experience with kindness and compassion? . . . Notice what your breath does, how your torso responds, whether you feel more relaxed or more expansive, and whether you are willing to take up more space . . . This is the self we want to bring with us on this time travel journey . . .

If you can't find a part of your own self to bring with you, consider bringing another person in your imagination . . . someone warm and understanding . . . someone you know . . . or someone who seems this way to you . . . even if you have never met them . . .

Now, picture your younger self . . . This could be a child self, or this could be yourself from the day before yesterday, when a difficult moment happened that is still sticking with you like glue . . . Ask your younger self if it is okay with them if you time travel back to when this memory happened. If you have your past self's consent, then step through time with your resonating self-witness. The first thing we need to do is stop time in the memory . . . These trauma memories can be on an infinite replay loop, and we need to stop the continual reinforcement of harm in order to move into the process. So, freeze time, and freeze everyone else in the memory except for your past self . . .

The next thing I invite you to do is notice your past self . . . What is happening in that self's body? . . . With the past self's posture? . . . What about your past self's facial expression? . . . and breath? . . . and voice? . . . and eyes? . . .

See how gentle and warm you can be as you approach your past self . . . acknowledging that any mistrust makes perfect sense . . . responding to any requests for distance with respect and care . . .

Noticing what is happening . . . and based on what you see . . . and feel . . . and know . . . first ask your past self if this self is frozen . . . Is there any need for acknowledgment that your breathing or heartbeat has stopped? . . .

Does your past self feel sad, angry, fearful, terrified, or lonely? . . . Is there shame? . . . Would it be sweet to know that you and your past self both matter? . . . Do you need to know that people must have needs in order to be alive? . . . And of course you would like to live in a world where other people are responsive and actually know you exist? . . . Is there a sense of collapse or immobilization? . . . Does your younger self need protection or advocacy or allyship? . . . Does your younger self need accompaniment in this moment? . . . To know that the feelings that are coming up make sense? . . . To know that the younger self makes sense in every regard and in every cell? . . .

Is there some way that you blame yourself or believe you are bad in this memory? . . . If there is something that is sticking, please make a note of it for the unconscious contract work that will need to be done . . . If the self-blame doesn't shift, pause here and do the unconscious contract work, and then come back to the memory to complete the process . . .

What happens when you ask these questions? . . . How does the younger self respond? . . . Follow the dialogue, ask more questions about what your younger self might be asking and what your younger self might be longing for, and watch what happens . . . How does your younger self change with these warm inquiries? . . . Is there new relaxation? . . .

As the body of your younger self relaxes, celebrate the changes and the relief that accompaniment brings . . . Once the body of the younger self relaxes entirely, find out if this self would enjoy coming back to the present time with you . . . and if the younger self would like this, step back together into the present moment . . .

If the answer is no, this simply means that more time is needed for resonant responses . . . Let your past self know that you will come back for them when you can . . . and make sure that the past self is safe before you leave . . .

If your past self came with you, how is it to have your past self with you? . . . Does your chest relax? . . . Do your shoulders drop? . . . Do you take a deeper breath? . . .

Now, review the intrusive memory again . . . Does it still suck you into the past? . . . Does it still have a sting? . . . Or is there more relaxation now? . . . Has it become just another memory in your life? . . . If the answer is no, it still stings, your work with this memory is not complete . . . just let yourself know you will return to this work, either with accompaniment or when you have a greater sense of understanding . . .

Return fully and completely to your sense of your own breath . . . following it in and out of the body . . . and let yourself return to the present time . . . bringing home with you whatever wisdom and peace you have gathered from this journey . . .

Welcome back! After you have settled back into the present, the next invitation is to learn the basics of this process and to try it out yourself.

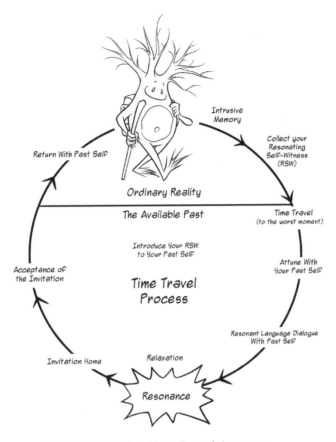

FIGURE 2.5 The Time Travel Journey

TIME TRAVEL PROCESS

1. Ask yourself, "What was the worst moment?"
2. Identify the age of your past self and where that self is.
3. Connect with your resonating self-witness or another warm and understanding witness in your imagination.
4. Ask consent from the past self you are travelling to.
5. Time travel to the past.
6. Freeze the past environment to make it safe.
7. Make any necessary introductions if the younger self doesn't know who has come to be with her. For example, "This is the grown-up part of you that understands everything about what happened and loves you completely."
8. What is happening with the past self's body?
9. The resonating self-witness makes resonant language guesses for the past self based on what is happening in the body in the memory, continuing the dialogue.

10. Check for and release any unconscious contracts.
11. Invite to return to the present time.
12. Arrive in the present time. Acknowledge, integrate, celebrate.

WORKSHEET
Time Travel Process

1. Ask yourself, "What was the worst moment?"

_____

_____

_____

_____

2. Identify age of past self and where that self is (in what room, in what house, lost in the dust of the universe, other).

   Age of past self: _____

   Where you are: _____

3. Find your resonating self-witness. (If you don't have a sense of being able to find this part of yourself, choose to bring a loving witness with you in your imagination.)

4. Ask consent from the past self you are travelling to: "Past self, are you willing for us to come to be with you in this difficult time?"

   Yes _____ (Go ahead with the travel.)

   No _____ (Time for resonant language reflection and connection with the past self—if this feels difficult, then support from outside the self might be needed.)

5. Time travel to the past. (Imagine yourself, in the clothes you are wearing now, stepping into the past environment. See yourself there, in that place.)

_____

_____

_____

_____

6. Freeze the environment to make it safe. If something is hurting the past self, make the harm stop.

   _____

   _____

7. Once everything is safe, make sure the past self and the witness know each other. If the past self is bewildered, make introductions. ("Past Self, this is your grown-up (or present-day) self, come back to be with you because this is a moment when no one should be alone.")

   _____

   _____

8. What is happening with the past self's body?
   Sensations: _____
   Posture: _____
   Facial expression: _____

9. The resonating self-witness makes resonant language guesses for the past self. (Shift between resonating self-witness and younger self in dialogue, tracking the younger self's changing body sensations until the body is calm.)
   "Younger self, are you feeling _____ ?"
   "Are you longing for _____ ?"

10. Check for and release any unconscious contracts. Is there an "always," as in "I will always . . ." Or a "never," as in "I will never . . ." (If you have the sense that you created behavioral patterns or avoidances based on this moment, or that you "learned a lesson" here or made an agreement with yourself, pause here and do the Unconscious Contract Release Process from Chapter 1.)

11. The resonating self-witness invites the past self to come to present time or another safe place. "Younger self, you have already survived this part of your life. You don't have to keep living it over and over again. Would you like to come to present time with me?" (If there is any reluctance to come to the present, it may be necessary to bring the people you love who might have been in danger from the past into the future, too, or to find out if the past self would prefer to go to a different safe place.

   _____

   _____

_____

_____

12. Arrival in present time. Acknowledge, integrate, celebrate. (Notice your body
    sensations, especially any energy, relaxation, or movement in your chest.)

_____

_____

_____

When human beings have a difficult time and are too alone, it is the nature of our brains to try to prevent this from ever happening again. So, we encode a behavioral agreement, a patterned behavioral response, as a kind of program to keep the difficult moments of danger, loss, shame, or vulnerability away. These agreements, or unconscious contracts, are the sea serpents we talked about, swimming in the sea of unconsciousness, triggered whenever we touch on anything connected with the difficulty. Rather than being an intrusive memory, they are more of an intrusive behavior pattern that can control us and prevent us from being our true emergent self. When the words *never* and *always* emerge in contracts, we can look for the seeds of trauma and explore whether time travel would be helpful in the release, as we experienced in Gwen's process.

As we consciously name these behavioral patterns in all their specificity and describe them in a contract form, we open to all we are, in this moment. The nebulous state of compulsions, prohibitions, and patterns that we believe define us starts to shift into a new way of seeing ourselves as whole people who have choice. From this place, we can find out whether our patterns are serving us, decide whether the price we are paying for them is too high, and then see whether we might like to release them.

Common contracts with "never" and "always" in them:

> *I will never forget . . .*
> *I will never remember . . .*
> *I will never forgive myself . . .*
> *I will never be like my mother/father . . .*
> *I will never relax and think I'm safe . . .*
> *I will never let myself play . . .*

I will never be on time . . .
I will always remember . . .
I will always turn away from myself . . .
I will always put others ahead of myself . . .
I will always be a good girl/boy/child . . .
I will always be vigilant . . .
I will always be working . . .
I will always be late . . .

In order to . . .

. . . preserve the memory,
. . . honor my mother/father/brother/sister/God,
. . . love my mother/father/brother/sister,
. . . survive,
. . . be safe,
. . . keep everyone safe,
. . . keep living,
. . . preserve my sanity,
. . . not be crazy,
. . . save myself from being harmed/ridiculed/shamed,
. . . be my own person and preserve my autonomy,
. . . have a place in my family,

no matter the cost to myself.

JOURNALING PROMPT FOR
Noticing Your "Always" and "Never"

One of the easiest ways to discover our "always" and "never" contracts is to journal or voice record a list. Write or say the words, "I will always . . ." and "I will never . . ." and see what comes. Try repeating these words, verbally or in writing, not trying to complete the contracts, but just to see what your landscape of prohibitions and compulsions is. If you come up with responses that seem connected to addiction, make special note of them so that you can return to them during the chapter on addiction. After you have a list, star the responses that seem to be the most charged (or upsetting) for work with the contract template.

I will always:

_____

_____

_____

_____

_____

_____

I will never:

_____

_____

_____

_____

_____

_____

Now that you have your list, bring the most emotionally charged items into the contract form, and discover what your body says about what the deep longings are that take you into the "always" and the "never." If a memory of a particular age or time arises for you in the discovery, pause to do your time travel connection with this younger self before you complete the contract process.

Always/Never Contract Template

1. I, _____, *solemnly swear to my essential*
    self (or mother, father, sibling, God, universe, etc.) that I will always/never

    _____

    _____

    in order to _____ ,
    no matter the cost to myself and those I love.

2. What is the good, historical, lived reason for this contract? When did you
    first make this contract? How does it make sense within the larger context of
    your life?

    _____

    _____

_____

_____

_____

3. *Essential self (or mother, father, sibling, God, universe, etc.), did you hear this vow?*

   Yes _____

   No _____

4. *Essential self (or mother, father, sibling, God, universe, etc.), do you want this vow to be kept?*

   Yes _____

   No _____

   (If the answer is "Yes, the vow should stay, no matter the cost," then it's time to use the Time Travel Process to go to the moment in your life in which this unconscious contract makes sense.)

5. The release: *I release you from this vow, and I revoke this contract.*

6. The blessing: *And I give you my blessing to:*

_____

CARRYING OUR PARENTS' VOWS

It is possible that you have a sense of what the contract is but are still struggling to release it. If this is true for you, see if you have made the contract to one of your parents or to your family line. If that feels true to you, the following worksheet may be supportive in your thinking about the traumas and difficult moments in your parents' or ancestors' lives, when they themselves were too alone. For example, one reader discovered that the root of her contract not to matter came from a tragedy in her mother's life:

> "I don't matter," Sylvia said, turning her head away from me.
> "How long have you not mattered?" I asked her.
> "Forever." She answered.
> "Did you matter when you were two?"
> "Oh, yes!" she said.

"How about when you were four?"
"No," she said.
"What happened when you were three?"
"My mother's mother died," she said.

Our ability to like ourselves can be shaped by difficult events that happened to the people we love, in addition to what happened to us. Sylvia's story may not seem like enough of an event to change the way she feels about herself, but when our parents lose their own parents, it can be like the bottom drops out of their world. These parents may no longer be able to enjoy their children, engage with them, or participate in daily life, and this present neglect can be a trauma for the child. When parental disappearance happens to children, it often impacts the child's ability to like themselves and to believe that they matter. Children don't have the brain capacity to see the big picture, so they make sense of these difficult moments by believing something is wrong with them. Events that happened before we were born, or even the difficult or lonely things that our grandparents lived through, can impact our lives and shape the contracts we carry.

If your "always" or "never" contracts don't make sense to you based on the events that happened in your life, consider whether you are making these contracts to honor what happened in your parents' lives. Below is a worksheet to help us explore how we may carry these intergenerational contracts.

WORKSHEETS
Our Parents' Lives

Circle and rank the events that happened to each of your parents in their lives:

Mother or Primary Parent (the one who took the most care of you)

Event	Your parent's age when this happened to your parent	Your age when this happened to your parent
Difficult birth		
Mother's postnatal depression		
Depression or mental illness of parents or siblings		

Death of parent		
Death of siblings, including miscarriages and abortions		
Lost love		
Hate crime		
Divorce/abandonment/infidelity		
Parent's military service		
Parent's PTSD		
Family separation		
Parent's career change		
Marriage to a previous spouse before the partnership that led to your birth		
Education changes		
Major injury, car accidents		
Death of a child, including abortions and miscarriages		
Migration		
Terminal or major illness in family		
Addiction		
Physical, sexual, verbal abuse		
Moving house		
Military service		
Famine/hunger/The Great Depression (1929-1939)		
Natural disaster		
Family bankruptcy/economic changes		
Personal bankruptcy/economic changes		
_____ _____		

Father or Secondary Parent (the one who interfaced most with the outer world)

Event	Your parent's age when this happened to your parent	Your age when this happened to your parent
Difficult birth		
Mother's postnatal depression		
Depression or mental illness of parents or siblings		
Death of parent		
Death of siblings, including miscarriages and abortions		
Lost love		
Hate crime		
Divorce/abandonment/infidelity		
Parent's military service		
Parent's PTSD		
Family separation		
Parent's career change		
Marriage to a previous spouse before the partnership that led to your birth		
Education changes		
Major injury, car accidents		
Death of a child, including abortions and miscarriages		
Migration		
Terminal or major illness in family		
Addiction		
Physical, sexual, verbal abuse		
Moving house		
Military service		

Famine/hunger/The Great Depression (1929-1939)		
Natural disaster		
Family bankruptcy/economic changes		
Personal bankruptcy/economic changes		
_____ _____		

TIME TRAVEL INTO OUR PARENTS' LIVES

The Time Travel Process that we do to provide ourselves with accompaniment when we've lived through difficult events can also be done for the parents we carry within us. We can tell we need to do this if we have the sense that we are carrying a frozen seed of trauma from one or both of our parents' lives.

The process is the same as the one we do for ourselves, except that we time travel to our parent's younger self at the worst moment of their trauma, and then create a resonant dialogue to discover what needs to be named that we or they have never given words to before. We can do this work effectively because, more than anyone else, we carry representations of our mothers and fathers within us. As magical as this sounds, neuroscience has shown it be so. Remember the words of the Canadian epigeneticist Moshe Szyf, "Our mother is in every cell of our prefrontal cortex."

In the next chapter, we are going to explore the difference between self-care through doing and self-care through being. We will consider self-sabotage and the ways in which we are meeting deeper needs than we ever imagined by doing things that might not be good for us.

CHAPTER 3

From Self-Sabotage to Self-Care in Everyday Life

How do I take care of myself?

Since there is confusion for many of us about the chasm between our intentions for self-care and the realities of our self-sabotaging actions (for example, we intend to exercise, but we stay on the couch watching videos instead), it can be essential to explore the role of our unconscious contracts in keeping us from carrying out our best intentions.

SELF-SABOTAGE: THE INSTRUMENTAL BRAIN VERSUS THE RELATIONAL BRAIN

All vertebrate brains have two hemispheres, two sides of the brain that specialize in different things to help us live more easily. The hemispheres are different in the shape and size of their neurons (brain cells), their main neurotransmitters (brain chemistry), in what they do for us,[1] and in their neural connectivity.[2] For example, our left hemisphere neurons grow more like orchards, and our right hemisphere neurons grow a little more like jungle vines.

Throughout the animal kingdom, the left side of the brain tends to focus on details and strategies, whereas the right side of the brain tends to see the big picture. Both hemispheres are always involved in supporting almost everything we do, but most of us have a tendency to see the world mainly through the lens of detail—either planning what we should do (our instrumental, or largely left-hemisphere, brain)—or through the lens of the global—feeling into how we can be with what is happening and what the big picture is (our relational, or largely right-hemisphere, brain).

The instrumental brain is not very good at integrating new information. Its best strategy for understanding difficult new information is blame. For example, we ask our partner to do something, they aren't able to, and instead of both of us becoming curious about why it's hard to take action, we both become irritated, the partner accuses us of nagging, and we accuse our partner of not caring. Being aware of unconscious contracts lets us become curious about our own and others' incapacity instead of just responding with irritation.

Additionally, the instrumental brain's inability to integrate feedback (information about the results of our actions) means that it just keeps trying the same old thing, like repeatedly making New Year's resolutions to go to the gym or lose weight instead of asking why what we are asking of ourselves is not doable. This signifies how important it is to awaken and bring our curious, relational, unconscious-contract-aware relational brains to bear on our difficulties. When the body sensations are within our awareness and are being integrated, then our relational, contextual brains have an easier time sorting things out.

One of the best ways to tell whether we are in our instrumental brain or our relational brain is by noticing whether we can feel any body sensations inside the torso—the heartbeat, sensations in the lungs, in the intestines. The information from these areas in particular comes up into the right side of the brain and, when we can feel it, lets us know that our relationality is available.

RESONANT LANGUAGE PRACTICE
Body Sensations

Take a moment to review the following chart and focus on the area 2-inches deep inside your belly, behind your belly button. Your shoulders, your neck, or your aching feet may want to be heard instead of the inside of your belly, so give a nod to all the other body sensations calling you, but focus on what is happening deep within you. This deep place in our bellies is a rich source of information about how our bodies are doing in the world. Bring to mind a difficult event that is still bothering you and circle the words that your belly says "yes" to.

When the body doesn't feel good:		
• Tender	• Tense	• Queasy
• Sensitive	• Tight	• Burning
• Bruised	• Constricted	• Knotted
• Throbbing	• Clenched	• Hot
• Pounding	• Sore	• Full
• Achy	• Nauseous	• Sweaty

When the body can't settle:

- Shaky
- Breathless
- Trembly
- Fluttery
- Shivery
- Wobbly
- Spacey
- Bubbly
- Dizzy

When energy feels wrong:

- Prickly
- Electric
- Tingling
- Nervy
- Twitchy
- Radiating
- Referring
- Buzzy
- Itchy

When the body is shut down:

- Wooden
- Congested
- Dull
- Dense
- Frozen
- Icy
- Disconnected
- Thick
- Empty
- Drained
- Blocked
- Contracted
- Heavy
- Suffocated
- Cold
- Numb
- Closed
- Dark
- Hollow

When the body feels good:

- Calm
- Energized
- Smooth
- Relaxed
- Streaming
- Flowing
- Fluid
- Warm
- Floating
- Cool
- Open
- Airy
- Light
- Spacious
- Releasing
- Expanded
- Expansive
- Radiant

Congratulations! If you were able to circle even one sensation in relation to your belly, you have invited your relational brain to awaken. When we haven't been held with warmth and resonance, awakening the awareness of body sensations can be tricky, because body sensations come with emotions, and we may not yet have the neural networks we need to hold the emotions. This is another reason that we rely very strongly on our instrumental brain to make it through with strategies and to-do lists. And instead of awakening our relationality (and the uncontrollable body and emotions) and turning toward ourselves with an offer of accompaniment, we tell ourselves what to do. This is safe in certain ways, but comes with the high price of sucking the life energy out of our lives.

Here is an invitation to begin to think about how you respond to difficulties. Do you "do" self-care, or "are" you in the spirit of self-care?

QUESTIONNAIRE
Doing Self-Care Versus Being Self-Care

Circle the letter of the response that is most often true for you.

1. You are getting ready to go to a party where you don't know anyone but the host. This touches on your social anxiety. You:
   a. beat yourself up for being anxious and force yourself to go.
   b. call and say you are sick and can't come.
   c. arrive very late, despite your intention to be on time.
   d. sit yourself down and acknowledge that yes, it is hard, and that you would love an automatic exit ticket that would whisk you home as soon as things got hard, with no social cost to you, and be with yourself until the anxiety eases a little with the accompaniment.

2. You have to finish a difficult work project under a deadline. You:
   a. tell yourself how stupid you are not to have completed more of the project earlier, and just keep working without eating or moving.
   b. quit your job.
   c. turn in the project late, or incomplete, and blame everyone else for the project's shortcomings.
   d. say to yourself, "Of course you are overwhelmed and it's hard to breathe. Would you like acknowledgment of the pressure?" and then continue the self-accompaniment until your heartbeat eases and you can make the best possible plan to proceed.

3. Your friend says or does something that hurts enough that you can't stop thinking about it. You:
   a. tell yourself not to be so sensitive and never say a word.
   b. stop communicating with your friend and avoid them as much as possible.
   c. accuse them of never having cared for you and shame them with your words.

d.   guess for yourself, "Would you like to live in a world where your needs mattered and where you could be sure that your comfort was important enough that you would speak up even when it was difficult?" and stay with yourself until you are ready to ask for a conversation that would feel good to you.

4. You have received news that your roof unexpectedly needs to be replaced, at a cost greater than you can easily pay. You:

a.   tell yourself that you are a fool to earn so little and that you are worthless, and you put it on your high-interest credit card, along with everything else that you can't afford.

b.   put off the roof repairs and put a bucket under the leak.

c.   start legal proceedings against the previous house owner or roof contractor in a spirit of bitter contempt.

d.   say to yourself, "Ouch," mourn the consequences of our atomized and unequal world, and stay with yourself until you have a good feeling about what to do next.

5. You notice a worrisome lump or other medical problem. You:

a.   tell yourself that you are too sensitive, criticize yourself for all your bad habits, worry about the condition every day, and never take action.

b.   immediately dismiss it from your mind whenever it comes to your attention.

c.   take yourself to the doctor, blame your past doctors for their lack of adequate care, and force yourself to do everything this doctor says, even if it feels wrong.

d.   say to yourself, "Of course you are afraid. Of course you wish it would go away. Of course you don't want to tell anyone. Do you long for perfect health? Do you need any acknowledgment that sometimes in the past, doctors have been dismissive or contemptuous? Or that health problems have been really scary, and you have been alone with them? Do you need accompaniment?" and then you stay with yourself until you are very calm and can make the best possible decision about what to do.

SCORING: For each A, B, and C, give yourself 5 points, for each D, give yourself 20 points. Self-accompaniment and being with oneself under stressful conditions is very rare, so if you have a score of 40 or greater, you have probably integrated others' care as emotional accompaniment for yourself (how to "be" caring toward yourself rather than "doing" self-care). You will enjoy this book for making that journey transparent. If your score is lower than 40, or you didn't score yourself because you dislike scoring, you may enjoy this book for the benefits it can bring to your body, brain, immune system, and overall sense of well-being.

If you are surprised that the D choices are even options, you are looking at the world through the instrumental brain's lens. Take a deep breath, let your eyes and your body soften a bit, see if you can feel the area deep in your belly, then read the D choices again to see if they make a little more sense. Most of us don't have a natural voice inside that turns to us and says, "Of course, Sarah. Of course you're anxious. Of course you need to know you make sense." When we don't have this voice, which we call the resonating self-witness, then we try to use our instrumental brain, which is often our critical inner voice, to take care of us.

JOURNALING PROMPT FOR
Noticing Your Instrumental Brain

Think for a moment about something you really want yourself to do, something you often return to: going back to school, telling your partner "no," buying or selling a house, getting a better job, finishing a project, pursuing a dream. First, allow yourself to become inspired by this recurring dream and write about it for several lines.

_____

_____

_____

_____

_____

Now, reread your words, allowing yourself to notice the sensations in your belly, your chest, your throat, and your face. Can you find any? If not, return to the table of words for body sensations and see if any apply.

_____

_____

_____

_____

_____

Now return to your dream. Spend 5 minutes just writing what your feelings and needs are in relation to the dream.

_____

_____

_____

_____

_____

And now, rereading your dream, what are your body sensations? Have they changed? Softened? Intensified? How do you like bringing brain integration to your strategies for yourself? (It can be a lovely experience, or it can awaken mourning that we haven't historically had the neurons to hold. If you are over-taken by mourning, see if you can let this book be with you in your mourning, saying to you, "Of course there is sadness here. You make sense.")

_____

_____

_____

_____

_____

GUIDED MEDITATION
Unhooking from the Instrumental Brain

Before beginning, bring to mind something that worries you, whatever you've been thinking about most often in the last 1 to 3 days.

Now, notice yourself as a breathing being . . . Where do you feel the move-ment of your breath? . . . Can you feel it in your nose, as a coolness in your upper sinuses, inside your mouth or your throat? . . . Can you feel it in the movement of your ribs? . . . Tap into your newly awakened awareness of the area deep inside your belly. Let your breath touch this area lightly.

Bring your awareness to your worry . . . Notice with gentleness what happens in your body as you bring your worry to mind . . . Do you stop breathing? . . . What happens to your ribs? . . . Do you tense up? . . . Does the inner consistency of your belly change? . . .

Whatever you find, tell yourself, "Of course your body is responding in this way," . . . and let the sensation of breathing touch your worry with warmth and acknowledgment . . . Name whatever your response has been over the past days . . . "Of course you've been grumpy . . . do you love it when things flow?" . . . "Of course you've been crying . . . would it be sweet to know that other people would be overwhelmed with this situation, too?" . . . "Of course you have felt lonely . . . this is a situation where accompaniment would be very helpful . . ."

Bring your attention back to your worry . . . how is your body now? . . . Start with your belly . . . What do you notice there? . . . Whatever you find, bring the warmth of your attention to it . . . Ask your belly, "Do you need acknowledgment that where there is worry, there is alarm? . . . And where there is alarm, the blood flow changes, and leaves the belly? . . . Belly, would it be sweet if someone else understood that bellies can't work well without a good flow of blood?" . . . Notice any changes . . . Now bring your attention up to your chest . . . How do your chest . . . your lungs . . . and your heart respond to your worry? . . . Whatever you find, let your breath bring it warmth . . .

See if you can hold the worry and the sensation of your breath and your own warmth for your attention together . . . How is it for you to both worry and feel kindness for yourself at the same time? . . . What happens with your overall sense of self? . . .

Now, bring your attention back to the live sensation of your breath . . . I will be silent for a moment, so that you can practice having warmth for your attention, wherever it goes . . .

And now, notice again where your attention has gone . . . Whatever it is doing, it is trying to take care of you as best it can . . . Make a small bow of gratitude to your attention . . . And bring your attention back to present time, back to reading this book, or back to your life . . . Bringing with you whatever learning or warmth has arisen for you, to use as you live your ordinary life.

Let's bring the warmth that you are awakening around to a daily applicability. Researchers use the word *self-management* to describe the way we use the instrumental brain for self-care. On the other hand, *self-regulation* is when we take care of ourselves with the help of our relational brain. Here is a questionnaire to help you discover what you do most often, instead of self-warmth.

QUESTIONNAIRE:
Your Own Self-Management Habits

Circle your favorite types of self-management.

Dismissal	*Nothing really happened to me.* *I just won't think about it.*
Shame	*I'm too sensitive.* *There's something wrong with me.*
Comparison	*Others have had it much worse than me.* *I have nothing to complain about.* *I have never gone hungry.* *I was never locked in a closet.* *Everyone else has this figured out.*
Proving ourselves wrong	*I should be healed by now—I'm 50 years old!*
Imagining death as a problem-solving strategy	*I wish I were dead.* *I shouldn't be here.*
Verbal self-abuse	*What kind of an idiot am I?* *I'm an asshole.* *I'm so stupid.*
Rehearsing strategies and conversations that will never happen	*And then I'll say . . .*
Merciless forward movement	*I will do this, no matter the cost to myself.*
Blaming others	*This all happened because they . . .*
Avoidance, withholding	*I just won't talk to them anymore.* *I won't share my joy.* *I won't start anything.* *I won't finish anything.* *I won't try anything.*
Not participating	*I will never be on time.* *I won't believe in my own contribution.* *I won't give it my all.* *I will withhold my life energy.* *I won't fully incarnate.*

There are attempts at self-care in all of these. And we can use our unconscious contract tools to find the roots of love in our self-management.

Common contracts of self-management that result in self-sabotage:

I will dismiss myself . . .

I will shame myself . . .

I will compare myself with others . . .

I will explain to myself how I am wrong . . .

I will imagine death as a solution . . .

I will call myself names . . .

I will endlessly rehearse conversations that will never happen . . .

I will drive myself without mercy . . .

I will blame others for my misfortune . . .

I won't start anything . . .

I won't finish anything . . .

I won't try anything . . .

I won't really participate . . .

I will never be on time . . .

I won't believe in my own contribution . . .

I won't give it my all . . .

I will withhold my life energy . . .

I won't fully incarnate . . .

In order to . . .

. . . keep hope away so that I'm not disappointed.

. . . keep others from shaming me more.

. . . be safe.

. . . understand how to live in this world.

. . . let my mother be right about me.

. . . belong to my family.

. . . not leave my father behind.

. . . make my father proud of me.

. . . keep the family alive.

CONTRACT EXAMPLES FOR SELF-MANAGEMENT

I, [*your name here*], solemnly swear:

that I will	in order to
take care of myself all by myself	stop people from finding me burdensome and leaving me
never let anyone see me cry/never cry again	protect myself from excruciating aloneness and despair
not exist	save my mother from burden and from death
not have feelings or needs	make sure that my siblings do not starve emotionally
never stop trying to make myself heard	honor my mother for never having been heard

These are just some possibilities; there are many others, and you will find your own.

In the following process, you will see how the strategy of self-blame often disguises great mourning and keeps us imprisoned.

ONE-ON-ONE WORK
Working With Fear of Death

SARAH: *So, Sadie, as we've been touching on these vows about the self, what are you sensing into here?*

SADIE: *It terrifies me that my family may disintegrate, that I won't have family once my father dies, that people will just lose contact with each other.*

SARAH: *How do you blame yourself?*

SADIE: *I blame myself for leaving my family. I feel that because I moved, I have not been able to be a positive force in my family members' lives in the way that I would like to have been. But I moved away because I didn't want to be around them.*

SARAH: *I just want to catch that: by leaving, you probably saved your own emotional life.*

SADIE: *Yes.*

SARAH: *Is there a contract? "I, Sadie, solemnly swear to you, my essential self, that I will hold myself responsible for the disintegration of my family, by blaming myself for moving away, in order to . . ."*

SADIE: *"In order to show them that I care and to recommit myself in order to make amends for having left." Does that make sense?*

SARAH: *It totally makes sense. Let me say it back to you and you can see how it sounds. "I, Sadie, solemnly swear to you, my essential self, that I will hold myself responsible for the disintegration of my family in order to make amends for having left."*

SADIE: *Yes. To hold onto some kind of hope. So it would be, "I, Sadie, solemnly swear to my essential self . . . that I will hold myself responsible for the disintegration of my family . . . in order to . . ." Ugh, I feel nauseous. "In order to have some hope that we can heal . . . no matter the cost of myself."*

SARAH: *So, Sadie's essential self. Did you hear the vow that Sadie made?*

SADIE: *Yes. I'm connecting with the ridiculousness of this vow right now, but I'm also connecting with the beauty of loving my family and wanting to hold them together. And I'm seeing how this strategy is skewed . . .*

SARAH: *The next question is, "Sadie's essential self, is this a good vow for Sadie?"*

SADIE: *No, it's not.*

SARAH: *Please tell her, "Sadie, I release you from this vow."*

SADIE: *"I release you from this vow." I don't know what the hell that means.*

SARAH: *It means you no longer have to hold yourself responsible for the disintegration of your family.*

SADIE: *Whew. Boy, I'm dizzy at that thought. Yes. I'm having a whole-body response. It's very interesting. I'm quite dizzy, with a pit just below my solar plexus. So, I'm no longer responsible for holding this family together.*

SARAH: *Now come back to regular Sadie, just leave the essential self for now. How is this body doing?*

SADIE: *A little less nausea, but still a sense of being punched in the gut, kind of strong.*

SARAH: *Yes. Is there a shock that needs to be acknowledged about how hard this has been on you?*

SADIE: *I think so, yes.*

SARAH: *Yes. And what happens with the sense of being punched? What does it do?*

SADIE: *It's moving outward a little bit, like it's not so concentrated. It's spreading out a little bit. There's a little bit of warmth in there.*

SARAH: *Is there a need for acknowledgment of the enormous love that you have for this family?*

SADIE: *Yes. The sensations are a little lighter. There's a bit more of a sense of tin-gly energy, gurgling, like water gurgling. A little bit more sparkly. It's saying, "I feel alive!" It's really nice. I don't have any other big insights, but there is an aliveness there.*

SARAH: *Wonderful. And Sadie, is there anything else that you'd like to say?*

SADIE: *Just that I just had a really nice breath. Oh, a very good breath that went deep down and felt really good.*

SARAH: *Oh, that's wonderful. I'm so glad.*

One year later, Sadie writes:

In terms of my work with the feeling of self-blame, I am still working with self-compassion practices, developing a kind voice toward myself. That's a lifelong journey, as we know! I am also doing some family systems healing in my immedi-ate family with my daughter so that patterns of self-blame and subsequent care-taking of others don't continue. I hope this work will extend to my ex-partner, so that healing in this chosen family of mine can happen in a bigger way.

I have considered approaching my brother with an invitation to do some reparative work. I don't know if he's up for it.

I continue to show up for my 95-year-old father with as much love as I can, which is quite easy now, after so many years of wanting to get as far away from him as I could. I continue to show immense gratitude to both my brothers, who, alternately, have been caring for and housing my father since my mother's death several years ago. This is all good work in the right direction.

JOURNALING PROMPT FOR
Finding Your Self-Sabotage Contract

Take a moment to think about promises you are unable to keep about things you will or will not do. (If your promises involve eating, drinking alcohol, taking drugs, or addictive behaviors like gambling, please note them but don't work with them in this chapter. We will be working with addictions in Chapter 11.) For this chapter, work instead with habits you would like to change, like being late, not exercising, never starting the book you would like to write, or putting every-one else's needs first.

What are three promises I have made to myself (or I wish I could make to myself) that I have been unable to keep?

_____

_____

_____

_____

What do I do instead of keeping my promises to myself?

_____

_____

_____

_____

And how do I treat myself when I'm unable to keep my promises to myself?

_____

_____

_____

_____

Before we go to work pulling together your self-sabotage contract, we're going to detour a bit so that you can learn how to give yourself a really good blessing at the end of your release from self-sabotage. Hold on to your discoveries, and we will circle back around to bring it all together in your contract work.

UNCONSCIOUS CONTRACT WORKSHEET
Working With the Blessing

As mentioned earlier, the blessing is an essential part of the contract. It is important that the blessing respond directly to the original contract. Sometimes people create a blessing that has nothing to do with the contract.

For example, if the contract is: *I, Sarah's tummy, solemnly swear to you, my essential self, that I will always be tight in order never to be taken by surprise by a punch again, no matter the cost to us.*

An incongruent blessing would be: *Tummy, I release you from this vow and I revoke this contract, and I give you my blessing to live well.*

That's a warm blessing, but it hasn't got much to do with the original contract. It may even be a round-about way for me, Sarah, not to actually release the
contract. In fact, even though the contract feels true, with that release my belly
stays tight.

What happens if the blessing is more congruent, more thorough, and more
generous? Let's find out.

A congruent blessing would be: *Tummy, I release you from this vow and I
revoke this contract, and I give you my blessing to understand that Sarah has
grown up and is no longer at the mercy of kids bigger than herself on the play-
ground. I give you my blessing to soften and expand and to know that Sarah lives
in a world that is usually safe and that you can rely on her core strength and her
flow instead of trying to create a suit of armor to protect her. I give you my blessing to let go of the past, to let go of the cellular memory that doesn't serve you,
and to see what it is like to move from your grounded, open center.*

With this blessing, my stomach starts to gurgle—energy is moving, and I
have provided my stomach muscles with a new, alternative way to live instead of
leaving myself in still-protected bewilderment.

Use this worksheet to practice noncongruent and congruent, generous,
blessing responses to imaginary contracts, and make sure you are offering a new
way to live that will take the place of the past contract.

Contract: *I solemnly swear that I will not complete projects that are important to
me in order to keep myself safe from ridicule and humiliation, no matter the cost
to myself.*

Incongruent blessing:

_____

_____

_____

_____

Congruent blessing:

_____

_____

_____

_____

Contract: *I solemnly swear that I will not tell the truth during conflicts in order to
survive, no matter the cost to myself.*

Incongruent blessing:

_____

_____

_____

_____

Congruent blessing:

_____

_____

_____

_____

Contract: *I solemnly swear that I will not let myself understand what is happening when people get angry in order to be nonthreatening, no matter the cost to myself.*

Incongruent blessing:

_____

_____

_____

_____

Congruent blessing:

_____

_____

_____

_____

Now that you have had some practice with the blessing, bring your attention to one of your own self-sabotaging contracts. If nothing is coming to mind, you can review the list of possible contracts included earlier in the chapter and see if any of them are alive for you.

Self-Sabotage Contract Template

1. I, _____, *solemnly swear to my essential self (or mother, father, sibling, God, universe, etc.) that I will always/never*

    _____

    _____

    in order to _____,

    no matter the cost to myself and those I love.

2. What is the good, historical, lived reason for this contract? When did you first make this contract? How does it make sense within the larger context of your life?

    _____

    _____

    _____

    _____

    _____

3. *Essential self (or mother, father, sibling, God, universe, etc.), did you hear this vow?*
    Yes _____
    No _____

4. *Essential self (or mother, father, sibling, God, universe, etc.), do you want this vow to be kept?*
    Yes _____
    No _____
    (If the answer is "Yes, the vow should stay, no matter the cost," then it's time to use the Time Travel Process to go to the moment in your life in which this unconscious contract makes sense.)

5. The release: *I release you from this vow, and I revoke this contract.*

6. The blessing: *And I give you my blessing to:*

    _____

It is stressful to live with unconscious contracts that leave us in self-sabotaging patterns. They are part of the inheritance of difficult childhoods. Resolving them is key to creating positive, interesting environments for ourselves as adults and to creating the kinds of homes that allow us to heal from early stress and abuse. This healing is hinted at by the research of Isabelle Mansuy and her team, who found positive transformation with supportive environments.[3]

CHAPTER 4

Healing Shame by Identifying Broken Contracts

While helping friends make dinner recently, I was trying to get the ice into the ice bucket. The cubes were frozen into a mass, so I banged the bag against the table to try to free them. One of the children ran in and asked, "What happened?" "Sarah hit me," said the hostess. She was making a joke about the noise—it clearly wasn't true, as I was all the way across the room struggling with the bag of ice. "I'm trying to free the ice," I said, but I stopped banging and got an ice pick and started working to chip the pieces free, cube by cube. If I even contemplated banging the bag again, I was felled by discomfort and collapse: shame. It as if the suggestion that I would hit someone, even though it was so absurd that I knew no one would actually believe it—which was part of the joke of saying it—was such an egregious violation of an unconscious contract I had that I couldn't even begin to move freely once the possibility of violation of that contract had been suggested.

As I explored the collapse I was experiencing, I had a sense of it being preverbal, from the time when a toddler does hit out at a mom in the throes of frustration. There was a sense of receiving absolute disapproval and experiencing a shame so deep that it excavated my sense of self. In that moment, I was separated from my mother, and it was unendurable. And in order to survive the unendurable, I separated from myself and collapsed into shame. (Not a good contract. I released it.) This leads us to:

THE MAIN QUESTION FOR THIS CHAPTER

What do I do, feel, or reveal that makes me leave myself alone?

RELATIONAL NEUROSCIENCE
CONCEPT: WINDOWS OF WELCOME

To better understand the early dance of intimacy, which constructs the level of emotion that we consider acceptable, I'd like to introduce you to Beatrice Beebe and her research. She and her team have spent the last several decades making separate video recordings of the mothering person (who can be any gender, but we'll call this person the mother, for simplicity's sake) and of the baby while they relate with one another, and then playing the two videos back, side by side, microsecond by microsecond. Through this work, she discovered that babies are born with the capacity to make every possible facial expression and that whatever expressions the mother can reflect back to the baby, the baby solidifies into their vocabulary of facial expressions by the age of four months. The baby edits out whatever the mother cannot reflect back. This means the baby will only become as sad or as happy as the mother can reflect. The baby will only move into fear if the mother's face can say to the baby, with a quick, passing facial expression, that acknowledges the fear, "You make sense. Yes, of course you're afraid." If the mother's face can't have this dialogue with the baby, then the baby stops using facial expressions connected with fear (or any other emotion that the mother can't respond to).[1] Throughout our lives we continue to monitor and edit the amount of emotion we or our relational partner can easily be with. These are our windows of welcome for emotions and motivations.

Sometimes people have the sense that if they have big emotions, someone will die. For babies, a mother's dissociation, dismissal, or lack of response feels like the loss of the mother, and so babies learn to tone themselves down at any cost in order

FIGURE 4.1 Windows of Welcome for Emotion

to maintain connection with their mother. The truth is that mothers do dissociate when the baby's energy is too much for them. Mothers blank out and become nonresponsive as a result of how they themselves were met (or not met) in their joy or their sorrow and the expression of their life energy. The baby makes a nonverbal contract with themselves to not go into the emotional expression that takes the mom out of relationship with them. We will learn more about this in Chapter 13.

We carry these internalized windows of welcome forward out of childhood, protected by unconscious contracts: "I will only be this angry," "I will only be sad when I am alone," "No one can know when I'm afraid." When we humans make an emotional expression that is more intense than other important people can respond to and they turn away from us, we experience a jolt of shame (a rise in cortisol[2] and a decrease in the endogenous opioids of attachment[3]) that is like an electrochemical shock. The shame is even worse when we are misinterpreted or when people misattune with us—thinking we are angry when we are scared or sad, or thinking we are joking when we are serious.

So, to recap, an infant experiences the limits of his mothering person's emotional capacity and learns to stay within them, and then carries these limitations forward. The presence of these internalized emotional boundaries has huge implications for us in terms of the ongoing limitation of our expression of life energy.

Let's take a look at the possible flavors of these limitations and losses.

RELATIONAL NEUROSCIENCE CONCEPT: THE CIRCUITS OF EMOTION AND MOTIVATION

According to neuroscientist and emotions researcher Jaak Panksepp, our life energy, in the form of emotions and drives, runs on circuits through the body, brainstem, limbic system, and cortex—structures that are shared with all mammals.[4] His work with these circuits will inform much of the rest of this book, as it is vital to our understanding of emotions, how the brain manages emotions, what kinds of information emotions are bringing us, and what balances and calms us. Panksepp outlined seven basic circuits (the names of which he capitalized to distinguish the circuits from discussions about ordinary emotions and motivations): SEEKING, CARE, PANIC/ GRIEF, FEAR, RAGE, SEXUALITY, and PLAY. After Panksepp's death in 2017, more research was published that led me to add DISGUST to his list of circuits.

Each of our words for emotions belongs to one of these circuits, and each of our emotional facial expressions belongs to one of these circuits. And so, if we integrate Beatrice Beebe's work into this material, the limitation of facial expression, which happens in infants by the time they are four months old, results in diminished access

CARE:
love, tenderness,
warmth, resonance

PANIC/GRIEF:
anxiety, sadness, sorrow, alarm,
shame, loneliness, abandonment

FEAR:
anxiety, worry, alarm,
terror, dread, horror

RAGE:
irritation, indignation,
exasperation, anger

LUST/SEXUALITY:
desire, jealousy, sensory pleasure,
maturation, deep self-connection

SEEKING:
wanting, pursuing, excitement,
taking action, satisfaction, pride

PLAY:
amusement, happiness,
delight, joy

DISGUST:
repugnance, aversion, revulsion,
distaste, detestation and horror

FIGURE 4.2 The Circuits of Emotion and Motivation

to the life energy that flows along these circuits. If we never permit ourselves to grieve, for example, then none of the life energy and information that would flow along the PANIC/GRIEF circuit is available to us.

Above is a drawing of the different circuits, with some of the emotions inherent in each of the circuits listed to the right.

Most of the feelings involved with the circuits are self-evident—fury is part of RAGE, terror is part of FEAR—but there are some that are a little less clear. For example, horror means different things to different people. For some, horror is an excess of fear, and for others horror is a huge amount of disgust. Anxiety appears on two of the circuits, according to Panksepp. He asserted that as mammals, when we are anxious, it can either be an activation of the FEAR circuit or of the PANIC/GRIEF circuit, but that we can't tell which from how it feels. So when we feel anxious, as we'll see in Chapter 5, we can make some headway by investigating which circuit is activated.

SEEKING is our get-up-and-go circuit, and it mixes with all the other circuits to give us motivation and drive. The feelings connected with this circuit include interest, curiosity, satisfaction, pride, wanting things, and the sense of being motivated or driven.

SEXUALITY can be a purely physical desire, but since it is also the circuit that carries us from childhood to adulthood through the sexual hormones, it appears to be where our emergent self, the birthright of self that we are always in the process of becoming, comes through.

It is important to make this information about the circuits personal in order to have a real sense of their meaning. The following exercise will give you a chance to do this.

WORKSHEET
Window of Welcome Scale

First, we will take a look at the emotional limitations created by our unconscious contracts by plotting a scale of how much of each emotion and motivation we find acceptable (in other words, how much can you reveal without experiencing shame), as well as how much you feel comfortable with other people expressing. This is a first, intuitive take on your sense of this, with 10 signifying your body says yes with ease, and 1 signifying your body's no. For example, if it's really easy for you to feel warm, and care flows out of you like a fountain, circle the 10 by *Warmth*. If you feel disgust when others are warm to you or when you feel it yourself, circle the 1.

CARE

Warmth	1	2	3	4	5	6	7	8	9	10
Affection	1	2	3	4	5	6	7	8	9	10
Love	1	2	3	4	5	6	7	8	9	10

PANIC/GRIEF

Sadness	1	2	3	4	5	6	7	8	9	10
Grief	1	2	3	4	5	6	7	8	9	10
Shame	1	2	3	4	5	6	7	8	9	10
Loneliness	1	2	3	4	5	6	7	8	9	10
Anxiety	1	2	3	4	5	6	7	8	9	10

FEAR

Worry	1	2	3	4	5	6	7	8	9	10
Anxiety	1	2	3	4	5	6	7	8	9	10
Fear	1	2	3	4	5	6	7	8	9	10
Terror	1	2	3	4	5	6	7	8	9	10

RAGE

Anger	1	2	3	4	5	6	7	8	9	10
Rage	1	2	3	4	5	6	7	8	9	10

LUST/SEXUALITY

Desire	1	2	3	4	5	6	7	8	9	10
Lust	1	2	3	4	5	6	7	8	9	10
Passion	1	2	3	4	5	6	7	8	9	10
Growth and Change	1	2	3	4	5	6	7	8	9	10
Emergence	1	2	3	4	5	6	7	8	9	10
Communion	1	2	3	4	5	6	7	8	9	10
Exploration of Self	1	2	3	4	5	6	7	8	9	10
Self-expression	1	2	3	4	5	6	7	8	9	10

SEEKING

Curiosity	1	2	3	4	5	6	7	8	9	10
Drive to accomplish	1	2	3	4	5	6	7	8	9	10
Drive to succeed	1	2	3	4	5	6	7	8	9	10

PLAY

Amusement	1	2	3	4	5	6	7	8	9	10
Happiness	1	2	3	4	5	6	7	8	9	10
Delight	1	2	3	4	5	6	7	8	9	10
Joy	1	2	3	4	5	6	7	8	9	10

DISGUST

Nausea	1	2	3	4	5	6	7	8	9	10
Disgust	1	2	3	4	5	6	7	8	9	10
Revulsion	1	2	3	4	5	6	7	8	9	10

Now that you have an initial sense of your windows of welcome for different emotions, it's time to put this information into the context of your own autobiography.

JOURNALING PROMPT FOR
Finding These Circuits Within Yourself

Take a moment to record a memorable moment in your life, positive or negative. After you've written about your experience, feel into which circuits are important in your memory and see if you can identify them.

My most commonly used circuits:

My least commonly used circuits:

What are your thoughts about how the presence and absence of these circuit energies have impacted your life story?

With your new sense of the way the circuits, your autobiography, and maybe even what you have always thought of as your personality interact, let's do a deeper dive into the actual contractual limitations that you are living within. Now, as we go through the circuits in more detail with a guided meditation, look for the blocks that could indicate the existence of unconscious contracts.

GUIDED MEDITATION FOR THE
Window of Welcome Contracts

Allow yourself to notice your breathing . . . Can you feel it? . . . The movement of the air in, expanding your stomach, or expanding your ribs, or moving your shoulders? . . . Or you may feel the movement of air through your sinuses, or your throat . . . Wherever you feel it, allow yourself to notice it . . . Now let another level of attention arise so that you can notice yourself noticing . . . and, if possible, bring affection and acknowledgment to your attention . . . and to where it goes . . .

Now, let your attention notice what your feeling state is . . . If you sink into your belly, what kinds of emotions do you find there? . . . We all have many things to have feelings about, all the time . . . once we begin to pay attention, we notice that our body carries the emotional truths about all our daily experiences . . . Notice if you feel sadness or grief for any losses, for anything or anyone, or for the world . . . Notice how much PANIC/GRIEF it's endurable to feel . . . Notice how quickly you shift away from the sadness, and how quickly you begin to think about something else . . . Bring your love and tenderness to whatever happens for you with sadness . . . Notice whether your body is holding any sense of shame . . . and if you find it, pay attention to the way that shame leaves us completely alone and stripped of support . . . See if it's possible to bring a warm gathering of resonant allies to stand with you . . . allies who understand you completely, who see the larger context of your life . . . who see your best intentions . . . and see if the shame becomes more bearable . . . Notice whether there are any blocks or stories that arise . . . that stop or cramp the grief in its tracks . . . or that amplify the shame . . . If you find that the shame becomes greater when you dip into grief, take note of it because it means there is a contract here . . .

Next, bring your attention to any RAGE that you carry . . . Everyone has things they feel angry about in this world . . . It's an emotion that belongs to all of us . . . It's an emotion that is important . . . and life-protecting . . . and life-saving . . . and that everyone has a right to . . . Notice if even the mention of anger makes your thoughts change their subject or gives rise to shame . . . There may be contracts . . . or, if you can't imagine anything that would possibly make you angry, it's very likely that you carry an agreement never to be angry . . . Whatever you discover, bring warmth to yourself for all the life-saving and family-saving agreements that you have made with yourself to limit your life energy . . . and make a mental or physical note for your contract explorations . . .

How about FEAR? . . . We will often feel fear in our bellies and in our chests . . . Is it acceptable for you to feel worry? . . . Anxiety? . . . Fear? . . . Is there any quaking terror that needs to be acknowledged? . . . Is it vulnerable or shameful to be afraid? . . . Do you stop yourself from feeling in order to survive?

Our next circuit is CARE . . . How okay is it for you to feel warmth in your heart? . . . Is it permissible? . . . Does it relax you to sink into warmth? . . . Can you radiate it outward, to people . . . or to nature . . . or to beloved animals? . . . Does it feel good to be in warmth? . . . Or does mistrust or skepticism rob you of your warmth?... How about when you feel it for yourself? Does CARE feel good? Or does that invitation bring shame?...

Now we'll look at whether it feels okay to be active... to be in your SEEK-ING circuit... to be in search of things... to reach for what you want... Is there shame when you start to gain traction?... Do you need to stop yourself, or slow yourself down... Do you want to make sure never to leave anyone behind?... Or is it good to accomplish things... Does it feel sweet to feel satisfied in what you've done?... Or is it never enough?... Notice the edges of what you can easily do... Notice what feels good to you...

And how about SEXUALITY?... Is it acceptable to have sexual energy?... Do you get to tap into it?... Can it be a source of pleasure and power and engagement for you?... Or does shame shut you down at just the mention?... Is there a part of you that believes that it has to be earned with beauty or strength rather than it simply being your birthright?... Do you deny yourself access to this life energy?... How about being yourself?... Is it good to be you?... Or do you not even know who that is?... Notice the edges of where you feel okay... Notice the limitations that your contracts make...

As we turn to exploring PLAY, take a moment to consider how your body responds to the invitation to spontaneity, freedom, and joy... Does your body come alive?... Or is there a shadow of shame... or of bewilderment... or incapacity?... Does play just seem impossible?... Remember where your body stops, because this means there is a contract here...

And finally, let's take a look at DISGUST... and whether it gets to give you the information you need from it... Feel into whether you get to welcome the direction that nausea gives you... Is it possible to say thank you to your lack of desire to digest or integrate what is not yours?... Disgust is here to help you know your boundaries and limits and to make you safe... Notice if you aren't allowed to have disgust... or to say no to invasion... or if these things are off limits for you...

As we finish this guided exploration... allow yourself to find your solid, grounded self again... your core being... and let yourself breathe again,... noticing your breath... and noticing your attention noticing your breath...

As you may have noticed in the guided meditation, shame is one of the signposts of the existence of our unconscious contracts. It is also a sign of loneliness, often of the suddenness of alarmed aloneness (the shock and emotions that arise when someone important to us disappears), which we will explore more in the next chapter. In the meantime, let's look at another way shame can arise as we break contracts that we don't even know about.

SHAME WHEN CONTRACTS ARE BROKEN BY OUR HEALING

In the last month, I've had the extraordinary experience of starting to be able to tell the difference between people being angry at me and my having done something wrong. In the past, when people would get angry at me, I would think, "Oh, of course I was wrong. I shouldn't have done that. Why did I do that? Why did I say that?" Now I have started to feel less alarm when people say they are angry at me. This leaves my hippocampus more online so that it can review the days or hours or minutes before this break in connection. With this access, I can see all kinds of things that have been happening that we are both responsible for, not just me. And it feels so different, and I can see why I took the action that I did. This is revolutionary for me and just started to percolate in the last month.

Yet at the same time, I was hit with the worst series of shame spirals that I have had in years. I was keeping track of it on the calendar: it went from October 22 to November 12. It was a long run of shame, day after day, almost unendurable. It really started to lift the day that I realized that I had a contract that I was breaking by having clarity about anger: "I, Sarah, solemnly swear to my essential self that I will believe I am in the wrong when my mother is angry with me in order to be able to stay connected with my mother, no matter the cost to myself."

When I released myself from that contract, the terrible shame started to lift. I believe that part of what was happening was that my healing had begun to outstrip my contracts. This can happen for all of us. We can find ourselves healing, seeing new things, and being able to do new things, yet there can be a backlash because we have an unconscious contract still in place that's telling our nervous system we're wrong to heal.

WHEN RELEASING CONTRACTS BRINGS EXHAUSTION

The release of contracts is meant to bring us new flows of life energy. If we get very tired after breaking a contract, rather than energized, this may mean there's a clause, a condition of the contract, that has not yet been named. For example, if I became tired after the release of a contract to believe that I was wrong when my mother was angry at me, there might also be a clause—"to believe I am in the wrong *and to punish myself by leaving myself* in order to be able to stay connected with my mother . . ." If this additional information feels true, release the vow again to see if more energy flows.

Another possibility, when we become exhausted when a release is made or if a release does not seem possible, is that the contract was made to a different party than the one that was named: perhaps the contract was with the mother rather than the self ("Mother, I swear to you that I will not stop working in order to accompany you so that you are not alone") or with the family line rather than the mother. If the "in order to" clause benefits the self ("I will never stop working so that *I can belong to my family*,"), then the contract is to the essential self. If the "in order to" clause benefits others ("so that *you are not alone*"), then the contract has been made with the other person or people. Try filling in a different person (or entity) in the blank space that shows who the contract was made with to see if life energy begins to flow again.

It may also be that we are breaking a contract by even talking about our issue. For example, we may need to let go of a contract like this one: "I solemnly swear to my essential self that I will never speak about my family of origin in order to protect them and myself from scorn and in order to belong to the larger world, no matter the cost to myself."

Another possibility, when tiredness results, is that we have released a contract that has kept us in a state of suspended alarm for decades. If this is so, we can bring a deep and warm curiosity and resonance to our tiredness, saying something like, "Body, are you exhausted? Do you need acknowledgment of the burden of this contract that has kept you in hypervigilance for all of these years and that, by letting go of this contract, you suddenly can tell for the first time how exhausted you are and how exhausted you have been forever?"

The following example, from work I did with another reader, will demonstrate the ways in which the unconscious limitations we carry can lead to decades of emotional insecurity and erode our confidence.

ONE-ON-ONE WORK
Working With Shame

SARAH: *Hi Nora. Tell me a little bit about what's percolating for you as we're working with this today.*

NORA: *I feel like my own life energy was shut down really early. What's coming* up for me a lot is that in first grade, when I started school, I knew I was really excited to go to school. And the first day I came home to the farmhouse—my mom and dad weren't there, but my aunts and uncles were—and I said I wasn't going back to school. From the first day I knew something wasn't right. It was a male teacher, and before Christmas that year, he was removed from the school because he had broken a kid's nose. I had sensed something was wrong from the first day. I think it was the verbal abuse that I was scared of. And I can't remember that year. After telling my aunts that I wasn't going back to school, I don't remember anything for the rest of the year.

SARAH: *But you do remember saying I'm not going to go back?*

NORA: *Yes. And I'm still afraid of talking. I've known about this for a few years, but I've never done anything about it, and just this last year it all came up. I could never share any of this. It wasn't okay to show emotions. I'm in my eighties now, and I had a very severe mother, and it was not okay to have emotions.*

SARAH: *So then, the first starting place is the big cap. Something like, "I, Nora, solemnly swear to my essential self . . . that I will be stoic?"*

NORA: *That I will be stoic and determined, and I will not stop for emotions in order to be safe . . ."*

SARAH: *"In order to be safe." Say a little more about what kind of safety it gives you.*

NORA: *Well, I'm afraid of the backlash if I say something.*

SARAH: *When you said the word backlash, I saw a hand coming, an actual hand coming through space. Is it that kind of backlash that your little body would have received?*

NORA: *No. I'm going to be made fun of. It was humiliation and shame.*

SARAH: *So, "In order to be safe from humiliation, ridicule, and shame. No matter the cost to myself."*

NORA: *"I, Nora, solemnly swear to my essential self that I will be stoic, and I will not stop for emotions in order to stay safe from humiliation, no matter the cost to myself."*

SARAH: *How is it for your body to say this explicitly?*

NORA: *It hurts that I've been like this for so long—that I've never been able to feel joy.*

SARAH: *Can we find out if you like the vow for this little girl from 75 years ago? We'll ask, "Essential self of Nora, did you hear the vow that the little one made to you?"*

NORA: *Yes.*

SARAH: *Yes. Is it a good vow still?*

NORA: *No.*

SARAH: *Will you tell her, "I release you from this vow"?*

NORA: *"I release you from this vow, and I revoke this contract, and instead I give you my blessing to enjoy life. To have emotions. To know that most of the people that were scary in the face of emotions are not with us anymore. I breathe.*

SARAH: *Breathing is good. Tell me anything you notice, because that was our big cap on joy, and now we're going to drill down just a little bit to work with joy, just a little bit. But what's it like to have the big cap off?*

NORA: *There seemed to be a bit of release. I'm not holding myself so tight.*

SARAH: *Ah, very nice. So now, what's something that you know of that tickles you a tiny bit with the possibility of joy? What comes to mind?*

NORA: *Yes, that's a hard question.*

SARAH: *Let me give you some examples of possible things that we could hold a little bit. It could be when a child shows joy. It could be the smell of a new-born baby. It could be an animal that you see in the woods. It could be the sight of the sun on fields. It could be snow falling; it could be snow melting. Anything tickle you a little bit?*

NORA: *When you talk about the baby, like with a friend of mine who had a grand-son, we used to play peekaboo. Something like that.*

SARAH: *Oh, very sweet. So just go into the peekaboo for a little moment and see if you can give me any body sensations that will help us to uncover what this next contract might be.*

NORA: *Well, yes, the body sensations are really hard. Because I've shut them down for so long.*

SARAH: *Of course, yes. You may feel more in the face. The face may be more accessible when you think of peekaboo.*

NORA: *Kind of, yes.*

SARAH: *When I see your face thinking about it, I see a very slight lifting here, which is the unconscious lift that comes with joy.*

NORA: *Yes. I was going to say it seems to be in the eyes.*

SARAH: *Yes. A little bit of clean crinkliness.*

NORA: *Yes.*

SARAH: *So just see what it's like. Is it scary that we're even talking about it or is it okay?*

NORA: *It's okay. It's scary, but it's okay.*

SARAH: *So then my wondering is—and we'll go in a different direction if you want* to—is there a contract that *"I will hide my joy and enjoyment so that nobody sees it?"*

NORA: *Yes. I will hide myself, everything, including my enjoyment, in order to not be seen, and in case I get in trouble, and in order to keep my mother from being angry or disappointed. "I, Nora, solemnly swear to my essential self to keep myself and my joy and everything else hidden in order to not be seen so that I will not be a burden and not disappoint my mother, no matter the cost to myself."*

SARAH: *And, so then, we'll ask your essential self, "Essential self of Nora, did you hear this vow?"*

NORA: *Yes.*

SARAH: *Is this a good vow for our Nora?*

NORA: *No. "Nora, I release you from this vow, and I revoke this contract, and instead I give you my blessing to be yourself."*

One year later, Nora writes:

I am feeling that the work we did was an opening to being heard and seen; my story was witnessed by others. It gave me permission to further get in touch with feelings. The feeling of joy along with other feelings that have been shut down for so long are a bit timid about appearing. Will they be accepted and honored? So now my work is to continue to encourage and open to the feelings in the body.

RESONANT LANGUAGE PRACTICE
Fresh Metaphor

Resonant Language

Fresh Metaphor

Here is a quote from Nora's example when we were looking for the way that joy can lift a body: *"It could be when a child shows joy. It could be the smell of a newborn baby. It could be an animal that you see in the woods. It could be the sight of the sun on fields. It could be snow falling; it could be snow melting."*

How does this quote land for you? Does it let you take a concept and feel it, embody it, live into it? If it does, this is because we're using metaphor (an integrative way that we use a concept from one area of thought to help us understand another thought). By using a meta-phor to describe our thoughts, feelings, or experiences, we can awaken ourselves to new meaning and depth. In this case, we're taking pictures, which are usually visual only and not felt, and inviting them to become visceral and felt within our body. We are inviting joy to enter the metaphoric world of what we see and feel.

These invitations, which surprise the brain into making new connections, occur fairly often in communication, especially when we are trying to check whether we are understanding someone else. When our metaphors are "fresh," or new to the brain (as opposed to tired phrases like "good as gold," or "it's not rocket science"), they awaken the right hemisphere,[5] and at their best, they delight us and give us a sense of being really understood by the other person.

Take a moment to allow your sense of wonder and curiosity to be awakened in response to the words that others use when they are describing their experience. This orientation will permit resonance to flow in every conversation and will bring depth and reverberating connection to your healing sessions. You can practice this in the real world, in any conversation, just by asking your conversational partner, "Is it like . . . ?" and bringing an image or fresh connection that comes to you in response to what they are saying. You can also practice here, in response to expressions from the different circuits:

SEEKING:

Friend: *I'm so curious about what's going to happen next in my mystery novel. I almost can't stop reading it.*

Response (sample): *Is it like your attention has turned into little iron filings and the book is the magnet?*

Your response: *Is it like . . .* _____ ?

CARE:

Friend: *I have a new puppy, and I don't want to go to work anymore.*

Response (sample): *Is it like trying to get yourself to walk away from a warm sunbeam into a cold, rainy day?*

Your response: *Is it like . . .* _____ ?

PANIC/GRIEF:

Friend: *I am so worried about the planet.*

Response (sample): *Is it like your love for our home gets tattered and frayed and blackened along its edges with horror and dismay?*

Your response: *Is it like . . .* _____ ?

FEAR:

Friend: *I am terrified about being able to pay my medical bills.*

Response (sample): *Is it like trying to live with constant earthquakes of insecurity shaking you every minute?*

Your response: *Is it like . . .* _____ ?

RAGE:

Friend: *I can't believe that the hotel treated my friend with such a lack of respect!*

Response (sample): *Is it like there is an acid bath of incredulity eating your body alive from the inside out?*

Your response: *Is it like . . .* _____ ?

SEXUALITY:

Friend: *That person totally lights me up. I think about them all the time!*

Response (sample): *Is it like you are a roadside flare that never goes out?*

Your response: *Is it like . . .* _____ ?

PLAY:

Friend: *I am so happy and excited!*

Response (sample): *Is it like being a wriggly puppy on a really soft rug?*

Your response: *Is it like . . .* _____ ?

DISGUST:

Friend: *I cannot bear that man. When I look at him, I feel nauseous.*

Response (sample): *Is it like your body wants to turn inside out and run away?*

Your response: *Is it like . . .* _____ ?

The most important thing with these metaphor guesses is not that you get them right, but that you are letting your friend know that you are willing to try to step into their world with them. Most often, when we make these guesses we aren't right, and our friends will respond with something like, "No, it isn't quite like that, it's more like . . ." and when you hear this response, instead of the shame of being wrong, you can feel a flush of satisfaction and think, "Ah, my friend knows that I am receptive to their experience!"

Resonance makes our contract work easier, because it provides the reassurance of accompaniment and warmth, both of which help to thaw our hearts so that we can start to see ourselves with compassion. Knowing what kinds of contracts others have can also make our explorations easier. Here are some of the contracts that I have run across in the years of doing this work with people.

CONTRACTS THAT STOP US FROM HAVING A RESONATING SELF-WITNESS

I, [*your name here*], solemnly swear:

that I will	in order to
not take care of myself	make my mother finally come and take care of me
give myself food (drugs) instead of warmth, as this is all I have of warmth	survive
not like myself	atone for the burden I was for my mother
never hope for or expect love	prevent disappointment and heartbreak

And here are some of the contracts that limit our windows of welcome, keep us from feeling our full range of emotions, and stop us from accessing all of our life energy. We will work more with these types of contracts as we learn about the circuits of emotion and motivation.

POSSIBLE WINDOW OF WELCOME CONTRACTS

that I will	in order to
never let anyone see me cry	keep people from leaving me
not have feelings or needs	make room for the people I love to survive
not let anyone know I'm afraid	save myself from humiliation and ridicule

As we explore these vows and the riddles we find around how much emotion it's okay to display, it's helpful to ask ourselves, "What do we believe we need to keep to ourselves? Is it not okay for anyone to see us cry? What *does* it seem okay to share so that we can be accompanied?" The results of a window of welcome contract might be that when you try to share how you feel, you end up sounding like this: "I don't know. I just feel like, I don't know. I don't know. I—never mind. I'm good." When we have a vow not to share our sadness or not to express our joy and it breaks through anyway, as it always does, because we are alive, there can be a terrible shame crash that accompanies the breaking of the contract. As we work with this material over time, we'll start to develop an awareness that says, "Oh, I'm experiencing a lot of shame right now. When did it begin?" When we realize this, we can trace it back and discover the broken window of welcome contract. For example, there might have been a moment at a party where we laughed much more loudly than anyone else in the room and in that moment, we broke a window of welcome contract about how much life energy we can express, and we have started to believe that we no longer belong.

JOURNALING PROMPT FOR
Discovering Your Own Window of Welcome Contracts

Now that you have a sense of how you might be limiting your own life energy and emotional expression, what thoughts are arising? Take some moments to reflect on ways that your emotional expression has become more whole and expansive since you were a child, or ways that you have restricted your expression as you have grown older. What would you like to invite yourself to focus on?

_____

_____

Next, take the opportunity to do a little work on one of the areas in which you would enjoy experiencing more flow, spontaneity, and energy.

Window of Welcome Contract Template

1. I, _____, solemnly swear to my essential self (or mother, father, sibling, family line, God, universe, etc.) that I will not

    cry/let anyone know I'm crying
    feel sad/let anyone know I'm sad
    feel lonely/let anyone know I'm lonely
    be afraid/let anyone know I'm afraid
    be angry/let anyone know I'm angry
    be ashamed/let anyone know I'm ashamed
    be hurt/let anyone know I'm hurt
    feel disgust/let anyone know I feel disgust
    feel helpless/let anyone know I feel helpless
    feel confused/let anyone know I'm confused
    be depressed/let anyone know I'm depressed
    go into shock/let anyone know I'm in shock
    laugh too loudly
    try/let anyone know I'm trying
    want things/let anyone know I want things
    in order to_____,
    no matter the cost to myself and those I love.

2. What is the good, historical, lived reason for this contract? When did you first make this contract? How does it make sense within the larger context of your life?

    _____
    _____
    _____
    _____

3. Essential self (or mother, father, sibling, God, universe, etc.), did you hear this vow?
    Yes _____
    No _____
    If no, then repeat the words of the vow.

4. *Essential self (or mother, father, sibling, God, universe, etc.), do you want this vow to be kept?*

    Yes _____

    No _____

    If the answer is yes, the vow should stay no matter the cost, then it's time for the Time Travel Process to the moment in your life which makes this unconscious contract make sense.

5. The release: *I release you from this vow and I revoke this contract.*

6. The blessing: *And instead, I give you my blessing to . . .*

    _____

    _____

    _____

In Chapter 5, we will expand our understanding of the roots of shame, by integrating it with alarmed aloneness and anxiety.

Revoking the
Five Contracts of Anxiety

NEUROSCIENCE CONCEPT: WHAT IS ANXIETY?

More than anything, anxiety is a bodily disquiet, a sense that something is wrong, that the future is in jeopardy, and that we may have some helplessness about what is happening.

Animal and emotions researcher Jaak Panksepp, introduced in Chapter 4, differentiated the seven Circuits of Emotion and Motivation[1] (to which I added DISGUST, making eight). They run through the human brain and body and light up as we experience different states. Mostly we know what they are. If we're angry, we know we're angry. If we're happy, we know we're happy. But when we say we're experiencing anxiety, which is one of the most commonly reported mental health issues in North America and in Europe, we can't actually tell from the way our bodies feel what, specifically, is happening emotionally. Mammal bodies feel the same anxiety whether feeling afraid or experiencing alarmed aloneness,[2] the shock and emotions that arise when someone important to us disappears. Like the words *pleasant* and *unpleasant*, the word *anxiety* is not definitive enough to allow the amygdala to be able to relax. We see this in the research that shows the amygdala calming when precisely correct words for emotions are used.[3] The body is giving us an alert sign that something is wrong, but it isn't clear what is wrong. The body is saying "I am agitated, and I cannot settle. There is something that stops me from being able to rest. My system is on edge."

In his research, Panksepp discovered that if anxiety was connected with fear, when benzodiazepines were administered, the anxiety sensations would go away. If the anxiety was connected with alarmed aloneness and opioids were administered, then that anxiety would go away. But if opioids were given for fear or benzodiazepines were given for alarmed aloneness, the anxiety would continue.[4] Does this mean that we should be taking drugs if we feel anxious? No. We have a medicine that Panksepp didn't know about—resonant language.

As students of resonant language, we can have a non-medication-based relationship with what's happening in our brains and bodies. Our bodies actually do respond to the speaking of needs that are appropriate to the circuits alive within us, which means that we get to explore our Circuits of Emotion and Motivation without having to alleviate feelings with drugs. Those of us who understand the medicine of resonant language are very lucky, as we can be our own neuroscientists for our brains and bodies. We can use the medicine of words, naming feelings and asking, "How do our bodies respond to these guesses? And what does that tell us about which circuits are involved in this situation?"

Another factor that leads to anxiety is that we humans have the capacity to worry about possible negative events and outcomes in the future. This worry can make our bodies agitated and our brains buzz with an inability to focus from the stress. Human bodies really need predictable stability to thrive. This anxiety about the future can also arise from more than one circuit.

The lack of direct connection between the word *anxiety* and specific circuits of emotion means that the roots of anxiety aren't innately known and calmed, and the body doesn't get to have the relief of having delivered its message to the brain, until they are named. This leads us to:

================ THE MAIN QUESTION FOR THIS CHAPTER ================
What is at the root of my anxiety?

There are a number of questions we can ask that help us feel into very good reasons for having anxiety, and they include the questions about fear. Have we had to live with violence? Have we received or witnessed harm, intrusion, violation, abuse, or neglect? Have we had to live with financial insecurity or active addiction? All of these things will very likely, but not absolutely, point to the FEAR circuit as the circuit to which we can bring empathy and process work. It's also possible in these moments that what's actually happening is not that we're so physically afraid, but more that we have a deep sense of aloneness. And our experiences with alarmed aloneness are equally important. Do we anticipate alarmed aloneness in the future? Are we living with it now? Have we lived with it in the past?

RESONANT LANGUAGE PRACTICE
Making Needs Guesses for Our Anxiety

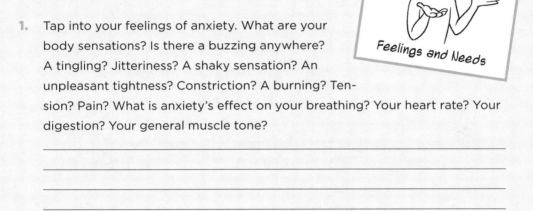

This exercise is a chance to experiment with the flavors of needs that touch your felt sense of anxiety.

1. Tap into your feelings of anxiety. What are your body sensations? Is there a buzzing anywhere? A tingling? Jitteriness? A shaky sensation? An unpleasant tightness? Constriction? A burning? Tension? Pain? What is anxiety's effect on your breathing? Your heart rate? Your digestion? Your general muscle tone?

    _____

    _____

    _____

    _____

2. Here are lists of needs that are connected largely with PANIC/GRIEF or with FEAR. Read through the lists to see which ones your body responds to. Circle the needs that seem particularly important or powerful.

PANIC/GRIEF	FEAR
Acknowledgment of alarmed aloneness	Acknowledgment of fear
Acknowledgment of shame	Acknowledgment of terror
Accompaniment	Physical safety
Presence	Protection
Love	To be safe
Comfort	To be able to see a good future
Tenderness	To be safe
To be known	Safety from emotional abuse and contempt
Shared reality	Peace
Shared care	Silence

PANIC/GRIEF	FEAR
For people, animals, and the Earth to be loved and cared for	Relaxation
Friendship	To know that loved ones are safe
Warmth	For the Earth to be solid
Emotional constancy	Predictability
Intimacy	Physical health and well-being
Acknowledgment of past loneliness	Acknowledgment of past danger

3. Which list seems more important? (It is possible that needs from both lists are equally important, in which case both circuits are involved in the anxiety.)

_____

_____

4. How does your body feel now, after connecting with these needs?

_____

_____

CONSEQUENCES OF ANXIETY

When we are anxious and no one has been with us with resonance, our adrenaline increases and the jittery feeling of anxiety can be hard to shift. We can stay anxious for decades, which creates its own imbalance. This is partly true because when stress increases and stays high for a long period of time, our balancing brain chemicals, such as adrenaline, serotonin, dopamine, and oxytocin, as well as the brain's own benzodiazepines[5] become depleted.[6] This depletion can then lead to depression, which is partly why anxiety and depression so often walk hand in hand.

OTHER ROOTS OF ANXIETY

Here are some other possible roots of anxiety:

- **Worry About the Future.** And the past, but very often people feel most anxiety about the future. We are always asking, *What can we anticipate? Does what we're anticipating make sense given what has gone before? Can we count on safety? Can we count on friendship?* It could help if we had a supreme capacity for trust. Another option is to build a constant, resonant relationship with our disquiet around being unable to actually tell what's going to happen in the future and to release any contracts we have that suggest we should know what to expect.

- **Health.** A physical sense of disquiet may arise when we wonder if our health is out of balance. When this happens and we name it ("Of course I feel anxious. I want to be healthy and well!"), even if we can't do anything about it, there's calming. Having a contract always to feel well can also give rise to anxiety, as we break this impossible contract whenever we feel ill.

- **Being Torn Between Two Authorities.** Another type of anxiety happens when we are caught between two trusted sources of truth or authority. When we're standing there at that Y in the road, the anxiety from being torn between two trusted sources may come from the following contract, "I will figure out how to integrate these two completely different ways of being within my own body. I will take these two completely different trusted sources, and be both of them at once, no matter the cost to myself."

- **Carrying Others' Anxiety.** We may carry our mother's or father's anxiety so that we belong, or so that they are not alone, or we may carry our family's anxiety with regard to some historical or family trauma. If we're a member of any social or physical group that does not hold power in our world, we experience being dismissed or marginalized or being the target of repression, attacks, or genocide. In the current political climate in much of the world, it can be life-threatening to not be part of the dominant power holder group. This fear is very tangible and something to hold with immense validation and tenderness for our vulnerability.

- **Worry About Another Person.** We may also experience not carrying someone else's anxiety but rather being anxious on behalf of someone we love. We may worry that someone we care deeply about is lonely or in danger of physical harm or death.

■   **Anxiety About Anxiety.** And then, of course, once we begin to feel anxious, it can be alarming enough to make us feel so out of balance that we then have alarm and anxiousness about the anxiety, and so anxiety escalates.

As you complete your reading of this list of possible sources of anxiety, take a moment to journal about your own personal experience of anxiety.

JOURNALING PROMPT FOR
Your Own Anxiety Story

How old were you the first time you remember feeling anxious? What were the circumstances?

_____

_____

_____

_____

Does your anxiety have the flavor of fear or loneliness?

_____

_____

_____

_____

What do you worry most about for the future?

_____

_____

_____

_____

What do you worry most about for people you love?

_____

_____

_____

_____

What do you worry most about for the planet?

_____

_____

_____

_____

What is the effect of your health on your anxiety?

_____

_____

_____

_____

How are you torn between two authorities?

_____

_____

_____

_____

Do you carry anxiety for others in your family?

_____

_____

_____

_____

Are you anxious about feeling anxious?

_____

_____

Rereading all these different roots of anxiety, I just want to spend a moment of silence being tender and warm with myself, so that I can say to myself, "Oh, Sarah, of course you would be anxious." This brings tears to my eyes. What happens if I sit with the little anxious one within me? I have a sweet sense of sitting down beside her and saying, "Yes, of course you worry." In this moment, one of the needs guesses I have for her is, "Do you need any acknowledgment of how widely we are spread out over the world?" There is a certain sweetness to reaching people, but I also want to acknowledge the alarmed aloneness in the separation from my family and closest friends. My body really loves being in the same room or the same town or the same neighborhood with those I care about. I love physical closeness. So I will guess for my inner little one, "Sarah, would you love it if you could conjure your beloved family and friends to have meals with you when you are traveling and working so that you could do what you love and be with the people you love at the same time?" Yes, I smile thinking of bringing everyone I love to my room to eat with me every day.

This kind of wondering is one of our resonant language skills—it is called an impossible dream guess.

RESONANT LANGUAGE PRACTICE
Impossible Dream Guesses

Impossible dream guesses are questions that usually begin with the words, "Would you love it if . . ." followed by a guess about something totally impossible that might be sweet for ourselves or our friend. The most important thing about these guesses is that they be completely impossible. If they weren't impossible, they would be advice, which would defeat the purpose, as it would not be resonance. For example, if I asked a busy friend, "Would you like to travel less?" instead of guessing, "Would you love it if everyone came to you?" then I would be couching some advice for her in the guise of an impossible dream guess.

And how about you? What are your impossible dream guesses for your anxious self? Reread your answers to the journaling questions on pages 94–95, and make an impossible dream guess for yourself for each of the anxieties that you listed. See if you are willing to use your own name to ask yourself the impossible dream guesses, and check to see if it feels warm to do this with yourself. How does your body respond to your impossible dream guesses?

_____

_____

_____

_____

_____

_____

_____

_____

_____

ONE POSSIBLE DIFFICULTY IN DECODING OUR ANXIETY

If our mothering figures were never acknowledged in their fear or alarmed aloneness, then they may not have been able to recognize and acknowledge our fear or our alarmed aloneness. And if we grew up without having our fear or loneliness acknowledged, we may be unable to even recognize the fear or loneliness we carry. Over the years that I've been working with emotions in these ways, I've started to recognize that there are cues about my emotions that I didn't even realize were indications of me feeling afraid or alone. I may notice that I have a dry mouth and then think, "Huh, I wonder if I'm feeling afraid?" Even now, I feel a bit startled when I think of all the times I did public speaking and felt how dry my mouth was, and how rarely I acknowledged that I was afraid.

In these moments, it's almost impossible for me to say to myself, with warmth and self-compassion, "Of course you're scared," or "Of course you feel utterly alone." If no one has ever acknowledged these things with us, then we won't be very effective at acknowledging them for ourselves. We may even have contracts against having these emotions or against noticing them, which means that our own bodies may be breaking contracts with us by even having a physical emotional response.

Some of the physical indicators of fear are: an increase in the heartbeat; blood pressure and breathing rate; dry mouth; heart palpitations; sweaty palms; and an increased startle response. Our overall skin temperature will fall and the skin temperature on our legs will rise because the body is sending the blood supply to the legs so that we can get the heck out of wherever we are. If you know you have an increased startle response, you might suspect that fear is foundational for you, and even this suspicion, in and of itself, can be startling and begin a healing process.

Some of the physical and behavioral indicators of alarmed aloneness are: heaviness in the upper back and shoulders; downturned mouth; difficulty smiling; difficulty meeting people's eyes; helplessness/hopelessness about accompaniment being possible; continual use of sarcasm; physical immobility; hypervigilance about mattering or being left; and sacrificing one's own needs in order to have company. And again, just starting to notice is the beginning of reclaiming self, self-warmth, and self-compassion.

OUR UNCONSCIOUS CONTRACTS AND ANXIETY

Here are five kinds of unconscious contracts connected with both FEAR and PANIC/GRIEF, as well as with the other roots of anxiety that we have mentioned. As you read them, put a star by the contracts that resonate for you in your life.

I, my nervous system, solemnly swear to you, my essential self, that:

FEAR

- I will be forever hypervigilant in order to stay safe and prevent harm to myself and others.
- I will never forget any element of what has happened and will keep the tension continually alive in my body so that I can stay alert and survive.
- I will never trust anyone in order to stay safe.
- I promise to take on my mother's nervous system in order to be loved and noticed.
- I will default to anxiety as a strategy for existing in order to feel that I exist.
- I will be forever afraid of the future in order never to be surprised by bad things that may happen.
- I will never relax my hypervigilance in order to be ready for whatever is coming.

FEAR for Others or in Honor of Others

- I will carry terror on behalf of others in order to keep them safe/be a good mother/sister/father/brother.
- I will share my mother's fear so that she will not be alone.
- I will be anxious in order to fit in with my family.

PANIC/GRIEF

- I will search forever for my love.
- I will never rest until I'm loved.
- I will always be watchful for any sign that I'm not loved.
- I will never allow myself to know how lonely I am so that I don't die of despair.

PANIC/GRIEF for Others or in Honor of Others

- I will erase myself in order to let my parents exist.
- I will carry constant heartbreak in order to accompany my mother/father.
- I will not allow myself to feel anything but grief in honor of my ancestors.

Health

- I will never relax into my full capacity for health in order to stay vigilant for whatever bad things are coming next, so that I'm not disappointed.
- I will forever feel like I'm not enough, even in my own capacity for health and well-being, in order to make my childhood make sense/make my mother right about me.

Torn Between Two Authorities

- I will resolve the impossible-to-resolve within my own body, so that I can live in a sane world.
- I will figure out how to integrate these two completely different ways of being within my own body in order to survive.

Anxiety About Anxiety

- I will live in a state of continual fear about my own anxiety in order to keep myself from being blindsided by its arising.

In order to be able to work with these contracts, it is important to disentangle the FEAR circuit and the PANIC/GRIEF circuit from other circuits with which they have become entangled through trauma. You may remember that the amygdala joins different parts of the trauma experience together with the power of superglue, and this includes the circuits. The two guided meditations that follow invite you into more differentiation and a smooth, flowing linkage between your circuits to help you find and work with any contracts you might have.

GUIDED MEDITATION
Disentangling Your FEAR Circuit

As you work with this meditation, remember that FEAR can include anxiety, phobias, panic, psychic trauma, and PTSD, as well the emotional ranges of worry and anxiety that are connected with physical or financial safety.

Allow yourself to notice your body . . . What do you notice first, as you bring your attention to being embodied? . . . Can you find the movement of your breath? . . .

As you begin to notice your own breath, let yourself begin a continuous remembrance of it as an ongoing, lifelong process . . . so that you continually invite your own attention back to your breath . . . and see what it is like to bring warmth . . . appreciation . . . affection . . . gratitude . . . and acknowledgment to your body . . . your body that has allowed you to live this lifetime . . . and has supported you . . .

Now, gently, imagine that you can see a tree of light that has roots in your belly . . . that reaches up to bring nourishment through a trunk that rises through your throat, and branches that spread up through your brain . . . Allow yourself to begin to envision this tree as your healthy FEAR circuit . . . able to keep you safe . . . only necessary to use when there is danger . . . Notice where there are tangles of branches . . . Notice where the circuit is blocked . . . or stuck . . . or caught in loops . . . Notice where the color turns from a supportive flow of available energy, which might show up as white light . . . or yellow light . . . into either a blocked or intensified flow . . . that might show up as red light or darkness . . . Simply allow yourself to see it . . . and to, as much as you can, bring affection and warmth to the tree of the circuit within you . . .

One of the things that creates the blocks or the loops in our circuits are ways in which our circuits are entangled . . . so we will check for entanglements . . . and invite the circuits to become free of one another . . . We will begin by separating FEAR from the SEEKING circuit . . .

Allow yourself to see another tree within you, the tree of the SEEKING circuit, . . . superimposed on the light of the tree of FEAR . . . Feel into whether you get to move freely . . . Do you get to pursue your dreams . . . or do the branches of the FEAR tree trap or restrain the movement of SEEKING? . . . Notice yourself in your search for love and connection . . . Do you get to follow your desire? . . . Can you reach for what you want? . . . Notice yourself in your career . . . Does FEAR hold you back? . . . Are you able to take action for self-care, or is it too dangerous? . . . Is there any way that FEAR paralyzes you . . . or makes you unable to move? . . . Does terror make your gut quake or twist . . . or your mouth dry . . . or does it make your heart pound when you try to move? . . . Do you need acknowledgment that there are always good reasons for our bodies to feel afraid . . . that scary things happen to people . . . that children and grown-ups often have to witness or receive violence . . . and that the cells of our SEEKING circuit may believe that the violence happened because we moved . . . or because we didn't move? . . . If these things are true for you, tell your SEEKING circuit, "Of course you believe it's dangerous to act . . ." or "Of course you are paralyzed with shame about not acting . . ." and gently allow the two trees to pulse in turn . . . so that you can see FEAR on its own, without SEEKING, and so that you can see SEEK-

ING on its own, without FEAR . . . Gently lift your SEEKING tree out of its past entanglement with FEAR . . . and let it know that it had very good reasons for being entangled . . . and that it doesn't need to be entangled any more . . . Now surround your SEEKING circuit tree with warmth and affection, and let it fade from vision . . .

Now invite yourself see the tree of your RAGE circuit within you . . . and to let yourself see the places where your RAGE and your FEAR trees are entangled and intertwined . . . Is there any part of you that is angry that you were once frightened? . . . Do you become angry at yourself when you are scared? . . . Are you angry at your own anxiety? . . . Are you always angry when someone else is afraid? . . . Are you terrified of others' anger? . . . Do you do anything possible to avoid it? . . . Feel into the ways that FEAR and RAGE are stuck together . . . and say to them, "Of course you are intertwined" . . . Say to these circuits, "Do you need acknowledgment that you have very good reasons to have your FEAR and your RAGE mixed up and blocked?" . . . And now allow yourself to see first one circuit, . . . and then the other, . . . and to perceive them as separate, . . . and to notice that they do not need to be entangled . . . How does your body feel with the thought that they do not have to be linked . . . that they each serve different purposes . . . that they each matter . . . that each voice of the circuits is important? . . . And let the tree of the RAGE circuit fade from your view . . .

Now bring forward a sense of the tree of the CARE circuit, so that you can see it simultaneously with the FEAR tree . . . Notice the places where these two trees are entangled . . . Is there any way that FEAR stops you from forming connections with others? . . . Do you protect yourself from the dangers of intimacy by stopping your reach? . . . When you love people, are you terrified that they will be hurt . . . by the world . . . by other people? . . . Do you worry that you will hurt them or that they won't be safe? . . . Does love terrify you so that you run away to stay safe? . . . Or when people frighten you, do you shift into caring for them in order to manage your fear? . . . Again, allow yourself to gently disentangle the branches of these trees . . . Let them know that love doesn't need FEAR to exist . . . that both can flow flexibly and responsively . . . that they do not need to be entangled . . . and let the CARE tree fade away . . .

Now bring forward the PANIC/GRIEF tree . . . and let yourself see this tree light up at the same time as the FEAR tree . . . What do you notice? . . . Where are these two trees entangled? . . . Is there a cyclone of FEAR and PANIC/GRIEF that runs together? . . . Has someone you've loved very deeply been harmed or died, keeping you in a state of chronic abandonment? . . . This entanglement can keep us from ever loving . . . from ever relaxing again . . . and can bring paralysis when *any loss or danger looms . . . It may also be that we are terrified of loss so we cannot mourn . . . or that grief so overwhelms us when we sense danger that we cannot take action to save ourselves . . . This is a common mixture for those of us who have survived domestic violence . . . Allow the trees to light up separately so that you can begin to tell the difference between them . . . to receive their separate gifts . . . and let PANIC/GRIEF fade . . .*

It's time for us to explore the ways that FEAR can be confused with PLAY . . . so allow the PLAY circuit to light up in your imagination so that you can see it . . . and see where your life has joined it with FEAR . . . If you lived in a house where someone became dangerous when people were happy, your PLAY circuit might have become entangled with FEAR . . . then when our own children are noisy, or moving quickly, or expressing life energy, we may become very afraid . . . Or if when someone is frightening, we always try to defuse it with PLAY, there may be an entanglement . . . Let yourself say to your playfulness . . . "Of course you become frightened . . . you have very good historical reasons" . . . and then let yourself see that these two circuits are distinct . . . let them light up in turn . . . and now let your PLAY circuit fade from view . . .

This time, let yourself see your SEXUALITY circuit . . . This tree might have a slightly different, lower shape . . . Let it be seen at the same time as your FEAR circuit so that you can perceive that there are two different circuits here . . . When these two circuits are entangled, often the person is frightened of sexual experiences or of intimacy . . . This can be the result of sexual violence or being engulfed in intimacy and having a sense of disappearing . . . We may also notice that these two circuits have been linked by trauma such that we need to be frightened or imagine being frightened in order to be sexual . . . Again, allow whatever knowledge you need about these two circuits to come to you . . . and allow them to light up separately . . . so that you can see that they are different . . . that it might be possible to be sexual . . . to enjoy sexuality . . . without the FEAR circuit having to contribute . . .

Finally, we will invite ourselves to see the FEAR circuit and the DISGUST circuit at the same time . . . DISGUST raises the body temperature of the torso, so the largest part of the tree that makes up this circuit may be in your abdomen . . . How are these two circuits entangled? . . . Do they get to work separately? . . . Or when you are disgusted, do you have to be afraid? . . . Does your disgust get to inform you that you are experiencing invasion . . . and let you take action? . . . Or are you paralyzed by FEAR when you experience DISGUST? . . . Are you terrified by your own DISGUST? . . . Does your terror stop you from being able to have boundaries? . . . Do you experience FEAR when others have boundaries, or can

*you celebrate them? . . . Or do you experience DISGUST with yourself whenever
you are afraid? . . . Allow yourself to see the ways that these two circuits have
been entangled, and invite them to disentangle themselves . . . Peel DISGUST
away from FEAR and let them exist separately . . . And let DISGUST fade away . . .*

*Now allow yourself to see your own FEAR circuit with its beautiful gifts
of awareness of and escape from danger . . . Allow yourself to imagine a fluid
response to times and people that feel scary to you . . . full choice, full movement . . . fully responsive but not hypervigilant awareness . . . Let yourself see the
beauty of this circuit tree within you, . . . and let it fade from your awareness . . .
so that the bones of its strength are within you . . . but you do not need to live
with its on-going message of anxiety.*

As you do the work of this and the following meditation, remember that sometimes these entanglements have arisen from our own personal experiences of trauma,
and sometimes we have inherited these entanglements from our parents or from our
family lines. We need to acknowledge this and hold ourselves with gentleness so that
as we're healing our own brains, we're also healing our parents' brains and systems
within us. This next meditation will take us on a similar disentangling journey for
our PANIC/GRIEF circuit.

GUIDED MEDITATION
Disentangling Your PANIC/GRIEF Circuit

*Allow yourself to notice your body . . . What do you notice first, as you bring your
attention to being embodied? . . . Can you find the movement of your breath? . . .
As you begin to notice your own breath . . . invite your attention to stay partially
with it at all times . . . so that you continually invite your own attention back to
your breath . . . and see what it is like to bring warmth . . . appreciation . . . affection . . . gratitude . . . and acknowledgment to your body . . . your body that has
allowed you to live this lifetime . . . and has supported you . . .*

*Now, gently, allow yourself to begin to envision your PANIC/GRIEF circuit . . .
Imagine that you can see it . . . a river system of sensation that joins your body
with your brain . . . Notice where there are tangles of pathways . . . Notice where
the river is blocked . . . or stuck . . . or runs in loops . . . Notice where the sensation
changes from a supportive flow of available energy, which might show up as a*

sensation of cool movement . . . to tumultuous rapids . . . or blocked or intensified flow . . . Simply allow yourself to feel it . . . and as much as you can, bring affection and warmth to the river system of this circuit within you . . . One thing that creates the blocks or the loops in our circuits is entanglements between our circuits . . . so we will check for entanglements . . . and invite the circuits to become free of one another . . . We will begin with the SEEKING circuit . . .

Allow yourself to see another river system within you, the river of the SEEK-ING circuit . . . overlaid on the sensations coming from the river of PANIC/ GRIEF . . . Feel into whether you get to move freely . . . Do you get to pursue your dreams . . . or does PANIC/GRIEF overflow or take over the SEEKING chan-nels? . . . Notice yourself in your search for love and connection . . . Do you get to follow your desire? . . . Can you reach for what you want? . . . Notice yourself in your career . . . Does PANIC/GRIEF wash you away and keep you from being effective? . . . Are you able to take action for self-care, or is it too lonely? . . . Does it separate you and immobilize you . . . Is there any way that PANIC/GRIEF par-alyzes you . . . or makes you unable to move . . . Does sorrow weaken you . . . or does loneliness freeze you in place . . . or do you stop moving and breathing in order to keep from crying . . . or letting people know of your loneliness? . . . Do you need acknowledgment that there are always good reasons for our bodies to feel lonely . . . that we are often alone in this world . . . that children often have to manage disappearance, neglect, or abandonment . . . and the cells of our SEEK-ING circuit can believe that the abandonment happened because we moved . . . or because we didn't move? . . . If these things are true for you, tell your SEEK-ING circuit, "Of course you believe it's threatening to act . . ." or "Of course you are paralyzed with shame and loneliness about not acting . . ." and gently allow the two rivers to pulse in turn . . . so that you can see PANIC/GRIEF on its own, without SEEKING, and so that you can see SEEKING on its own, without PANIC/ GRIEF . . . Gently lift your river of SEEKING out of its past entanglement with PANIC/GRIEF . . . and let it know that it had very good reasons for being entan-gled . . . and that it doesn't need to be entangled any more . . . Now surround your SEEKING circuit with warmth and affection and let it fade from vision . . .

The next invitation is to let yourself see the river system of your RAGE circuit within you . . . and to let yourself see the places where your river of RAGE and your river of PANIC/GRIEF are entangled and intermingled . . . Is there any part of you that is angry that you were once abandoned? . . . Do you become angry at yourself when someone leaves you and you suffer? . . . Do you expect to be left if you reveal your longing for connection? . . . Are you angry at your own lonely anxiety? . . . Are you always angry when someone else is lonely? . . . Do you run from the word needy? . . . Are you terrified of others' dependency? . . . Do you do anything possible to avoid it? . . . Feel into the ways that PANIC/GRIEF and RAGE are stuck together . . . and say to them, "Of course you are intermingled; you are still loved." . . . Say to the circuits, "Do you need acknowledgment that you have very good reasons for your loneliness and your anger being mixed up and blocked?" . . . And now allow yourself to see first one circuit . . . and then the other . . . and to allow yourself to perceive them as separate . . . and to notice that they do not need to be entangled . . . How does your body feel with the thought that they do not have to be linked . . . that they each serve different purposes . . . that they each matter . . . that each voice of the circuits is important? . . . And let the river system of the RAGE circuit fade from your sensation . . .

Now bring forward a sense of the river of the CARE circuit, so that you can see it simultaneously with the GRIEF river system . . . Notice the places where these two rivers mix together . . . Is there any way that GRIEF stops you from forming connections with others? . . . Do you protect yourself from the dangers of intimacy by stopping your reach? . . . When you love people, do you mourn all the ways that they cannot reach you? . . . Do you mourn for the loneliness of the people you love? . . . As soon as you love someone, do you see their sadness? . . . Is that your job, to see people's sadness? . . . Or when people leave you, do you shift into caring for them in order to manage the abandonment, thus never letting yourself grieve? . . . Again, allow yourself to gently disentangle these two river systems . . . Let them know that love doesn't need sorrow to exist . . . that both can flow flexibly and responsively . . . that they do not need to be entangled . . . and let the CARE river fade away . . .

Now bring forward the FEAR river system . . . and let yourself feel this system flowing at the same time as the PANIC/GRIEF river . . . What do you notice? . . . Where are these two rivers running together, entangled? . . . Is there a cyclone of FEAR and PANIC/GRIEF that runs together? . . . Has someone you've loved very deeply been harmed or died, keeping you in a state of chronic abandonment? . . . This entanglement can keep us from ever loving . . . from ever relaxing again . . . and can bring paralysis when any loss or danger looms . . . It may also be that we are terrified of loss so we cannot mourn . . . or that PANIC/GRIEF overwhelms us when we have a sense of danger so we cannot take action to save ourselves . . . This is a common mixture for those of us who have survived domestic violence . . . Allow the rivers to run separately so that you can begin to tell the difference between them . . . to receive their separate gifts . . . and let PANIC/GRIEF fade . . .

It's time for us to explore the ways that PANIC/GRIEF can be confused with PLAY . . . So allow the PLAY river to begin to flow in your imagination so that *you can feel it . . . and feel where your life has joined it with PANIC/GRIEF . . . If you lived in a house where delight and joy made someone sad or lonely or feel excluded, your PLAY circuit might have become entangled with PANIC/GRIEF . . . Then if our own children are noisy, or moving quickly, or expressing life energy, we can become very sorrowful or ashamed . . . If when someone is sad or lonely, we always try to defuse it with PLAY, there may be an entanglement . . . Let yourself say to your playfulness . . . "Of course you become sad . . . you have very good historical reasons" . . . And then let yourself see that these two river systems are distinct . . . Let them flow in turn . . . and now let your PLAY circuit fade from perception . . .*

This time, let yourself see your SEXUALITY circuit . . . This river system might have a slightly different, lower shape . . . And let yourself feel it at the same time as your PANIC/GRIEF circuit, so that you can perceive that there are two different circuits here . . . If these two circuits are entangled, people are often lonely when they are connecting in sexual experiences or during intimacy . . . This can be the result of sexual violence or the result of being engulfed in intimacy and having a sense of disappearing . . . We may also notice that these two circuits have been linked by trauma if we need to be shamed or imagine being shamed in order to be sexual . . . Again, allow whatever knowledge you need about these two circuits to come to you . . . and allow them to light up separately . . . so that you can see that they are different . . . that it might be possible to be sexual . . . to enjoy SEXUALITY . . . without the PANIC/GRIEF circuit having to contribute . . . and let SEXUALITY fade . . .

Finally, we will invite ourselves to see the PANIC/GRIEF circuit and the DISGUST circuit at the same time . . . DISGUST raises the body temperature of the torso, so the largest part of the river system that makes up this circuit may be in your abdomen . . . How are these two circuits entangled? . . . Do they get to work separately? . . . Or when you are disgusted, do you have to be ashamed? . . . Does your disgust get to inform you that you are experiencing invasion? . . . And let you take action? . . . Or are you paralyzed by shame when you experience DISGUST? . . . Does your shame stop you from being able to have boundaries? . . . Do you experience PANIC/GRIEF when others have boundaries, or can you celebrate them? . . . Or do you experience DISGUST with yourself whenever you are lonely or ashamed? . . . Allow yourself to see the ways that these two circuits have been entangled, and invite them to disentangle themselves . . . Peel DISGUST away from PANIC/GRIEF and let them exist separately . . . And let DISGUST fade away . . .

Now allow yourself to see your PANIC/GRIEF circuit with its beautiful gifts of awareness of and reaching into the experience of times when others have been distant . . . allow yourself to imagine a fluid response to times and people that feel distant to you . . . full choice, full movement . . . fully responsive but not hypervigilant awareness . . . Let yourself see the beauty of this circuit within you . . . and let it fade from your awareness . . . so that the strength of its river of valuing connection is still flowing within you . . . but you do not need to live with its on-going message of anxiety.

In completing these two meditations, we can experience many "aha" moments, so take some time now to review the meditations and note where you feel stuck.

JOURNALING PROMPT FOR
Discovering Blocks to Releasing Vows of Anxiety

And now, take some time to journal about and contemplate which circuits were especially difficult to separate, as those are places where contracts may be limiting your life energy and your choices.

_____

_____

_____

_____

_____

_____

ONE-ON-ONE WORK   When Contracts and
Anxiety Dissolve with Trauma Work

KATE: *It's hard for me to find my voice. I'm aware of the anxiety, the way it lives in me. The way I sense it is, it's like something trapped inside, running around, furiously trying to find a resting place and just not able to. And I know there was a time when I had a resting space inside my heart. And I lost it.*

SARAH: *I want to begin by asking, does this sensation running inside of you need acknowledgment for its frantic search?*

KATE: *Yes. Frantic search. Yes. I just want to breathe on that. I can sense some soothing of that acknowledgment. It's like almost slowing down. Just hearing that. Yes, ever so slightly slowing down. It's like, "Oh wow, somebody sees this, the frantic search." It's slowing down even more. It's so exhausted, it just wants to cry.*

SARAH: *So, speaking to the part of Kate that's been running and running and running and running, "Are you so exhausted?"*

KATE: *Yes, and I also notice a worry about the sustainability of the body when it's under such constant stress. I'd better find a peaceful place before this body expires. It's like being at the door of death and being all frantic about it. Now just calm down. It's just the doorway. Relax a little, you can do this. I can do this. I'm noticing how when I calm down, the frantic energy picks up again, like a cycle.*

SARAH: *We may be touching a vow, because one of the signs that we're in the presence of a contract is there's a body reaction to the resonance, but it doesn't really land. That's a sign that there's another process going on besides just the need for resonance. Does that feel like it might be a direction for us to explore?*

KATE: *Yes. I can feel it in my cells.*

SARAH: *Does the franticness feel like a fear for physical safety, or does it feel more like alarmed aloneness? Which does your body relax into more . . . a longing for protection and safety? Or a longing for warm presence, people, connections, and community?*

KATE: *Both. I feel like it's 50/50.*

SARAH: *Let's start with the physical fear one, and then see what might be there for the loneliness. Start with "I, Kate's nervous system, solemnly swear to you, Kate, that I will . . ." and see what kind of words might come.*

KATE: *"I, Kate's nervous system, solemnly swear that I . . ." Oh my God, I feel so many tears coming up, and it reminds me of this song that I made up this week about being alone in the terror. "I, this nervous system, solemnly swear to seek community so that I'm not alone. A cabin in the woods where I'm safe or a warm community where I feel safe. So that I never experience terror or loneliness again, no matter the cost to myself." And now I feel the franticness moving all up my back. It's like it's trapped. It stays in the body, it moves, up and down, up and down.*

SARAH: *Now we want to check with Kate: "Kate, did you hear the vow that your nervous system made to you? "*

KATE: *I feel like we made it together.*

SARAH: *Then we'll say, "Essential self of Kate, do you like the vow that Kate and her nervous system made to you?"*

KATE: *Do I like this vow for her? I feel something getting tight, like somebody is about to tell us to let go of it because it doesn't work for us. Yes, I like it.*

SARAH: *To be specific, we want the essential self to hear the words "relentlessly" and "no matter the cost" because we can certainly let Kate continue to search for any kind of safety, but the question is, does the essential self want her to search relentlessly, no matter the cost?*

KATE: *No, it actually wishes I would just give it up and live in the moment and enjoy life. Yes. Now I can see I want to enjoy life, but then there's my nervous system here and it's got this contract with me. It's saying, "I know you want to enjoy life, but I have something important." Oh wow, it's like a monster that has found its way inside of me.*

SARAH: *Let's find out then, "Essential self of Kate, do you want Kate and the nervous system to keep this contract?"*

KATE: *No, keeping it isn't sustainable.*

SARAH: *Thank you. Will you please tell Kate, "Kate, I release you from this contract."*

KATE: *This is the hardest part for me. I release myself from it, but then what happens when we end the call? I'm going to be back with it. I release myself from the contract. What does that mean?*

SARAH: *I think we need to do a little bit of time travel. Can you touch the moment when your nervous system took this on? You used the words, it's like a monster entered your body. Can we touch that moment? What was that moment?*

KATE: *Yes, I remember that moment.*

SARAH: *You can say what the moment was or we can just work together without mentioning what the moment was. Whichever you prefer.*

KATE: *I can describe it. It was a moment when there were some scary people at my door and I picked up a phone and called a few friends, local friends, and asked if they could be with me, just come over to my home and be with me, so that I wouldn't be scared alone. And each of them said no. That was so big for me. I want to breathe through that because that's where I feel like this monster became attached.*

SARAH: *Right. So just go ahead and breathe and tell me when it's okay for us to ask about consent for time travel.*

KATE: *Yes. Wow. I can just feel in that moment something in here went—it's almost like it attached itself to me and it hasn't let go since then.*

SARAH: *Yes. Is it okay for you and me to time travel to Kate in that moment as she receives the nos? Is it okay for us to go to her?*

KATE: *Yes, it's all those nos that did it.*

SARAH: *So, you and I are stepping through time and space, stepping into your apartment. Coming in. Standing right beside her.*

KATE: *Yes. Just now as you say this, I can feel in my body, like that monster doesn't have an opportunity to attach because I have someone there. It's like, oh gosh, if I just had someone there. I feel you there now. If I could attach that moment to my nervous system.*

SARAH: *With our presence, we're making the guess of, "Kate, do you really need accompaniment and presence and a sense of not being alone?" We're making that guess with our very presence.*

KATE: *Yes. I like that. It's not just a verbal guess. It's actual presence. As if with you there with me, I can just breathe through whatever's happening. The terror doesn't attach itself because I've got company. I just need more time to be with it and not rush away from it. The cells, centimeter by centimeter, a one-by-one domino effect, they just get revived. They soften or something. I just want enough time for all of them to come back to life, or as many as possible.*

SARAH: *Yes.*

KATE: *I made these calls to people to try to get help, one by one. One was to my brother, and I said, "I have these people at the door and I'm very scared, could you just come and be with me so that I'm not alone in it?" And he didn't come. Doing time travel—does it mean I'm lying to myself? No, that's not true. What I'm aiming for is to get that with the help of time travel that I actually called, and someone said yes.*

SARAH: *Yes. We can say that you called me through time and that I just picked up the phone. You say, "Would you get on a flight and come over?" And since we're time traveling, I can time travel back to you.*

KATE: *I'm noticing my nervous system has a vow to call on people to see if they'll be here for me.*

SARAH: *Is it a vow that has a cost to you?*

KATE: *I don't see the cost. I don't see a big cost to it.*

SARAH: *Then it's not one to worry about.*

KATE: *Okay.*

SARAH: *I wonder if the Kate that we are in contact with has enough relaxation now to want to come to present time with us, or if we want to leave us there with her, so that she gets to have more time?*

KATE: *Yes. Leave us there forever. It feels very soothing to be in that time with people with me. It's like I just want to soak it in and marinate in it for as long as I need it.*

SARAH: *Very good. We'll leave that happening and we'll check back in about the vow that we started out with, where the nervous system made a contract with you to relentlessly search for either community where there's safety, or aloneness in security and solitariness where there's safety, no matter the cost to you. Does it still feel like that vow is present in your body?*

KATE: *Not at the moment.*

SARAH: *Very good.*

KATE: *Right now, I have all of you here. It's kind of like the cat that's laid down on the floor. It's not active at the moment.*

SARAH: *Thank you, Kate. So much gratitude that we get to touch this then. And this is one of the things that we need to know as we begin to work with these processes. When we get stuck with time travel, it'll take us into unconscious contract work. When resonance soothes things temporarily, but then the sensation or upset comes back, we're touching either the trauma tangle connected with a particular moment in time or an unconscious contract. In this work, we can start anywhere and go anywhere, and if we stay connected with the body of the person who's receiving and what they hold as their intention, then we're just in service and we have these tools and we offer them and we follow and we listen. So, we have such sweet possibilities.*

One year later, Kate writes:

A year later . . . Come to think of it . . . I haven't "complained" saying, "I called . . . and nobody came," for quite a while. I remember a time when the grief of those moments was so raw, so shrill and searing and very heavy. And it feels to me the grief of that specific moment in time has been deactivated, it's no longer active, its charge has dissolved. In fact, the other week I was retelling my story to someone who'd never heard it before . . . and I failed to mention that "I called . . . and nobody came." My failing to mention that moment is an indication to me that something has shifted since a year ago.

In reading the transcript I can see that having let the experience of having you with me in those moments of time travel really rest in me helped to integrate the experience of accompaniment. It's so important to allow my system to bring it in until it feels it has fully charged, like a battery that is plugged into a charger and is allowed to "fully charge." I'm glad you offered me that option at the time.

Now that you have a sense of these types of entanglements and contracts, go ahead and try an anxiety contract out for yourself.

Anxiety Contract Template

Try doing one for each root of anxiety that you have identified.

1. I, _____, solemnly swear to my essential self (or mother, father, sibling, family line, God, universe, etc.) that I will/will not

    _____

    _____

    _____

    _____

    _____

    _____

    in order to _____ ,
    no matter the cost to myself and those I love.

2. What is the good, historical, lived reason for this contract? When did you first make this contract? How does it make sense within the larger context of your life?

    _____

    _____

    _____

    _____

3. Essential self (or mother, father, sibling, God, universe, etc.), did you hear this vow?

    Yes _____

    No _____

    (If no, then repeat the words of the vow.)

4. Essential self (or mother, father, sibling, God, universe, etc.), do you want this vow to be kept?

    Yes _____

    No _____

(If the answer is "Yes, the vow should stay, no matter the cost," then it's time to use the Time Travel Process to go to the moment in your life in which this unconscious contract makes sense.)

5. The release: *I release you from this vow, and I revoke this contract.*

     _____

     _____

6. The blessing: *And I give you my blessing to:*

     _____

     _____

Now that we have an understanding of the roots of anxiety, we're also beginning to have a deeper understanding of the way that the circuits function, which opens the door for us to delve deeply into RAGE and the contracts we may have that prevent us from accessing this important source of life energy, advocacy, and protection. Chapter 6 takes us into this exploration.

CHAPTER 6

Claiming Anger's Life-Giving Force

All over the world, people have heard of the concept of "fight, flight, and freeze," but even though these words point to natural nervous system states, people believe that they are wrong to be angry, wrong to be afraid, wrong when they experience alarmed aloneness, and wrong to collapse when they experience helplessness. People are often very surprised to learn that they have a RAGE circuit, and that it is their birthright, and that one of its main neurotransmitters, Substance P[1], is key in mood disorders, anxiety and stress.[2] Many people have considered their tendency to become angry as a character flaw rather than as a vital life energy that regulates our nervous system, permitting us to be protective and to advocate for what is needed.

However, when RAGE is aimed at people who have less power, it's frightening and can be traumatic. It isn't meant to be used against those we love or who are dependent on us. Often people who experience others' anger develop memories of real harm having been inflicted when the anger was expressed. People who were powerless to avoid receiving others' rage may have made contracts with themselves never to be angry in order to keep themselves from doing harm. These are unconscious contracts that deny people their boundaries, their ability to say no, their powerful protective advocacy, their capacity to take action, and their ability to access life energy in support of protection, self-defense, defense of others, and in support of their world.

If people have made a vow to constrict themselves and stop their anger, it's as if they're turning down the volume on their life energy. The RAGE circuit responds when resources are threatened—resources like food, family, love, or money. The whole body responds to RAGE. The upper body in particular becomes fully energized. As we become more familiar with rage as a protective life force, we begin to feel the ways in which our body has created different blockages to try to compress us and keep us from expressing something that either was not acceptable or that we feel would go against our commitment to do no harm. Most of us carry a deep commitment to do no harm, and as we come into relationship with our own longings to do no harm, we can start to see our vows even more clearly.

Another possible contract connected with RAGE is when people swear to themselves that they will always be angry in order to be the powerful one. It may be the case that their child self was not felt or heard unless they were in a RAGE. Or they may have discovered that they could keep someone else from moving into RAGE and becoming scary by being in a RAGE themselves. When people have needed their RAGE circuit for protection in a dangerous world and they have made it their primary circuit for problem-solving, they lose the life energy that could be flowing in the CARE or FEAR or PLAY or PANIC/GRIEF circuits. When circuits are not used, their life energy is lost. As people do this healing work, they reclaim and balance their circuits, bringing their bodies and immune systems more energy, flexibility, and possibility.

Sometimes people ask if RAGE is addictive, and according to Panksepp, it is not. It lands for mammal bodies as an experience they would rather not repeat. If someone is getting pleasure out of frightening another person, Panksepp says it is not the RAGE circuit that is active but a particular expression of the SEEKING circuit, a state called predatory aggression, which is very pleasurable, or rewarding, for mammals—an experience that people want to repeat. If people take pleasure, comfort, or relief from expressing anger toward others, it is more likely that they are using their SEEKING circuit, dumping stress (and decreasing cortisol) by passing on aggression, rather than actually becoming angry and activating their RAGE circuit.[3]

And if we have received someone else's SEEKING circuit predatory aggression and in our misinterpretation we made a vow against our own RAGE, we are closing the wrong door anyway. It is absolutely essential to separate powerful, life-serving RAGE from predatory aggression.

TUNING IN TO HEALTHY RAGE

THE MAIN QUESTION FOR THIS CHAPTER

Can I embrace the power and wisdom of my anger and still do no harm?

In addition to contracts, another factor that can make RAGE frightening is if we never learned how to let it flow through us—how to harvest it in a healthy way. Once we do learn to take what we need from RAGE's power and assurance, this circuit becomes a resource rather than a harmful liability.

When we are learning to be with our anger in this way, we let it travel through us as energy rather than letting our muscles seize it and turn it into motion. (This includes the muscles of the face, since the RAGE facial expression can be terrifying for others.) Take a moment to try this out. Think about a resource of yours or of someone or something you love that is under threat. Now feel any anger or RAGE that is there. The sensation will almost immediately turn into a muscle contraction. Intentionally release the contraction and let the energy of the rage continue to travel through you, moving into your arms and out your extended fingers. If there is fury in your face, bring it out through your arms and your extended fingers. What is there that needs to be said, and how do you phrase it?

See if you can turn your expression into a sentence that has both of the words you and I in it. For example, "I am so angry at you that you didn't come to your daughter's play!" This takes us out of name-calling and gets us closer to the heart of the matter. (We will work more with I–You language in a later chapter—it is one of our resonant language skills.) As you hear your own expression, name the resource that is under threat with warmth and affection for yourself along with your love for that resource. It might sound something like this, "Of course you are angry—do you love the ecosystems of this Earth so passionately?" If it's money, connect it to what money can do for you: "Of course you are angry that you were fined $350 for that traffic violation! Do you love all the food and comfort and warmth that $350 can bring to your family?" What happens in your body with the naming?

JOURNALING PROMPT FOR
Autobiography of Your RAGE Circuit

Now that you have a safe way to work with the activation of the RAGE circuit in your body, take this opportunity to journal your RAGE circuit's autobiography.

When was the first time you felt mad/angry in your life?

_____

Are you always angry?

_____

Are you never angry?

_____

Was your anger welcome in your family home?

_____

Was there one particular person who got to be "the angry one"?

_____

Were other people terrifying when they were angry?

_____

Now that you know the difference between RAGE and predatory aggression, who in your life do you now see as using predatory aggression to manage their stress?

_____

When was the most recent time you felt mad/angry?

_____

When was the first time you felt outrage?

_____

When was the most recent time you felt outrage?

_____

What makes you angry?

_____

Which of your expectations are not being met?

_____

Do you rant?

_____

How often/what do you rant about?

_____

How long does it take for things to build up enough to make you angry?

_____

Even if you have never been angry, what are some very good reasons to have been angry in your life?

_____

_____

_____

_____

QUESTIONNAIRE
Identifying Threats to Resources That Activate the RAGE Circuit

If it is true that our RAGE circuit is awakened when different resources are threatened, it is important that we start to identify which resources are connected with which surface reasons for RAGE so that we can hold ourselves and others with more compassion and deep understanding when anger arises. By surface reasons, I mean whatever first comes to mind, like a belief that you are being disrespected or taken advantage of. As you look at the surface reasons for RAGE in the left-hand column of the table at the end of the list shown below, see if you can feel into the actual resources that are under threat. There are also more blank spaces here for you to add other surface reasons for RAGE that are personal to you.

Here is a partial list of resources. Before you work with the table, review the resource list and see if there are any you would like to add.

Life	Social Capital
Air, Food, Water, Home	Influence
Energy	Money
Health and Well-Being	Self-Concept
Existence	(Sense of Self as Good)
Freedom	Family Concept
Inclusion, Belonging	(Sense of Family as Good)
Love	Group Concept
Attention	(Sense of Group as Good)
Good Name	

Surface reason for RAGE	Actual threatened resource
People not contributing	
Disrespect	
"I'm not going to take this shit."	

Surface reason for RAGE	Actual threatened resource
Disobedience	
Obstruction of progress/something causing lateness	
Someone being mean	
People being late	
Not being heard	
Not being taken seriously	
Being lied to	
Being lied about	
Being taken advantage of	
Feeling naïve or foolish	
Having one's personal will thwarted	
Jealousy	
Being misled	
Gossip	
Impugning integrity of self or someone I love	
Child, animal, or helpless being endangered	
Misuse of power	
Thinking someone else is doing something "wrong" on purpose	
Closed mindedness	
Being pushed into a corner, not having a choice	
Receiving/witnessing contempt	
Receiving/witnessing predatory aggression	
Treating kids badly	
Personal unfairness (seeing a person, self or other, being treated unfairly)	

Surface reason for RAGE	Actual threatened resource
Systemic unfairness (systems making rules that stop people from having equal access to power, like changing voting boundaries to make sure a particular party will win an election or setting an unrealistic or unequal threshold for receiving parole or loans or scholarships)	
Racism or other isms	
Police brutality	
Police negligence	
Inaction on climate crisis	
Putting party well-being over the well-being of the country as a whole	
Nepotism	
Favoritism	
Righteousness	
Destruction of ecosystems/planet	
Sloughing of responsibility	

WHEN RAGE IS ENTANGLED WITH OTHER CIRCUITS

As shown in Chapter 5, circuits can be entangled by trauma. This leaves people with less flexibility and driven more by automatic reactivity than they might enjoy. You will remember from the section above that people can confuse and entangle SEEKING (predatory aggression) and RAGE. SEEKING can also be entangled with RAGE if we go right to frustration and anger whenever our forward progress is being blocked. (This is one of the roots of road rage.) It is also possible that people have mixed up the PLAY circuit and the RAGE circuit if they always had to smile when they were angry. If you notice that you get really nice when you or someone else is experiencing rage, it could be an entanglement of the RAGE circuit and the CARE circuit or the RAGE circuit and the PLAY circuit.

Or if our mothers couldn't bear RAGE but could handle GRIEF, we might shift all our anger energy into the GRIEF/PANIC circuit and cry every time we are angry. This can be a confusing experience.

If we become terrified or disgusted every time someone pulls their eyebrows together or raises their voice a couple of decibels, we may have a traumatic entanglement of FEAR and/or DISGUST with RAGE. Traumatic entanglements of SEXUALITY and RAGE are also possible and can lead to unexpected explosions and ruptures around sexual experiences.

This understanding of circuits allows us to explore how contracts are connected with this enormously important circuit of rage or anger. Are we able to step fully into a sense of our own power and be responsible and self-connected while we're mobilizing a protective and strong and even sudden and powerful expression of protection and life energy in the RAGE circuit? Is this accessible to us? As we clear the vows that keep us from this power, we open a new pathway for our life energy. It is important and beautiful work, and sometimes we need to be supported to move out of a freeze to do this work. Time travel empathy can be essential for the movement out of freeze.

QUESTIONNAIRE Entangled Circuits

Here are examples of my RAGE circuit entanglements with other circuits. What are the results of your entanglements?

RAGE	SEEKING	I get angry when I'm trying to get things done and someone interrupts me.
RAGE	RAGE	I get angry at people when they are angry at me.
RAGE	FEAR	I am frightened of people slamming cabinet doors when they are angry.
RAGE	CARE	I try to take care of people when they are angry and anticipate and prevent what makes them angry.
RAGE	GRIEF/PANIC	Sometimes I feel so lonely when someone close to me is angry.
RAGE	PLAY	When my son was young, I would be frighteningly rough when I was playing.
RAGE	SEXUALITY	I become enraged when consent is not part of SEXUALITY.
RAGE	DISGUST	I become enraged (usually after a 1–3 day delay) when people are disgusted with me.

Now you take a turn:

RAGE	SEEKING	
RAGE	RAGE	
RAGE	FEAR	
RAGE	CARE	
RAGE	GRIEF/PANIC	
RAGE	PLAY	
RAGE	SEXUALITY	
RAGE	DISGUST	

Recognition of all these facets of anger and RAGE are important for self-knowledge, for self-responsibility, and for growth. Different people become angry about different things, and the energy of their anger shows up in the following four areas:

PERSONAL – at self
IMPERSONAL – at others
ACTIVE PARTICIPATION – at systems you are actively participating in; e.g., families, schools, universities, employment
PASSIVE PARTICIPATION – at systems you are passively participating in; e.g., medical and insurance systems, government

WORKSHEET
Plotting Yourself on the Anger Grid

Circle your response to each comment, gradating along the continuum from false to true:

1. When I make a mistake, I become angry at myself.

   False   4   3   2   1   True

2. When things go wrong, I blame others.

   False   5   6   7   8   True

3. When my career is not going well, I become angry at my employer or my family.

   False   D   C   B   A   True

4. When I'm scared about the future, I become enraged about the government's decisions.

   False   F   G   H   I   True

Now, draw circles on the grid around each of the letters and numbers that match your answers, and draw lines connecting each of the circles around the grid to see the shape of the dimensions of your anger.

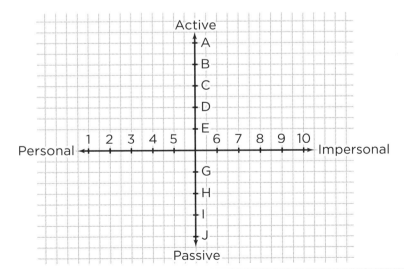

OTHER TYPES OF CONTRACTS
CONNECTED WITH RAGE

Another common contract that people make about RAGE is the contract to punish themselves or others for getting angry at all. This is often an inherited contract: our mother punished our father for becoming angry, either returning the anger or not speaking to him for days, so we punish the people around us or ourselves in similar ways when they become angry.

Other transgenerational contracts include compensation for a parent's inability to touch their own RAGE. In such cases, the child may carry the parent's RAGE for them.

Vows of loyalty are also possible, where the child makes a contract never to be angry in order to keep from terrifying their mothering person or always to be angry in order to accompany the mother or father.

WHEN OTHER PEOPLE'S ACTIONS
BRING US TO A POINT OF BREAKING
OUR CONTRACTS, RAGE RESULTS

One of the most confusing sources of RAGE is when we are stuck between an unconscious contract that we have and the actions of someone else that result in us breaking our contracts. An example of this is if we have a vow to always be on time and our child is dawdling, so we are getting to the child's school late. Or we have a contract never to return anything we've purchased and a beloved partner asks us to bring back a pair of trousers. Or we have made a work commitment and a doctor tells us we're going to be admitted to the hospital due to an urgent health issue, so we have a temper tantrum. Our vow to keep our commitments is being broken, and we have no control over it—these types of broken contracts give rise to RAGE. If you find yourself having a temper tantrum or a RAGE fit, ask yourself which of your contracts you are being forced to break, and then go through the contract release process. Finally, check to see whether that changes your RAGE at all. If you were raging as a result of a broken contract, your RAGE will dissipate.

RESONANT LANGUAGE PRACTICE
Bringing in Poetry

Resonant Language

Poetry and the Poetic Visual

Anger is one of the sinews of the soul.
                    –THOMAS FULLER

One of the most mysterious ways we can use language
to begin to touch experience is by speaking poetry.
These days, poetry often stays in its own world: a
world of books and readings and poets quietly writing submissions
and sending them off to journals and competitions or saving them in folders and
never sharing them. But poetry brings the right hemisphere to life. Poems point
toward the idea that life cannot be reduced and put into neat boxes—it is more
alive than that. And the language of poetry can put words to the mystery of our
experience so we can make a bridge to the experiences of others rather than feeling separate, on our own continent. We can write it for people we care about in
honor of their experience, and we can quote poems written by others.

For example, let's say a friend is struggling with hidden anger. We might say,
"Is it like Shakespeare said, *My tongue will tell the anger of my heart, or else my
heart concealing it will break*?"

Or what if a friend can't stop thinking about something difficult that has happened. We might say, "Let's go out together for some fresh air, like Shakespeare
says, '*A turn or two I'll walk to still my beating mind.*'"

We can collect bits and pieces of language that move us and share them in
conversation or emails. If we have a friend who has just burned their bridges in
rage, we might send them something like this:

> *Anger be now your song, immortal one,*
> *Akhilleus' anger, doomed and ruinous,*
> *That caused the Akhaians loss on bitter loss*
> *And crowded brave souls into the undergloom,*
> *Leaving so many dead men—carrion*
> *For dogs and birds; and the will of Zeus was done . . .*
>
> – Iliad 1.1-8

Poetry has a particular power to create a resonant response to anger, as it is
packed with metaphor, and it is not everyday language. This is important since
anger is usually larger than comfortably fits into everyday language.

Just because it's surprising doesn't mean it isn't resonant. One of my favorite memories of resonance was one night after a workshop when I said to a friend, *I'm so tired,* and she said to me, *Do you need the sleep that knits up the ravell'd sleeve of care?* (a quote from Shakespeare).

RESONANT LANGUAGE PRACTICE
Write Your Own Poem About Anger

Resonant Language

Poetry and the Poetic Visual

Choose a moment, for yourself or a friend, that involves a huger anger than you can easily handle. Write down the images from nature that come to you as you con- sider the effect of this anger on you or your friend (e.g., a cracked desert landscape, molten lava, the relentless equatorial sun, etc.).

_____

_____

_____

_____

Notice if there are any images that aren't from nature that arise for you (e.g., empty sidewalks, a burning house, an atomic bomb, etc.).

What verbs or action words hold something of the quality of this anger (e.g., scorching, destroying, etc.)?

_____

_____

Let yourself feel whether these words and images are satisfying for you. Put them together in any way that feels good. Poems can rhyme or not rhyme. They can say what happened to start the anger process, or they can begin in the middle of the experience. See what happens if you let yourself pull these things together in phrases or in sentences.

_____

_____

_____

_____

GUIDED MEDITATIONS FOR RAGE

GUIDED MEDITATION #1
Being With Personal RAGE

To prepare for this meditation, review your writing for this chapter so that you have a sense of a moment when you were powerfully angry about something that happened to you.

Begin this meditation by breathing . . . Notice yourself as a breathing being . . . Invite your attention to rest on the sensation of breath, wherever you feel it . . . See if you can invite your upper belly, around the bottom of your ribs, to move out when you inhale . . . and bring yourself back to breathing however your body breathes on its own, just allowing yourself to notice your breath . . . Where do you feel the sensation of breathing? . . . Is it in the rise and fall of your belly? . . . Is it in the small movements of your ribs and shoulders? . . . Is it the passage of air, a slight coolness, through your nose, sinuses, mouth, or throat? . . . Breathe for a moment, and allow yourself to notice the thoughts and memories that accom-pany the anger about what happened to you, taking you away from the sensation of breath . . .

What happens in your body when you allow yourself to touch the mem-ory? . . . Does the pressure increase anywhere in your body? . . . If your mind wants to shift your thoughts away from the unbearableness of anger, tell your mind thank you for trying to take care of you . . . and remind it of all the knowl-edge and tools in this chapter that are helping anger to become livable and to make sense . . . and see what it's like to bow with respect for the anger . . . and to say to your body, "You can let go . . . You can let the anger flow . . . flow through you, without catching you up." . . . See what it's like to say to yourself, "Of course you're angry! . . . Would you like a little acknowledgment that you love the resource of trust . . . of integrity . . . of free access to relaxation . . . of easy access to security . . . to dignity . . . to knowing that your needs matter?" . . . As you notice how much you love the flow of life, see how that noticing affects your breathing . . . do you take a deeper breath? . . . What happens with your hands? . . . Do they become softer, more relaxed? . . . How is it to say to yourself, "My anger makes sense . . . I can feel its power . . . I can feel its importance . . . I understand myself . . . and I make sense . . . My anger matters to me . . . It tells me about the resources that may have been under threat when I was younger . . . and those that my body believes are under threat now . . ."

Again, touch into the memory . . . and if you are angry at someone else, check to see if you have any anger at yourself that needs to be acknowledged . . . And if you are angry at yourself, check to see if there is any anger at others that needs to be acknowledged . . .

Return to the anger memory and notice any constriction that you are feeling . . . Is there any loneliness or fear in this emotion? . . . Would it be sweet if someone else understood the importance of this event? . . . In another universe where we were all accompanied in our anger . . . not into action, but simply accompanied . . . in an understanding of anger as an important message . . . Would your body finally get to relax? . . .

Now, in this moment, see if you can connect to something larger than your own anger and your own body, something at the very center of your being that appreciates your own vulnerability and your persistence, that brings affection and gratitude for the journey you have been on, for what it has felt like to be you . . . Is it possible? . . . If it is, celebrate. . . . If it isn't possible yet, allow your brain to do whatever it needs to, to distract you and care for you and make the world's edges a little less sharp . . .

Taking a moment to reconnect with your breathing . . . allow yourself once again to notice that you are a breathing being . . . that you are here . . . that you exist . . . Touch your hands together gently . . . touch your face with gentleness . . . stroke the back of your neck . . . and allow yourself to come fully back to the present time.

GUIDED MEDITATION #2
Being With RAGE About Systems

To prepare for this meditation, choose a larger issue that brings you toward your outrage. This can be a political issue or an environmental issue or an issue of privilege or prejudice or integrity.

Begin this meditation by breathing . . . Notice yourself as a breathing being . . . Invite your attention to rest on the sensation of breath, wherever you feel it . . . See if you can invite your upper belly, around the bottom of your ribs, to move out when you inhale . . . and bring yourself back to breathing however your body breathes on its own, just allowing yourself to notice your breath . . . Where do you feel the sensation of breathing?. . . Is it in the rise and fall of your belly? . . . Is it in the small movements of your ribs and shoulders? . . . Is it the passage of air, a slight coolness, through your nose, sinuses, mouth, or throat? . . . Breathe for a moment . . . and then allow yourself to notice the thoughts and memories that make up the outrage, taking you away from the sensation of breath . . .

And bring yourself back to your breath . . . so that you can notice what happens to you with these powerful thoughts and memories . . . Does the pressure increase anywhere in your body? . . . If your mind wants to shift your thoughts away from the unbearableness of your RAGE or your outrage, tell your mind thank you for trying to take care of you . . . and remind it of all the knowledge and tools in this chapter that are helping anger to become livable and to make sense . . . and see what it's like to bow to the anger . . . and to say to your body, "You can let go . . . You can let the anger flow . . . flow through you, without catching you up . . . without making you do anything" . . . Let the energy of the anger flow out through the tips of your fingers . . . and see what it's like to say to yourself, "Of course you're angry! . . . Would you like a little acknowledgment that you love being able to trust the systems and groups that you belong to . . . to be able to trust their integrity and commitment to equity . . . that you want free access to resources for everyone, no matter who they are . . . and easy access to security for all . . . and to know there is enough . . . and to know that everyone's needs matter?" . . . As you notice how much you love the flow of life and resources, see how that noticing affects your breathing . . . Do you take a deeper breath? . . . What happens with your hands? . . . Do they become softer, more relaxed? . . . How is it to say to yourself, "My anger makes sense . . . I can feel its power . . . I can feel its importance . . . I understand myself and my frustration as a part of this group or this system . . . and I make sense . . . My anger matters to me . . . It tells me about the resources that may have been under threat when I was younger . . . and the resources that my body believes are under threat now . . .

Return to the anger memory and notice any constriction that you are feeling . . . Is there any loneliness or fear in this emotion? . . . Would it be sweet if many other people understood the importance of this difficult memory or thought? . . . In another universe where we were all accompanied in our anger . . . not into action, but simply accompanied . . . with an understanding of anger as an important message . . . would your body finally get to relax? . . .

Now, in this moment, see if you can connect to something larger than your own anger and your own body, something at the very center of your being that appreciates your own vulnerability and your persistence, your love of equity, your desire for open-mindedness, for willingness to learn, that brings affection and

gratitude for the journey you have been on, for what it has felt like to be you . . .
Is it possible? . . . If it is, celebrate. . . . If it isn't possible yet, allow your brain to do
whatever it needs to, to distract you and care for you and make the world's edges
a little less sharp . . .

Taking a moment to reconnect with your breathing . . . allow yourself once
again to notice that you are a breathing being . . . that you are here . . . that you
exist . . . Touch your hands together gently . . . Touch your face with gentleness . . .
Stroke the back of your neck . . . and allow yourself to come fully back to the
present time.

Now we'll take a look at the work that one person did with contracts and see the importance of time travel around RAGE when a person has reactivity to others' anger.

ONE-ON-ONE WORK
Working With RAGE

ROSE: *I think the experience I would like to choose is where recently somebody responded angrily to me in a kind of shutting-down-the-conversation way. I was stunned and I couldn't think of anything to say. And that's a pattern. Yes, I'm stunned.*

SARAH: *When we say we're stunned, we're talking about the nervous system shifting into immobilization. Most people freeze into a hardened immobility or collapse when they have less power in a situation and someone uses contempt or anger in relationship to us. Is that what happened?*

ROSE: *Yes. When I recently felt into this situation to find where it might have started, what I found was a picture of me sitting at the dinner table when I was two or three, with my father sitting next to me. He and my mother were having an argument and he was slamming his fist on the table and I remember that being very frightening. The paradox is that he was often my safe space. I was the youngest of three and my memories are of a lot of teasing and humiliation from my siblings. My mother was usually busy, and if I went to her, she would often respond with irritation or be cross with all three of us rather than be gentle and help us sort it out. My father was usually around, sitting somewhere reading a book or the paper, so I would crawl onto his lap* *and he would just acknowledge me, without trying to fix it. He would tuck me in and allow me to be there. So he was usually a very safe place for me to go to. And yet here he was—the anger wasn't directed at me, but it was scary to have this kind of snarling bear energy and to be so frozen, because the safe place I would go to, that should have been him.*

SARAH: *As you're remembering this, how does your body respond, if it's all right to ask?*

ROSE: *My palms are a bit sweaty. My shoulders are tight. I feel tense and tension in my legs.*

SARAH: *So it's quite alive. Is it okay if we time travel to this little one?*

ROSE: *Yes.*

SARAH: *Then you and I will step through time and space and freeze your father and freeze everybody else at the dinner table. We will put them inside floating golden bubbles, so everybody is taken care of. Then maybe we would say to this little 2-year-old person, "Was that really scary? And are you so confused because this person who's such a safe place for you suddenly expressed this intensity and moved so quickly with such loud noises? Were you so startled that you stopped breathing?"*

ROSE: *Yes.*

SARAH: *Are you just waiting for it to be over?*

ROSE: *Yes. Yes.*

SARAH: *You need your mom to be safe and your dad to be safe? Is it almost like you can tell that there's something wrong and you want things to be put right?*

ROSE: *Yes. I don't understand where it comes from. How could this kind, gentle person suddenly become a snarling, dangerous animal?*

SARAH: *What happens for this little one? Can she tell we're there?*

ROSE: *Oh, yes. She knows you're there. That's so much easier—her shoulders loosen and her leg muscles loosen and she can breathe and her forehead kind of untangles. But it's like she's removed herself a bit. Being in that chair, sitting there, it's so tense and scary and confusing. Could we go sit somewhere else?*

SARAH: *Oh, yes. Would she like to go outside? Or would she like to come to the present time? Or would she like to go to the sea? Where would she like to go?*

ROSE: *Well, she would like to go downstairs and sit on the two steps that go to the back door.*

SARAH: *We'll go downstairs and sit with her there.*

ROSE: *And the other people in the house, they're frozen too, aren't they?*

SARAH: *Well they're not just frozen, but we put them in nurturing golden bubbles of care. Yes.*

ROSE: *Yes. Yes. Because there are more people there; there's my grandmother, too.*

SARAH: *We've got them all floating, being completely nourished and nurtured in every possible way.*

ROSE: *Oh yes. Well, you know, if we could have angels with us, maybe I can go back and we could all sit around the table with the angels there and they can help us.*

SARAH: *What a good idea.*

ROSE: *Well, I can be there and it can be nice. Yes. We could take turns at talking.*

SARAH: *That would be nice too.*

ROSE: *Yes. And we say how we feel, and the others will listen and be kind. Sarah, I wonder, could you talk to my daddy?*

SARAH: *We can give him his own Sarah who says, "Of course you're angry. Are you so worried? Are you so overwhelmed? Do you just need acknowledgment that, in this moment, you are frustrated, and you have no other recourse than to yell and bang?" How's the little one doing?*

ROSE: *It's kind of interesting to watch. She finds it interesting to watch his interaction with somebody who's calm and understanding, who's not scared of his anger. It's like she's seeing an example and realizing, oh, so it could be like that? It can be so difficult to imagine anything except freezing.*

SARAH: *It's nice to have a different possibility.*

ROSE: *Yes. That brings relief from the tension and a role model.*

SARAH: *I also want to acknowledge that anger is most often an expression that a person has a sense of, in some way, being cornered and choiceless.*

ROSE: *Yes, that's something I would really like to take with me. A permanent reminder of that. That I don't mistake it for power.*

SARAH: *Yes, just check in with the little one. You said you'd like to take it with you, and one of the things we can do is to invite the little one, with the knowledge that she has now, to come be a part of us. We can see if she would like to come to the present time and be in your heart.*

ROSE: *There's something stopping her, something not acknowledged.*

SARAH: *Just stay with her and I imagine it'll emerge from her body.*

ROSE: *Sadness.*

SARAH: *Ah, sadness. Does she need acknowledgment that in this moment there's a terrible loneliness? That when her father becomes angry, it's the terrible loneliness of losing a person she loves.*

ROSE: *It's less personal than that. It's a loss of an illusion, a dream of safety and harmony? A hope? Yes, that fist breaks something. It smashes a possibility, it smashes the illusion, like realizing, oh, so this is the reality? It isn't like I imagined.*

SARAH: *This is where we're touching what might be a contract. Does she have a contract to never trust her sense of possibility? Is it like that? Instead of there being a sense that this is one survivable moment in time, where she can have resilience and everything will return to being okay, there's a sense of things being irrevocably changed?*

ROSE: *Yes. It's difficult to grasp. I'm holding the pieces of, "I was wrong. I was wrong to believe in the possibility." It's like a loss of trust in myself, or my inner wisdom, or self-connection.*

SARAH: *Does she now have a sense that she can't trust herself?*

ROSE: *Yes.*

SARAH: *Yes. Does it feel like her nervous system making a little bit of a contract that sounds something like, "I, Rose's nervous system, solemnly swear to you, Rose, that I will never trust myself again, so that we're never taken by such shock and surprise ever again"?*

ROSE: *Yes. That I will never trust myself again. I always need to ask other people whether I'm right. I will never trust myself again so that . . .*

SARAH: *So that I never have to live through the horror and shock of disillusionment again?*

ROSE: *Yes. I was wrong. I was wrong. I had this precious thing inside me, and it was wrong.*

SARAH: *"I will never believe in the precious thing inside me again"?*

ROSE: *Yes. I can't rely on it. We can't rely. Rely on . . . what to call it? A heart-knowing? I don't know, that seems like a strange term.*

SARAH: *Heart-knowing is a beautiful term. Is it love?*

ROSE: *No, not quite.*

SARAH: *And, is it instinct?*

ROSE: *No. Oh, it all sounds so pretentious. You know, it's like a seed that was planted that I brought here.*

SARAH: *A seed that was planted that I brought here. Like this is what this little one came with from before birth, from before conception?*

ROSE: *Yes. Brought this from somewhere else or from passed along ancestors.*

SARAH: *Something that was bigger than her or more than her? In this moment, is it like a bubble that popped?*

ROSE: *It was something that was smashed. It's like I'm holding these pieces and it's broken, so I cannot rely on this heart-knowing.*

SARAH: *It's very interesting that it's smashed. I wonder if we need to give a little acknowledgment directly to the heart-knowing, as its own being? Do we need to say, heart-knowing, do you need acknowledgment that you were smashed?*

ROSE: *That's funny, it doesn't land at all. The heart-knowing is not smashed.*

SARAH: *How does the little one respond to that?*

ROSE: *It's not something that can be smashed. It's like the trust was broken.*

SARAH: *Yes. And so then look for, "I, little Rose, swear to myself to no longer trust." Just see.*

ROSE: *"I, little Rose, swear that I will no longer trust . . . or rely on my heart-knowing to guide me in order to not be separate, in order to belong with my family. No matter the cost to myself or my connection with my heart."*

SARAH: *And Rose's essential self, did you hear the vow that Rose made?*

ROSE: *Yes.*

SARAH: *Is that a good vow for her?*

ROSE: *No.*

SARAH: *Will you please tell her, "Rose, I release you from this vow."?*

ROSE: *"Little Rose, I release you from this vow and I revoke this contract. And instead you have my blessing to live from your heart-knowing."*

SARAH: *I feel a glow through my whole body. How is it for you?*

ROSE: *Yes, it feels like something has settled. It feels more grounded, calmer.*

SARAH: *And, as we continue to work for a little bit, just see if the little one wants to come back with you now.*

ROSE: *Oh, yes.*

SARAH: *Okay, then, and just enjoy her for a breath or two. Enjoy her presence. Yes?*

ROSE: *Yes, yes. She's nestled in my heart.*

SARAH: *And now let's test what we'd been doing and see how it does in present time. If you imagine this experience, with this person bringing in anger, contempt, and shutting down the conversation, with the result that you were unable to respond last week, what's it like to think of that memory now?*

ROSE: *Ah, there's a gentleness and curiosity. You know, I might not have a reply straight away, but that's ok.*

SARAH: *Wonderful. Wonderful. Rose, is this a good place for us for today? I want to express a need that was met for me, feeling a sense of awe in the understanding that we give up our access to heart-knowing in order to have belonging with our families and our family systems. It just feels like such an important truth to be able to talk about. So I'm very, very grateful for our work today. Thank you.*

One year later, Rose writes:

I am speaking up for myself more, and I am no longer willing to put myself down the way I used to or give away my space. I am getting better at hearing my inner voice, and paying attention to it, taking it seriously, tending to what it says. The other day, in conversation with a relative, I interrupted her when she started to give me unsolicited advice, and I told her I didn't find her comments helpful, and that I love being understood. I have always been too terrified of her to do that, but this time I didn't even think about it. It was still scary, but there was no hesitation. I still sometimes freeze, or don't manage to catch my voice in the moment, but I can see I'm getting better at retracing my steps and bringing the part that got frozen or steamrollered in the moment back to be heard. So yes, I trust myself more!

Now that we have made it through many of the possible contracts connected with RAGE, take a look at the following list of unconscious contracts to help you decide what you would like to work with.

POSSIBLE UNCONSCIOUS CONTRACTS CONNECTED WITH RAGE

I solemnly swear to my essential self that:

I will . . .	In order to . . .
never be angry	keep from doing harm/being like my parent/ save my parent from terror/keep from expressing predatory aggression
use rage to be heard or seen	wake my parent up to me/bring my parent back to life
always be angry	be the powerful one/never show my weakness/carry my parent's RAGE out of loyalty/be angry when my parent could not
carry anger on behalf of my mother or father	honor them

I will . . .	In order to . . .
change my anger into grief	belong/be acceptable
always be nice/make jokes when people are angry	alleviate tension/make sure everyone survives
always be afraid/disgusted/hypervigilant when people are angry	be loyal to my parent, who was always afraid/disgusted/hypervigilant when people were angry
punish myself when I am angry	make sure I don't destroy the world with my RAGE
punish others when they are angry	make them pay for my pain/for scaring people/make them pay for the pain I felt with my mother or father

RAGE Contract Template

Try doing one for each anger-related vow that you have identified.

1. I, _____, solemnly swear to my essential self (or mother, father, sibling, God, universe, etc.) that I will always/never

    _____

    _____

    in order to _____ ,
    no matter the cost to myself and those I love.

2. What is the good, historical, lived reason for this contract? When did you first make this contract? How does it make sense within the larger context of your life?

    _____

    _____

3. Essential self (or mother, father, sibling, God, universe, etc.), did you hear this vow?

    Yes _____

    No _____

    (If no, then repeat the words of the vow.)

4. *Essential self (or mother, father, sibling, God, universe, etc.), do you want this vow to be kept?*

    Yes _____

    No _____

    (If the answer is "Yes, the vow should stay, no matter the cost," then it's time to use the Time Travel Process to go to the moment in your life in which this unconscious contract makes sense.)

5. The release: *I release you from this vow, and I revoke this contract.*

6. The blessing: *And I give you my blessing to:*

    _____

CHAPTER 7

Coming Back From Dissociation

Have you ever been unable to think or struggled to find words in a stressful situation? When you get into a testing situation, are you sometimes unable to remember the answers? When things get overwhelming, do you become spacey and find it impossible to make decisions or to plan things? When people become demanding, do you collapse and comply? When you feel helpless do you lose all your energy and sense of personal power? All of these responses come from the immobilization response of the nervous system (which people often call *freeze* from the phrase *fight, flight, or freeze*).

Stephen Porges, the main researcher into the vagus nerve, uses the word immobilization instead of freeze, because freeze implies a frozen hardness, a hard shell of immobility. But when we use the word *immobilization*, it can include a kind of a slack, absent collapse—it doesn't have to be a *freeze*.

THE MAIN QUESTION FOR THIS CHAPTER

How do we know when we are immobilized, and how is that different from being dissociated?

When we become immobilized, we have moved into the rearmost channel of the vagus nerve—the part without the nerve insulation that brings us speedy thought and action. On a physiological level, our heartbeat, blood pressure, and breathing rate all decrease.[1] Immobilization and dissociation are two linked circles of a Venn diagram. We can be immobilized without losing connection with our bodies (without being dissociated), and we can be dissociated without losing our mobility. Part of dissociation is that we lose connection with our bodies, so we may not notice any of this, but some of the cues of dissociation are:

- a separation of conscious awareness of self from the body,
- confusion/spaciness,

- an inability to track thoughts,
- heaviness/collapse,
- an inability to move or take action/lack of energy.

There's a reason that we feel slow when we're immobilized: the nervous system switches from its fast track (120 meters per second[2]) to its slow track (2 meters per second[3]). We lose some of the oxygen supply to our brain. Additionally, endogenous opioids flood various parts of our brain and make thinking hard or even impossible. As mentioned in previous chapters, we can turn off certain circuits with our unconscious contracts or as a result of trauma, but dissociation and immobilization disable our entire system and turn down the life energy in all the circuits. This is most often a response to trauma, to moments when we didn't have a sense that action was possible, or to a series of events that left us helpless and without agency. We can often feel this as a general loss of life energy and a lack of capacity to take action. People sometimes say that they feel like they're "not really here," or they're "only half-alive."

It's also possible to experience a shift to the left hemisphere (the left shift) that takes us into a dissociative state. We often use the same word *dissociation* for both dissociation that's a full-body shutting down traumatic dissociation and for the dissociation that comes from being left-shifted, but there is a difference. When we shift out of our relational brain into our instrumental brain, we're dissociating from and leaving the right hemisphere's integrated map of the body, but we're not losing energy or cognitive capacity. We aren't becoming immobilized. Instead, we're losing access to emotion, self-connection, and relationality. Often, we're shifting gears in order to move more fully into seeking, and being only in the SEEKING circuit is its own special kind of body disconnection, because the SEEKING circuit makes up a lot of the instrumental brain and has no access to the integrated body map. Many people live this way for their entire lives.

Dissociation is like a lever that disengages our drive wheel, lifting our observing self out of its capacity to act. There's a spinning-in-place that we can experience as nothing really working anymore. Being dissociated isn't wrong, it's a survival strategy. Our system downshifts into immobility or shock to save our energy and our lives until it becomes safe to move or to participate. We can learn to have profound tenderness with our dissociated selves. If our dissociation is left-shifted, rather than traumatic, we can remember that our relational selves are right there waiting for us, actually informing our dissociated selves. They simply need to be rediscovered and reintegrated into our daily lives. Here is a questionnaire to help you understand the degree to which you may live in either dissociated state.

QUESTIONNAIRE
How Often Do You Dissociate?

As you go through these questions, don't worry about how you answer, simply let your body answer quickly, off the top of your head, and then see how the results feel to you.

LEFT-SHIFTED DISSOCIATION

1. I have no idea what's happening for me emotionally.

   Never   Rarely   Sometimes   Often   Always

2. I don't like to talk about what's happening for me emotionally.

   Never   Rarely   Sometimes   Often   Always

3. I don't know what's happening with my body sensations in my gut, chest, throat, and face.

   Never   Rarely   Sometimes   Often   Always

4. I enjoy talking about ideas, concepts, or thoughts more than feelings, sensations, and emotions.

   Never   Rarely   Sometimes   Often   Always

5. I like to tell people the names of the airports I have visited on my journeys.

   Never   Rarely   Sometimes   Often   Always

6. I feel most comfortable in my conversations when I'm talking about something I know a lot about.

   Never   Rarely   Sometimes   Often   Always

7. I tend to speak about myself rather than ask others about themselves.

   Never   Rarely   Sometimes   Often   Always

8. I like to know people's professions and levels of education.

   Never   Rarely   Sometimes   Often   Always

TRAUMATIC DISSOCIATION

1. I don't see people's faces or notice their facial expressions.

   Never   Rarely   Sometimes   Often   Always

2. I can't take action. I feel paralyzed.

   Never   Rarely   Sometimes   Often   Always

3. I feel helpless.

   Never   Rarely   Sometimes   Often   Always

4. I have no energy.

   Never   Rarely   Sometimes   Often   Always

5. I often gaze off into space and disengage from the present moment.

   Never   Rarely   Sometimes   Often   Always

6. I feel alone, lost, and unreachable.

   Never   Rarely   Sometimes   Often   Always

7. I can't think or organize my thoughts.

   Never   Rarely   Sometimes   Often   Always

8. I never know how I feel about things or what my opinion is.

   Never   Rarely   Sometimes   Often   Always

SCORING

Give yourself a 1 for each Never, a 2 for each Rarely, a 3 for each Sometimes, a 4 for each Often, and a 5 for each Always. Count up the number of each type of answer for each type of dissociation. Which type do you score higher for?

JOURNALING PROMPT FOR
Noticing Present-Time Dissociation

Right now, in this moment, how completely are you aware of your body as yourself? How much does it seem to you that your mind and your body are separate? How clear are your thoughts? How much access do you have to movement or to being able to carry out your intentions? Is it easy to write about your experience, or do you lose your path when you try to write? Do you find that even reading these questions leaves you confused, as if you are drifting away? Can you feel yourself breathing? Do you notice your own heartbeat? What are the fine muscles of your face doing? Can you tell if you are carrying any emotions in your facial expressions?

_____

_____

_____

DISSOCIATION AND THE CIRCUITS

It's possible for us to dissociate in response to different cues from the different circuits. For example, if PLAY was dangerous, we might dissociate anytime people around us are happy, joyful, or playful. This kind of trauma comes from a moment when we were playing and something dangerous happened. For example, if we experienced being attacked or something else that was dangerous, or if when we lost focus while playing while we were also taking care of a younger sibling and they got hurt. In the latter case, we may believe our PLAY could be dangerous to others.

Dissociation can happen in relationship to the RAGE circuit if we feel that our anger makes us dangerous to others or others' anger is dangerous to us. If we believe that this circuit is life-threatening and we shut it down, we leave ourselves immobile and perhaps unable to tolerate anger in ourselves or others. In these moments, we can dissociate or become immobile in order to be able to survive the experience of RAGE.

Another possibility is that our FEAR can trigger a kind of predatory aggression in siblings or parents or school mates or teachers. We may learn to turn off the FEAR circuit with dissociation if these people attacked us when we showed fear, and then we may end up not even knowing how terrified or frightened we are in the experience of danger.

It's also possible to dissociate with SEEKING, so that whenever we begin to feel our own life energy, we close ourselves down so that we don't leave anyone behind, or so that we protect ourselves from the shame and humiliation of trying and failing. We may also dissociate if we've experienced other people having very toxic SEEKING circuits, with a huge desire to win, for example, which would mean that they have a huge desire for us to lose. It can be terrifying to be on the receiving end of such competitiveness.

An aspect of contracts in relationship with the SEEKING circuit is the tendency we might have to sacrifice everything else in honor of SEEKING. When we put all of our life energy into the SEEKING circuit, we shift into the left-hemisphere dissociation, separating the thinking-mind from the body, which we spoke about earlier in this chapter. This way of life is most often rewarded in technologically based societies where achievement and success are valued highly.

We can shut down PANIC/GRIEF in order not to be sad or recognize sadness if we have a sense that showing our sadness is threatening to ourself or others. For example, if our mother turned away or changed the subject when we were sad, we knew that this meant our sorrow was too much for her. If this circuit is shut down, then we may not be able to mourn the way we need to when we experience a loss. We also may not receive social support because we are not able to reveal our sadness to others. This might look like going back to work right after a family member dies and hearing comments about how well we are handling things, only to fall apart years later with delayed grief.

And of course, we can shut down our SEXUALITY, or our sense of self, if we've ever experienced violence or intrusion in connection with our sexual being or in connection with existing at all.

With the CARE circuit, dissociation can come on very strongly if we've had to be the parent to our parents. Caring for big ones when we are a little one is something that turns our nervous systems upside down and turns us inside out. This doesn't mean we took care of them in their old age. This means that, starting from early childhood, we were looking after them or committing our nervous system to their well-being or stabilization. If a mother says, "I didn't raise my child, my child raised me," this is probably a sign that this mother used her child's nervous system to stabilize herself. If we dissociate in response to receiving CARE, or being asked to give CARE, we may very well be in the presence of relational history and intrusion or abandonment that have been almost impossible to survive. This might lead to us avoiding close relationships, finding it difficult to take care of our own children, or finding it difficult to receive care from others. We may also find ourselves feeling numb when someone expresses vulnerability.

WORKSHEET
The Color of Your Dissociation

First, assign a color to each of your Circuits of Emotion and Motivation.

Circuit	Color
SEEKING	
CARE	
GRIEF/PANIC	
FEAR	
ANGER	
PLAY	
SEXUALITY	
DISGUST	

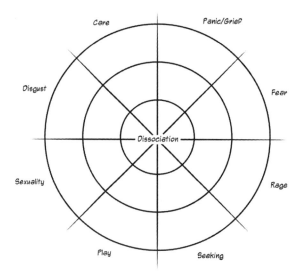

Now, put your colors into the outer ring of the Circuit Circle provided underneath the table shown above. Bring the colors that seem connected with your dissociation into the center in lighter shades, so that you can get a feel for the contribution of the various circuits involved in your dissociation. For example, if you have a sense that your SEXUALITY circuit and your FEAR circuit are very linked with your patterns of dissociation and you made SEXUALITY fuchsia and FEAR green, then you may find that your dissociation (inside the circle in the middle) will be a combination of light pink and light green. There are no right answers here, this is just your own personal exploration that lets you move your felt sense of things into the visual field. If you don't have colored pens, you can hatch different patterns with a pen; or if this doesn't appeal to you, you can contemplate what is true for you: What is the flavor of your dissociation? Which circuits take you into dissociation most consistently?

HOW BREAKING CONTRACTS LEADS TO DISSOCIATION

Far more common than the direct contracts that take us into dissociation is the phenomenon of breaking contracts unrelated to dissociation, which then immobilizes or puts us into dissociation.

Let's look at how contracts relate to dissociation. There may be some contracts that directly involve dissociation, such as, "I vow never to feel sexual feelings in order to protect my family from judgment." More often, though, it is when contracts are broken that we dissociate. One way this could show up would be if I have a contract not to be angry but anger starts to rise anyway, I would dissociate in order to keep the anger unfelt and unacknowledged.

All of our nervous system states are vulnerable to broken contracts, as shown in Chapter 6 on anger. Breaking through these behavioral prohibitions, which are the essential structure of our unconscious contracts, is very stressful. For example, if a person has a contract not to exist, but here they are, breathing, the very act of existing may put them into a state of dissociation. If a person has a contract not to be the person they are—if people believe they aren't supposed to be smart, or funny, or fast, or strong, or insightful, or large-bodied, or red-haired, or unathletic, but they are, the stress of being wrong for our families can put us into a semipermanent state of immobilization or dissociation.

Finding the Broken Contracts That Lead to Dissociation

How are your personality and your body different from what your father or your father's line would have liked you to be?

_____

_____

_____

Do you have an impossible and just-starting-to-be-conscious contract to be what they wanted, which is different from who you really are? If so, what is it?

_____

_____

_____

How are your personality and your body different from what your mother or your mother's line would have liked you to be?

_____

_____

_____

Do you have an impossible and just-starting-to-be-conscious contract to be what they wanted, which is different from who you really are? If so, what is it?

_____

_____

_____

How are you as a person and as a body different from what would have made you safe in your school years?

_____

_____

_____

Do you have an impossible and just-starting-to-be-conscious contract to be what the people in school wanted, which is different from who you really are? If so, what is it?

_____

_____

Do you have any guesses about contracts that may lead to dissociation when they are broken? If so, what are they?

RESONANT LANGUAGE PRACTICE
Acknowledgment of What Is

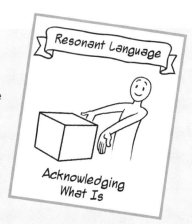

Resonant language allows us to name things that have never been named. When we turn these messages, which have been held in an uncompleted form in our bodies, into words, we can finally receive the meaning of these messages. Simply receiving and acknowledging them is an important aspect of healing. The form of resonant language that we are practicing in this chapter is "Acknowledging What Is."

Different people enjoy framing this type of resonance differently, with some readers liking the question, *"Would you like some acknowledgment . . . that the terror made your breath stop . . ."* or *"that you always were competing with your sibling to be seen?"* Others preferred the question, *"Would it be sweet if someone else understood . . . how the outrage turns you inside out?"* or *"the depth of your love that was never received?"* or *"that your mother had no idea how to be a mother?"*

To practice this type of resonant language, begin by deciding which question works better for you:

"Would you like some acknowledgment that . . ."

or

"Would it be sweet if someone else understood how . . ."

and then fill in the blanks for yourself for the following sentences.

. . . the fear was _____ ?
. . . the anger was _____ ?

. . . your mother was _____ ?
. . . your father was _____ ?
. . . the grief is _____ ?
. . . the sense of abandonment was _____ ?
. . . the shame is _____ ?
. . . the joy was _____ ?

Try to complete the questions so that your answer to them is yes.

When you are asking others these questions about acknowledgment, they may or may not answer yes. If they don't offer a yes, they may respond by telling you what they would enjoy accompaniment in or acknowledgment of. This type of question sets the stage for self-resonance and the naming of experience, so we don't need to ask correctly, we just need to ask with resonance.

Let's take a moment to experience a gentle, guided meditation to support the return from both kinds of dissociation.

GUIDED MEDITATION TO
Invite the Return From Left-Shifted Dissociation

This meditation addresses a possible tendency to live apart from having a sense of the body and is a gentle invitation to begin to notice the emotional body and to awaken our own right hemisphere's capacity to bring us meaning and a rich life.

Allow yourself to notice your sense of self . . . Do you exist? . . . Are you participating in your body's existence? . . . Or is your body just a carrier for your doing? . . . Did you know that you are always breathing? . . . What do you notice first, as you bring your attention to being embodied? . . . Can you find the movement of your breath? . . . Can you feel it at the edges of your nostrils? . . . Inside your nose? . . . In the back of your throat? . . . Does all internal body sensation disappear below your collar bone? . . . If it does, notice if you can feel your arms, hands, legs, or feet . . . These feelings don't bring us back from left-shifted dissociation, but they do help to anchor us in our bodies . . . Come back to your breath . . . Look for sensations of breathing in your chest . . . Notice how your heart feels . . . your stomach . . . your intestines . . . your pelvis . . .

Consider that it might be possible that you and your body are one . . . that your essence is arising from every cell of your physical being . . . that every cell is contributing to you being alive and being exactly who you are . . . that each cell carries epigenetic information about the systems you are embedded in . . . that each cell is doing its own microbreathing while you are doing your macrobreathing . . . that you need all the breathing to be happening to support your life . . . Thank your cells for their breathing . . . Let the gratitude rise up in you . . . Can you feel your heart growing larger with gratitude? . . .

Allow yourself to come back to your breath . . . What do you sense with your breath? . . . Can you feel your chest move? . . . Can you feel your abdomen move? . . . Touch your belly to see if it's moving . . . Allow your attention to sink 2 inches into your belly . . . inside you . . . What do you notice there? . . . The sensations there are usually feelings of constriction . . . immobility . . . cramping . . . or of relaxation . . . openness . . . gentle pulsing . . . and all of them are linked to emotion . . . as you begin a relationship of openness and communication with your emotional body, you will experience more relaxation, ease, and connection than ever before . . . Try it out for a moment . . . Ask your belly, "Are you sad?" and see if any sensation shifts . . . Try "Are you angry?" . . . "Are you afraid?" . . . "Are you lonely?" . . . "Is there someone you miss?" . . . Do the sensations in your abdomen shift in response to your guesses? . . . Add needs . . . "Do you long for deep, satisfying friendship?" . . . "Do you love safe havens and refuges, even if you've never really relaxed into one?" . . . "Do you love to be alone?" . . . "Do you love to be with people?" . . . "Do you long for a tribe?" . . . Do your belly sensations shift? . . .

Would it be sweet to have some acknowledgment of how odd it is to be invited to focus here . . . on the sensations inside your body? . . . How baffling? . . . Acknowledgment that your mind doesn't even know why it would be asked to do this? . . . That it keeps popping out to work on something it finds more productive? . . . That during this lifetime you have never really been here, with this focus combined with affection, before?

Gently and with warmth, acknowledge your attention, wherever it wants to take you . . . Thank it for trying to guide you toward what it thinks is meaningful . . . and let it know that this connection with body is essential for healthy living and satisfaction . . . and see if your attention is willing to come back to your breath . . .

Now, let your attention spring back into engagement with your everyday life . . . Notice if there is any relief in releasing the request to notice the emotional body . . . and be in the normal flow of your regular life . . . Hold any relief with affection, too . . . "Of course it's a relief to relax" . . .

GUIDED MEDITATION TO
Invite the Return From Traumatic Dissociation

As you read or listen to this meditation, you may find that you drift in and out or that you dissociate entirely. Allow yourself to notice what is happening, and if it feels pleasant to leave and allow the meditation to continue, drift along with it. If there is a cost that you pay, stop the meditation immediately and skip ahead, past the meditation. It may be that listening to a meditation that invites you to have a body breaks a contract, or several, that you have to not have a body.

Allow yourself to notice your body . . . What do you notice first, as you bring your attention to being embodied? . . . Can you find the movement of your breath? . . . If you are noticing that you can't feel anything . . . or that you are already dissociated . . . invite yourself to surround every bit of your diffuse, dissociated self with affection and warmth . . . Your affection does not have to be limited by gravity . . . It will find you wherever you are . . . If you are dissociated and dispersed, you have very good reasons to be . . .

If you begin to notice your own breath . . . let yourself start a continuous remembrance of breathing as an ongoing, lifelong process . . . so that you continually invite your own attention back to your breath . . . and see what it is like to bring warmth . . . appreciation . . . affection . . . gratitude . . . and acknowledgment to your body . . . your body that has allowed you to live this lifetime . . . and has supported you . . . even if you live somewhat dissociated from it . . .

And now bring your attention to your sense of your whole body as your very own . . . that it is not here for anyone else's demands or even requests . . . that it is here for you and you alone . . . Allow yourself to notice that within your own relationship with your body, it might be safe for you to fully inhabit it . . . that you might be able to enjoy your own hands . . . arms . . . shoulders . . . chest . . . heart . . . throat . . . face . . . Follow a breath down into your belly . . . your intestines . . . your pelvis . . . your hips and bottom . . . your sexual organs . . . your legs . . . your knees . . . your ankles . . . your feet . . . they are all yours and no one else's . . . You may have lived through events in which you experienced your body as not being your own . . . But no matter what has happened . . . your body belongs to you . . .

Come back to your breath . . . Know that your breathing is supposed to help you survive and thrive . . . that your blood is pumping for you . . . that your brain is, for at least this small moment, just for you . . . and that you can have a great affection for your body . . . for your being . . . for your existence . . . It isn't here to make you vulnerable . . . It is worthy of protection . . . and love . . . No one else is supposed to be able to touch it or even think about it unless you want them to . . . Put a magic bubble around yourself to see if it helps . . . a bubble that prevents intrusion . . . and prevents judgment . . . even your own . . . And let your body be fully supported . . . and protected . . . And know that if you aren't able to live fully in . . . and enjoy . . . your body, then there are probably very important contracts you have that disconnect you from yourself . . . and that you can always create a circle of warmth . . . and affection . . . and love . . . for your whole being . . . that extends around your body . . . and around your consciousness . . . even if it is separated from your body . . .

And now, follow your breath again . . . if you can find it . . . and allow yourself to return fully . . . or as fully as your contracts permit . . . to the present moment . . . Notice what you are seeing . . . Notice what the external world wants from you . . . and remember what you have discovered about what has caused you to leave this body . . . or to turn away from it . . . or to judge it too harshly to remain connected to it . . .

Through the process of these meditations, you may have discovered new insights into the contracts that prevent you from living fully in your body. Review the following contracts that might take a person directly into dissociation, and underline those that speak to you.

POSSIBLE CONTRACTS THAT TAKE US DIRECTLY INTO DISSOCIATION

I will . . .	In order to . . .
not stay in my body	stay safe
not participate in life	protest my lack of choice about existing
not exist in the present moment	manage pain
not move	keep from attracting attention and being a target

I will . . .	In order to . . .
dissociate with my mother	keep her from being alone
not go where I am not wanted	keep from being rejected
not feel	lighten the load on my parents
never fully incarnate	stay with my prenatal twin who died

What comes up for you? What might your contracts be?

ONE-ON-ONE WORK
Working With Dissociation

The following process shows a very gentle way of being with dissociation.

SARAH: *Lucy, hello. As I'm talking about dissociation, I wonder if there's anything that's coming to mind for you.*

LUCY: *It's hard even to know how to choose. I often get very confused and don't know what to do next. I know that's a form of dissociation. And I think I'm dissociating right now. I think I have a vow somewhere around not allowing myself to heal. When I'm given the opportunity to heal and surrounded by all kinds of healing energy, I either dissociate or go into shame. Right now, I'm experiencing anxiety and dissociation.*

SARAH: *I wonder, do you need acknowledgment that the dissociation comes a bit like a wave over which you have no control and that suddenly almost everything disappears?*

LUCY: *Yes, but I can't describe it as separation from my body. I can feel the anxiety in my body, and my thinking gets confused.*

SARAH: *Yes, that's a flow of endogenous opioids going right to your prefrontal cortex. We can just say, "Hello, endogenous opioids in Lucy's prefrontal cortex." We could even say, "Welcome, we know that you are protecting Lucy, and we are grateful for all of your devotion and protection for her."*

LUCY: *I would like to have that much compassion.*

SARAH: *Do you need a little acknowledgment that you get annoyed with this process? Do you want some choice about what floods your brain? And that sometimes you would wish for clarity and self-connection and articulateness?*

LUCY: *Yes! Absolutely.*

SARAH: *If your brain goes completely blank and we sit with you in warmth, then we're doing exactly what we need to do. And if we discover a vow, then we're doing exactly what we need to do.*

LUCY: *Thank you. I'm very intrigued by the idea that there is a vow involved. I remember as a younger adult that I would go completely into dissociation. If I were with a group of people, probably when I was a teenager as well, or even younger, I would often wake up suddenly and think, I don't remember anything that went on for the last half hour. Then I'd be very embarrassed, because I didn't know what was happening and didn't know how to participate. That rarely happens these days, so I'm seeing that as progress, but there's also a lot more frustration and anxiety because I'm more aware of the tendency to dissociate.*

SARAH: *When do you notice it most? Is it most noticeable when you are social?*

LUCY: *Definitely, and social is a broad category. For example, in a workshop where there's some activity to participate in, it's social because there are other people involved. I just get, not so much spaced out as confused. It feels frozen in a way, but there's enough of me left to be very frustrated about it.*

SARAH: *Yes. Do you remember this from being a little one in school, or do you ever remember it with your parents, or do you mostly remember it from other environments?*

LUCY: *I don't remember it from being little. I remember things from childhood that I imagine are relevant, but I'm not remembering that sensation. I know I was bullied by other children. I was teased and I didn't know how to defend myself.*

SARAH: *There was a bewilderment there?*

LUCY: *Bewilderment and simply resignation. Like I was doomed and there was nothing I could do. It didn't feel like confusion at that time, though.*

SARAH: *So then let's check in about middle school. Is there any sense of confusion in middle school?*

LUCY: *I think by the time I was in middle school, I'd already learned how to dissociate and not feel confused, because I wasn't present. I also remember an episode of total humiliation, but I don't see the connections between these things.*

SARAH: *Okay. Let's move forward. We're looking for when the confusion begins, just to see if there's a vow that is specifically connected with the confusion. If we tune into you when you were a little bit older, where were you between 18 and 22?*

LUCY: *I started college a little early because I skipped a year, and then from the ages of 20 to 22, I was studying in Europe. I was very isolated. The confusion then was about how to simply be a normal person in the world. How to be sociable, have friends, and have activities with other people. I see everyone around me doing it and I don't have a clue how to do it. I'm confused right now even trying to answer your questions, because I'm not finding . . .*

SARAH: *The clear beginning to the confusion?*

LUCY: *Yes. I started college taking art classes and that's the one area in which I was not confused. I didn't know how to do social.*

SARAH: *No.*

LUCY: *But it started before that. That was very lonely. I was convinced that I was the one that was peculiar.*

SARAH: *Okay. So, let's start there. "I, Lucy, solemnly swear to my essential self that I will believe that I am the peculiar one."*

LUCY: *Yes. I'm still holding that vow today. I will believe that I am the peculiar one, and I will take the blame for how confusing everything is.*

SARAH: *In order to?*

LUCY: *Maybe it's so that the world will make sense.*

SARAH: *So that the world will make sense. If I can blame Lucy, the world will make sense. No matter the cost to myself. And is the vow also, "I will be angry at Lucy"?*

LUCY: *"I, Lucy, solemnly swear to my essential self that I will be angry at Lucy and I'll blame Lucy for her peculiarities. I will make Lucy the peculiar one in order to make the world make sense, no matter the cost of myself." It's a huge cost.*

SARAH: *Yes. Lucy's essential self, did you hear the vow that Lucy made to you to get angry at Lucy and blame her and hold her responsible?*

LUCY: *She heard.*

SARAH: *Okay. Is this a good vow for Lucy?*

LUCY: *No.*

SARAH: *Would you please tell her, "Lucy, I release you from this vow."*

LUCY: *Lucy, I release you from this vow and I revoke this contract, and instead you have my blessing to find out who you are.*

SARAH: *Mmm, what a beautiful blessing. How does your body do?*

LUCY: *Lots of grief. I don't think I'm ready to fully release that vow. I think there's a whole complex of vows involved.*

SARAH: *Okay. I'm going to ask you something radical and then we'll get to find out what your response to it is.*

LUCY: *Okay.*

SARAH: *What if you belong because you are Lucy and because you are right here and because, even more radically, you are loved? What if there's absolutely nothing that you have to do or say in order to belong?*

LUCY: *Well, there's a part of me that gets that, that's heard it many times. But I can't fully believe it.*

SARAH: *Is it because belonging has a particular quality for you?*

LUCY: *Fitting in.*

SARAH: *Somehow feeling like you're like everybody else?*

LUCY: *Yes. And I rebel against the idea of being like everybody else. It's not about conforming in a boring kind of way. I saw people around me, who I admire and who I think are more advanced than I am, and I have proved, with every breath I take, that I'm not up to that.*

SARAH: *Does your body need acknowledgment that your parents were enormously intelligent?*

LUCY: *My father was, definitely. Yes. And that was what he admired most in me, when he could see it. In fact, he attributed some kinds of intelligence to me that I didn't really have. He also was greatly supportive of my artistic self because that I did have. But it's people who are doing things I admire that my father would have had contempt for. You know, like healing work, woo-woo stuff. The sort of things that my father had contempt for, yet I wanted so much to be a part of.*

SARAH: *So then, we also want to look for any vows of loyalty. If there's a way that your spirit's longing for one thing but your father would have contempt for it, then it would lead directly into dissociation.*

LUCY: *"Father, I will never betray you."*

SARAH: *"I will never betray you." Yes. Can you feel that?*

LUCY: *Yes. "I'll never betray you by becoming more flexible and open-minded than you are."*

SARAH: *Lucy, did you hear this vow that you made? Check to see if it's to your father?*

LUCY: *I hate it.*

SARAH: *You hate it. Did you make it to Lucy? "I, Lucy, solemnly swear to you, myself, that I will . . ."*

LUCY: *"I will never betray my father." Oh yes, no, I don't like that vow at all.*

SARAH: *Yes, would you like to release Lucy from that vow?*

LUCY: *I would like to. "Lucy, I release you from this vow and I revoke this contract and again I give you my blessing to find out who you are."*

SARAH: *And, maybe, to know that your father has died and that his contempt was part of his mortal life and isn't with us anymore?*

LUCY: *Yes. I'm feeling a little bit of relief.*

SARAH: *Oh, very good. Very good.*

LUCY: *Like, before my shoulders were around my ears, and now, they can relax a little more.*

SARAH: *And of course, these kinds of vows of loyalty would leave us in very confused and dissociated places. What's happening in this moment with the confusion?*

LUCY: *My father has come in again in a different form. It's like a skepticism. Like, okay, this was great, but as soon as we're done with this session, I'm going to go right back.*

SARAH: *Let's just see if there's something there that wants to be released today. "I, Lucy, solemnly swear to my essential self that I will be a skeptic like my father."*

LUCY: *Yes, I'll be a skeptic like my father until the day I die, whether I want to or not.*

SARAH: *In order to . . .*

LUCY: *In order to protect myself from disappointment.*

SARAH: *Oh, very good vow. Maybe, "just as he did"?*

LUCY: *Just as he did. No matter the cost to myself.*

SARAH: *Lucy, did you hear the vow that Lucy made to you?*

LUCY: *Yes.*

SARAH: *Is that a good vow for Lucy?*

LUCY: *No.*

SARAH: *Would you please tell her, "Lucy, I release you from this vow."*

LUCY: *"Lucy, I release you from this vow to be skeptical until the day you die. Yes, I release you from that vow and I revoke the contract."*

SARAH: *And "Instead you have my blessing to . . ."*

LUCY: *You have my blessing to live until you die. Yes, one of the vows that you had as an example was to not participate in life. That rang a bell for me. I will not participate in life in order to avoid disappointment and failure and humiliation. No matter the cost to myself.*

SARAH: *And do you like this vow?*

LUCY: *No, no, I don't like it at all.*

SARAH: *Please tell Lucy, "Lucy, I release you from this one too."*

LUCY: *"I release you from this terrible vow, and I revoke this contract and give you my blessing to live."*

SARAH: *Oh, I feel that in the bones of my spine. How is it for you?*

LUCY: *Yes, I feel it in the bones of my spine. Sinking into the chair. Not quite believing it, but it feels good.*

SARAH: *Oh, very good.*

LUCY: *That vow was held for 70 odd years.*

SARAH: *Yes, I know. We have that habit.*

One year later, Lucy writes:

Reading the transcript of our session now, I'm surprised how much richness there was in the exploration of the relationship with my father. I think, though, that the ongoing intensive one-on-one therapy has been necessary for me to really absorb and benefit fully from the work, because my vows are so firmly entrenched that doing a few sacred vow sessions often left me feeling hopeless and skeptical. I also am simply unable to do the process on my own, at least so far, because I still go into dissociation/confusion. I am definitely making progress now, finding clarity, dissociating less, and embodying my feelings more.

Dissociation Contract Template

Try doing one for each dissociation-related vow that you have identified.

1. *I, _____, solemnly swear to my essential self (or mother, father, sibling, God, universe, etc.) that I will always/never*

    _____

    _____

    in order to _____,
    no matter the cost to myself and those I love.

2. What is the good, historical, lived reason for this contract? When did you first make this contract? How does it make sense within the larger context of your life?

    _____

    _____

_____

_____

_____

3. *Essential self (or mother, father, sibling, God, universe, etc.), did you hear this vow?*

Yes _____

No _____

(If no, then repeat the words of the vow.)

4. *Essential self (or mother, father, sibling, God, universe, etc.), do you want this vow to be kept?*

Yes _____

No _____

(If the answer is "Yes, the vow should stay, no matter the cost," then it's time to use the Time Travel Process to go to the moment in your life in which this unconscious contract makes sense.)

5. The release: *I release you from this vow, and I revoke this contract.*

6. The blessing: *And instead I give you my blessing to:*

_____

CHAPTER 8

Discovering and Dissolving the Contracts That Block Secure Attachment

Imagine a baby. The result of this request can be quite absurd, since people in the United States and Western Europe tend to visualize a baby lying alone on a blanket or in a crib, as if it were possible for babies to exist on their own. Babies are entirely dependent on relationship, as much as they are on oxygen, food, water, and temperature control, and if they are left alone for long, their brains become damaged. So, it makes sense that the qualities of the relationship that babies are nourished by shape babies' brains and the way they learn to run their own nervous systems. The qualities of early relationships change how we take care of ourselves, the way we see ourselves, and what we expect from others. The bonding within these relationships is called attachment, and the pattern we develop in response to the way we are treated is called our attachment style.

======= THE MAIN QUESTION FOR THIS CHAPTER =======

How can we heal our attachment styles so that we have an easier, more nourishing life?

RELATIONAL NEUROSCIENCE CONCEPT: ATTACHMENT

Attachment is how we expect to connect with our closest people and animals. It includes what we expect from others and what we automatically do when we are anticipating relationship. Is the relationship safe? We'll react one way. Is the relationship unpredictable or dangerous? We'll respond another way. (We don't necessarily react the way we'd expect to—sometimes we become more distant when things are safe, or we move closer when someone is unpredictable, or sometimes something inside us relaxes when things are dangerous.) The way we respond depends on what things were like when we were little, on what is familiar (family-like). For example, if we grew up in a home with people who had exploding tempers, it might make us too nervous to be around someone who never explodes—that might feel like waiting for the mother of all bombs to go off.

Our patterns of attachment show up most in our intimate relationships and not at all in distant relationships. We aren't looking for danger, nor are we stimulated or triggered with a grocery store clerk or a work buddy.

One way to look at this is to ask ourselves who we find boring and who we find compelling in our closest friendship and partnership relationships.

The most solid, stable, complex result of attachment is, as Daniel Siegel says, integration[4]—the experience of being able to have both linkage and differentiation in a relationship. Then both we and the other person can say, "I'm with you, we affect each other, and I know you're a separate being from me." This is a fluid, moving target because people are never just one way. We're changing all the time, and in order for people to be able to be responsive, both people need to have a resonating self-witness and to be securely attached to each other. What does *securely attached* mean?

OUR EARLIEST DAYS

The way that our parents managed their own emotions becomes the way that we manage ours. If our mom has an insulation layer between herself and her emotions, we learn from her as children to insulate ourselves, and we carry the learning with us as we grow up. We learn that we can't rely on others for emotional support and that we just need to get used to being alone. In children, this is called *avoidant attachment*. If our mothering people believe that there is no separation between them and us, we are merged with one another. For example, there are mothers who make a child put on a sweater if the mother is cold. There are mothers who cannot recover if the child is sad. This kind of attachment can make it difficult to separate from others. This is called *ambivalent*, or *anxious*, *attachment*. The names for the attachment styles that I'm working with are most often used with children, but I find them equally helpful when thinking about our adult selves.

If, on the other hand, our mothers have moments of communion, connection, joy, and shared emotional experience with us and moments when they are entirely separate and comfortable in that, but still caring, even when we are sad or angry, then we're getting the kind of interactions we need in order to know that we have a self (to be embodied, to know what we feel and what we think and who we are) and that others also exist, and we become securely attached. *Secure attachment* is like in the Goldilocks story: not too little togetherness, not too much, but just right.

Secure attachment requires predictability. As infants, we have a remarkable ability to detect regularities in events, to perceive how congruent behavior is, and to expect when events will occur by estimating probabilities of "if–then."[1] For example, if I do this, my mother will do that. If I smile, my mother will smile. Or if I smile big, my mother will smile smaller. We start to make these predictions. If I cry, my mother will turn away. Or, if I don't cry, my mother will turn away. However, we also want there to be some surprise and dance of relationship, some moments where we get to exist all on our own and some moments when we are completely enfolded. There's a need for variability that allows secure attachment to grow. Remember, we're in the Goldilocks story: not too tight, not too loose, not too cold, not too hot. Just right. And our secure attachment lies in the mid-range of responsiveness, which can be so relieving for those of us who want to be perfect. We cannot do it by formula. We have to do it in relational connection; finding just right is about what's good for the other and also what's good for us.

We can think about tendrils unfurling in the growth of a plant to provide some idea about the way that attachment works, specifically with the neurons that grow from the prefrontal cortex to the amygdala to support self-regulation. In secure attachment, these fibers are really able to hold, nurture, and nourish the emotional self with stability, commitment, and understanding. We know we are complex beings, and whatever is happening, we are able to say, "Of course you're having this emotional experience." The right hemisphere is very happily holding our emotional self and saying, "Yes, you make sense."

If we move into avoidant attachment, it's as if there's some insulation between ourselves and our emotional experience. There are neural fibers in place, but they are entirely self-referencing, which makes warmth elusive. We've learned to live here on our own, largely in the left hemisphere, without depending on others to comfort us, and it's a pretty stable thing. This insulation from our own emotional experience allows us to have what feels like emotional stability, but we're stable because the whole right hemisphere system of emotions is removed from us. We're removed from our own emotions and our partner's emotions. While that can seem stable, it can also be a bit distant and lonely, and it can make our imaginations poorer and rob us of a sense of meaning and worsen our health, which can shorten our lifespan.[2]

In contrast, anxious/ambivalent attachment can be described as never quite getting to exist as one's own independent being and never quite having the sense of being seen and fully understood. Sometimes people describe this as a feeling of always reaching for relationship. On a nervous system level, when things are fine, there is a lot of responsiveness and aliveness in the nervous system. When things go wrong, there are no regulating neural fibers to keep us calm. Instead, there is a lot of stress. In order to get any connection at all with our mothering people, we may have had to join with them or they may only have been able to locate themselves in relationship to us. If we had to join our mothers or they had to join us, it means that we might believe we have to give up ourselves in order to have connection with others. If we're a little bit sad, our mother becomes devastated. Or, if we're angry, our mother either gets angrier or is lost in her own emotional experience. If we're terrified, our mother is terrified with us, or she may be terrified and inconsolable separately from us. There's no movement back into herself or acknowledgment of us as differentiated beings—a point of view which would allow stability, resonance, and calming.

And then, *disorganized attachment*, which can also be called *traumatic attachment*, is brought about when the fibers of our brains are tattered and torn by experiences of our parents being either terrified or terrifying. If our parents have disorganized attachment, then they may very well pass it on to us, even if they avoid passing on the violence and trauma of their childhoods, because their nervous systems are carrying the mark of the trauma that they experienced. We learn from them and model ourselves upon them, even if they are not hurting us. It's possible that our parents tend to dissociate or go into rages, and these are direct transmissions of trauma.

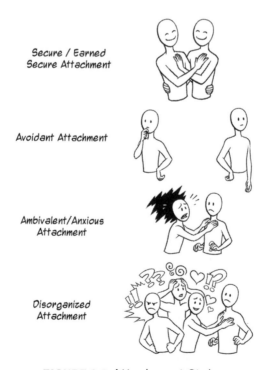

Secure / Earned
Secure Attachment

Avoidant Attachment

Ambivalent/Anxious
Attachment

Disorganized
Attachment

FIGURE 8.1 Attachment Styles

But one of the things that can be really confusing about disorganized attachment is that we can have a very kind parent who is terrified, and that terror in their nervous system moves into our nervous system and so we also become disorganized. Disorganized attachment is essentially unpredictable. We never know what's going to come. We never know when the heart will be seized with a spasm of terror. One of the beautiful outcomes of doing this work is that as we increase the capacity to hold our own emotional selves and learn how to soothe a heart that has been seized by spasms of terrors, we gradually begin to be able to hold the enormity of what we lived through and what our parents lived through when they were children. As we gradually see the system with the eyes of our resonating self-witness, we become more compassionate, and we have the opportunity to hold our disorganized selves and parents with great gentleness.

Most of us have all the different styles of attachment: there's a little bit of attachment that's disorganized, some that's ambivalent, some that's avoidant, and some percentage is securely attached. One of the nourishing things about journeying toward healing is having a sense of what your attachment percentages are to begin with and tracking your growth toward more secure attachment over time.

EARNED SECURE ATTACHMENT

These changes for the better in our attachment style are called the movement toward *earned secure attachment*. We can be born with secure attachment, a result of the luck of our mothering person being securely attached. Not all of us are this lucky, so it's good to know that we can gradually heal over time, as we do with the *Your Resonant Self* journey. When we start out insecure and we move toward security, it's called *earned secure attachment*.

A child can use warmly resonant parents and other significant figures to decrease stress, even when those people are not physically present, by carrying them as an internalized image. If we're securely attached, we get to lighten our load by outsourcing our stress. Happily, we can also learn this later in life on our healing journey. People decrease their stress levels more and more as they move further into earned secure attachment. As we form connections with others and develop a sense of them as resources, then we can be walking down the street and think, "Oh, I'm just so worried." And then we can think about someone we have learned to trust, "Caroline would really understand this. Caroline would get this if she were here. She would be saying, 'Of course you're worried.'" Then our stress and cortisol decrease, because we can think, "Okay, I'm in a world that's comprehensible. I make sense to my friend

Caroline." Much of the benefit of secure attachment is about making sense of the world and making it manageable.

Are you starting to get interested in what your attachment style might be? Here is one way to explore possibilities.

QUESTIONNAIRE
What Are Your Attachment Style Percentages?

This questionnaire is not official nor precise—it will give you an impression of what your attachment percentages might be and a sense of what you can work on if you want more earned secure attachment and less stress. Your results will come out differently depending on which relationship you have in mind when you answer the questionnaire, so choose one relationship to keep in mind as you answer all the questions. Many of these questions are about partnership—if you aren't partnered, your best friend or sibling can stand in where the word *partner* appears.

Each question is worth four points. If the question regards sex and you aren't sexual, simply give yourself 4 points for the question. If you are split between 2 answers, circle both and give yourself 2 points each for them. If you are split between 4 answers, give yourself one point for each.

1. I wake up liking myself
    a.   most of the time.
    b.   sometimes.
    c.   I don't think about it.
    d.   never.

2. When things are hard I
    a.   reach out for help.
    b.   melt down for a while, have a hard time moving forward, then do my best to keep going.
    c.   work harder OR withdraw (or both).
    d.   hurt myself or others, physically or emotionally, OR dissociate.

3. I believe that people who know me can feel genuine affection for me.
    a.   I believe this most of the time.
    b.   I believe this sometimes.

    c.   I don't think about it.

    d.   I believe this rarely.

4. When I'm talking with people in casual conversation, I
   a. most often both share my own experience and ask about theirs.
   b. often am caught up in emotions and/or am very curious about others' emotions.
   c. am most comfortable talking about myself or telling stories.
   d. charm people and I'm charismatic; people want me to like them and/or I'm too afraid to take up space.

5. When I'm talking or writing in professional contexts, I
   a. share openly, appropriate to the company and my comfort level.
   b. worry about what other people think too much to share openly. I usually say what I think others want to hear.
   c. usually just say what I think and don't worry about it.
   d. tailor my expression according to what I want from the people I'm with OR self-expression is terrifying to me.

6. I prioritize my intimate connections over other experiences, that is, I choose to spend my day off with my partner or a good friend, or on self-care, rather than filling all my time with projects
   a. most of the time OR I balance my days off between intimacy and self-care.
   b. always, even at the cost of self-care.
   c. rarely OR I spend my days off watching shows or playing video games.
   d. I never know what I'm going to prioritize OR when my partner doesn't choose me, I feel urgency or panic.

7. I do what I say I'm going to do
   a. mostly, and I adjust agreements when needed.
   b. sometimes, and it's hard for me to say no.
   c. almost always.
   d. rarely OR always feel panic or urgency if I can't.

8. I feel afraid
   a. very rarely or not very often. I have good resources to reach out to when I'm afraid.

    b.   often.

    c.   I don't think about whether I'm afraid.

    d.   always or never.

9. When other people say they are sad, I

    a.   say something to acknowledge what they are going through.

    b.   feel so sad for them.

    c.   don't really notice, change the subject, or point out how they caused it themselves.

    d.   sometimes I dissociate OR I become angry; sometimes I'm deeply supportive.

10. When other people are happy, I

    a.   celebrate with them.

    b.   am happier for them than they are themselves.

    c.   feel slightly uncomfortable and often help them get grounded again with reality OR I feel resentful, or a little uncomfortable because I am not happy so it's hard to be happy for them.

    d.   can become angry OR scared OR dissociate without real reason.

11. When people are angry at me, I

    a.   have a flexible, fairly calm response depending on the situation.

    b.   get angrier OR am frightened OR sometimes I cry.

    c.   attempt to shut them down with logic or contempt.

    d.   have an unpredictable, sometimes frightening response OR I dissociate or feel shaky.

12. When someone starts speaking quickly and doing a hard sell (pushing me to agree or trying to convince me of something), I

    a.   leave if I want to, stay if I'm interested.

    b.   collapse and do what's being asked OR make friends in defense.

    c.   don't really notice OR shut down and endure OR become slightly irritated and defend my position.

    d.   become confused and dissociate and/or I rage.

13. I feel most comfortable and secure with a partner or good friend who is

    a.   engaged and attentive, with periods of disengagement for rest.

    b.   very calm and solid.

    c.   alive, responsive to life.

    d.   unpredictable and a little dangerous.

14. When my partner or good friend asks me to talk about emotions, I
    a.   feel connected and interested.
    b.   have a lot of resentment and pain that has never been heard.
    c.   have a sense that the time is wasted, and the conversations seem to take forever.
    d.   can become angry and/or dissociated and confused.

15. When discussing the personal history of our relationship with a partner or good friend, I
    a.   remember anniversaries and events with clarity.
    b.   can tend to recall old pain.
    c.   have a hard time remembering nuances and details.
    d.   can become angry and/or dissociated and confused.

16. The more intimate I become with my partner or good friend, the more I
    a.   feel warm and close and happy and recognize my edges.
    b.   want something that feels unattainable and/or feel like we are the same person.
    c.   fear losing myself and/or am afraid of getting too close.
    d.   dissociate and/or become unpredictable, terrified, or terrifying.

17. When something is promised and my partner or good friend doesn't follow through, I
    a.   ask my partner or good friend what happened and come up with a different strategy.
    b.   make excuses for my partner or good friend and/or lose my temper and/or have a sense of abandonment.
    c.   know that I am right and the other is wrong and I judge and blame and express contempt.
    d.   respond with emotional or physical violence and/or with dissociation or self-harm.

18. My to-do list is
    a.   a helpful support to my days.
    b.   what to-do list are you talking about?

   c.   my entire life.

   d.   something to beat myself up about.

19. When someone who is not my partner or good friend expresses love and affection, I feel

   a.   warm and happy. I can easily express love and affection in return.

   b.   anxious, doubtful that it's true and/or indebted.

   c.   uncomfortable. And it's hard to say it back.

   d.   either satisfied that I have the power I need and/or terrified.

20. When I'm asked how I feel by people who are important to me, I'm most likely to answer

   a.   with emotion, words, and some understanding of why I feel the way I do.

   b.   with my best guess of the emotions I am having that are most similar to the person who is asking.

   c.   with information about what I'm thinking.

   d.   by dissociating and/or getting angry.

21. When my partner or good friend is angry or upset with me, I

   a.   sometimes pursue them to work it out, sometimes leave the person alone, and I decide based, at least in part, on what that person has told me is wanted.

   b.   become even more angry or upset, can't leave the person alone and/or can't be calm until that person is also calm.

   c.   always leave my partner or good friend alone to work it out.

   d.   try to reach my partner or good friend and then if it doesn't work I dissociate and/or become angry or hopeless and/or try to do anything to soothe them and have their warmth again.

22. When my partner or good friend threatens to leave me or talks about thinking about splitting up, I

   a.   listen carefully and express what's alive for me.

   b.   panic and maybe even melt down with the threatened abandonment.

   c.   ignore my partner or friend until things are calm again.

   d.   lash out with emotional or physical violence, can become very controlling, and/or I dissociate.

23. When my partner/friend or I travel separately or spend time apart from each other, I

   a. enjoy my alone time and stay connected and committed with my partner via text, email, or phone calls. If it is a committed partnership, and monogamy is our shared intention, it is easy for me. If polyamory is our shared intention, I remain committed to our agreements.

   b. struggle with feelings of abandonment and aloneness.

   c. don't have much contact with my partner or good friend while we're apart. Sometimes the separation is very relieving or pleasurable.

   d. forget my partner or friend exists. If the partnership is sexually intimate, I can enjoy connections (sometimes sexual) with old friends or strangers that my partner would not consent to if my partner knew about them and/or I may experience jealousy, despair, depression, suicidality, or extreme anxiety.

24. My sexual relationship with my partner is

   a. mutually satisfying or we've decided together not to be sexual. I know this because we have conversations about it where both of us express what is true for us.

   b. sometimes good and sometimes not satisfying—I often want my partner to be more engaged and present.

   c. satisfying for me.

   d. unpredictable. Sometimes I'm prone to flashbacks and dissociation, and sometimes I don't realize my partner is actually my partner.

25. In my important relationships,

   a. I have a sense of an inherent balance between giving and receiving.

   b. I always give more than I receive.

   c. my partner says I take more than I give.

   d. I swing intensely between giving and taking.

SCORING: Each question is worth 4 points. If you have chosen more than one answer in any question, divide your 4 points equally among your answers. Add up your totals by letter and put the amounts in the blanks shown below.

A = Secure/Earned Secure Attachment _____ %

B = Ambivalent/Anxious Attachment _____ %

C = Avoidant Attachment _____ %

D = Disorganized Attachment _____ %

Now that we have a sense of our percentages, what can we do with this information? How can we use what we are learning about ourselves to move toward earned secure attachment?

WHAT TO DO TO HELP HEAL OUR AVOIDANT ATTACHMENT (AND WHY WE WOULD WANT TO)

Avoidant attachment can shorten our lives by leaving us lonelier than our hearts would like and with less of a sense of meaning than really sustains us. Remedies for avoidant attachment include each step along the *Your Resonant Self* healing journey, including all of the exercises in this workbook and all of our efforts to catch and understand our bodies' messages for us. We also gradually reclaim the body as indivisible from ourself, so that we aren't just *understanding our bodies*, we are instead *being* our bodies and living as well-loved bodies and beings in this life. In addition, we can learn about and release our own vows of separation, which keep us apart from ourselves and from other people.

WHAT TO DO TO HELP HEAL OUR AMBIVALENT ATTACHMENT (AND WHY WE WOULD WANT TO)

With ambivalent attachment, we don't have much stress resiliency. It is important for our ambivalently attached parts to have a daily practice of self-resonance. This practice puts into place the ability to rebound from stressful situations by mobilizing our internalized sense of support instead of having to call upon our cortisol resources to survive. Our ambivalently attached parts will often have contracts not to be separate from others, and it can give us immense freedom and energy to release these contracts.

WHAT TO DO FOR YOUR DISORGANIZED ATTACHMENT STYLE

We will be focusing on healing from disorganized attachment in Chapter 9, as our unhealed trauma experiences affect our ability to be safe and secure in intimacy.

JOURNALING PROMPT FOR THE
Journey Toward Earned Secure Attachment

What is your own attachment journey? We all start in an attachment style that is very influenced by our mothering people. Trauma tends to knock us further from security; love and healing tend to move us in the direction of security. Where did you begin, and what kinds of traumas may have moved you out of secure attachment? What kind of healing work have you done that has moved you toward security?

My sense of my mothering person's foundational attachment style is

_____

_____

And so that was where I started. But my style wasn't exactly like hers, the way that attachment showed up in me before I was five years old was

_____

_____

Then I started school, and the effect of school on me was probably

_____

_____

When we enter puberty, we are often rerunning attachment issues from our toddler days. When I think about myself in relationship with both parents and peers in my years of puberty, what occurs to me is

_____

_____

As an adult we tend to live through traumas and but to meet people who love us and to have healing experiences. How have both experiences affected your attachment journey?

_____

_____

GUIDED MEDITATION
Holding Ambivalent Attachment

Take a moment to remember and find yourself as a breathing being . . . Is the greatest place of aliveness in your breath still the same as the last time you noticed? . . . Find the place of aliveness, and invite your attention to rest there . . . as your attention ebbs and flows in its ability to stay focused, hold it with gentleness and warmth . . .

Now bring your attention to any places in your current life where you have a sense of being off balance . . . any relationship where you are giving more than you are taking . . . or where you are focused on or worried about how someone else is doing or what that person is feeling . . . and notice your body . . . how do you know you are off balance? . . . What is happening in your chest as you think of this situation? . . . What is happening in your belly? . . . Be very gentle with yourself . . . and ask, "Do I exist? . . . Am I the center of my own world, no matter what is happening with others? . . . Do I matter and belong to life?" . . . If your answers are yes, let yourself enjoy the sense of belonging and existing . . . If your answers are no, do you need acknowledgment that others' well-being is very important to you . . . that you have a sense of the linkage of all beings . . . and that you may never have had another person simply delight in your existence without expecting anything in return? . . . Just for a moment, let yourself imagine your essential, central self turning to look at you and enjoying that you exist as your own being . . . no matter how hard a time others are having . . . They also exist . . . . They also matter . . . But their well-being is at least partially in the hands of life itself, rather than in your hands . . . Just for this moment, let life hold them . . . Let their own mitochondria give them fuel . . . and see if you can feel your own tiny cell powerhouses giving you fuel . . . Because you exist . . . and you are being held by life . . . and you matter, just as yourself . . . And you are just right, radical as that idea may seem . . . See what it is like to breathe as a being who is just right . . . and who matters . . . Even one breath is a radical act . . .

And allow yourself to return to your breath, and to yourself as a breathing being . . . and to come back to this moment . . . and your life . . . and what it is asking from you . . . and carry with you the possible delight of your own existence.

GUIDED MEDITATION
Holding Avoidant Attachment

Take a moment to remember and find yourself as a breathing being . . . Is the greatest place of aliveness in your breath still the same as the last time you noticed? . . . Find the place of aliveness, and invite your attention to rest there . . . As your attention ebbs and flows in its ability to stay focused, hold it with gentleness and warmth . . .

Now bring your attention to any conceptual thought that you think of as just plain fact . . . it could be something about mathematics . . . and very gently . . . open the door to your body . . . let yourself feel your chest . . . your belly . . . your throat . . . or your face . . . Let the fact and your body coexist in this moment . . . How is it to be you? . . . An embodied being . . . not just a mind . . . How is it to be a breathing . . . existing . . . feeling . . . being? . . . Can you feel your breath? . . . Can you remember the fact? . . . Can you feel your body? . . . Can you feel any pleasure in the existence of the fact? . . . Can you feel any pleasure that you exist . . . while thinking about the fact? . . . Can you reach the sense of enjoyment? . . .

And now, letting go of the fact . . . let yourself notice any sensation in your face . . . any area where your muscles are constricted . . . or tight . . . or pulled together . . . Do you have any worries? . . . Use your own name as you speak to yourself . . . I'll use my name to model this . . . Ask yourself . . . "Sarah, are you so worried? . . . Do you need acknowledgment that it impacts you? . . . That you carry it with you all the time? . . . Is there any grief connected with the worry? . . . Are you in touch with the need for mourning? . . . Or is there any anger, or irritation, or contempt that needs naming? . . . Is there anything connected with integrity . . . or truth . . . or flow . . . that wants to be acknowledged? . . . Is there any fear nibbling at your body? . . . Do you wish for safety for all beings?" . . . Bring your attention back to your body overall . . . and particularly your face . . . Is the sensation there the same as it was when we started this meditation? . . . How is it to be a living, breathing, sensing being?

And allow yourself to return to your breath . . . and yourself as a breathing being . . . and to come back to this moment . . . and your life . . . and what it is asking from you . . . remembering the doors we opened gently in this meditation . . . Can you remember yourself as a participant in sensation?

PATTERNS OF PARTNERSHIP: A LIFE'S BALANCE

We're starting to get a feeling for some of our attachment tendencies. Are we always the same in all our relationships? No. And sometimes we can trace an alternating pattern of ambivalent and avoidant partners in our relationship history. For example, first we'll have a relationship where we're the pursuer (a more ambivalent attachment pattern) and then one of us will get tired of that and we'll break up. Then someone else will come and they'll lean toward us and we'll say, "Oh, it feels so nice to have somebody lean toward us." And then it gets a little sticky, and we will think it's too close, and we will move away (a more avoidant attachment pattern) until we get tired of being pursued and break up with that partner. And then we go back to being the pursuer. In the next worksheet, you will get a chance to trace these tendencies in your own relationship history. Do you see an alternating pattern, or do you have one main tendency?

WORKSHEET
Patterns of Partnership

Partner Name	With this partner, I felt largely:			
	Avoidant	Ambivalent	Disorganized	Secure

RESONANT LANGUAGE PRACTICE
Swearing

Only work with this form of resonant language if you actually enjoy swearing. If you find it offensive or have trauma responses to swear words, skip this section. We include swearing in our list of resonant language because it has been shown by research to light up our right hemispheres and to convey emotion.

Swearing

As you learn about your attachment style and your patterns of self-protection or of hanging on or merging for survival, you may experience some intense emotions. You may be experiencing overwhelm, helplessness, preemptive exhaustion, dissociation, anger, loneliness, or fear. For example, sometimes it can seem like attachment was done to us rather than it being something we had much choice in. Whatever you are experiencing, first see if you can find the sensations in your body that are connected with your emotions.

Now, one of the juiciest ways to express the hugeness of things with swear words in English is to combine religious words with the old Anglo Saxon words for body parts, body fluids, and sexual acts. If your connection to spirituality is through Christianity and you find it difficult when people swear or use the Christian names for spiritual personages as parts of swear words, please skip this section.

If you do find swearing satisfying, choose your favorites from each list below, put them together, hold your body sensation and your emotion with your attention, and say the combined phrase aloud. See what happens with your body in response to your acknowledgment of enormity.

Holy	Fuck
Holy Mary	Shit
Jesus	Tits
Sainted	Cunnilingus (not Anglo-Saxon, but fun to add)
Blessed	Cock
Divine	Cunt
Angelic	Twat
Mother of God	Piss

Now that you have had a chance to release some of the tension that may come with learning about attachment, it's time to take a look at what kinds of contracts we may have that we are unwittingly using to keep old and outdated attachment patterns in place.

With resonant healing, we are all moving into earned secure attachment. Every time we have a sense of being known and understood for our complexity, for our emotions, for our contradictory experience, we are moving into secure attachment. So the more healing and dissolution you do of old and unhelpful attachment contracts, the easier you will find life.

Before we move into journaling and working with some of your own attachment contracts, take a moment to witness the work that someone else did in this area.

ONE-ON-ONE WORK
Working With Attachment Contracts

SARAH: *Emma, hello! How is it to be looking at this material together?*

EMMA: *Well, when you put up the contracts for avoidant and ambivalent attachment just now, I felt so much grief. Also fear and terror come up with all of this, because it's not just in the past, but it's happening in the present and impacting the future.*

SARAH: *Of course, these contracts can have enormous consequences. What would you like to give yourself as a gift from our work together today?*

EMMA: *Some support for the transition I'm going through, which is divorce. It's painful and it just took a turn for uglier. My husband's avoidant and I'm ambivalent, but we've gone beyond being able to heal that between us. So I'm looking at the pattern with my son and connecting to the ache in my heart.*

I've got a place that I'm moving to at the end of the month, and I have all this confusion about having to figure out how to support myself and needing the space to do that and yet not abandoning my son. It's almost easier to be away from him because then I worry about him less. There's enmeshment, and then there's the pull toward distance, and then there's fear about how I've been enmeshed and the impact of that. The thought of leaving is terrifying. The thought of staying is impossible, too.

SARAH: *Yes. If you check in with your heart—what visual do you get if you imagine us being able to look at your heart?*

EMMA: *It does seize sometimes, like it goes cold and then other times it beats out of my chest. It's sometimes frozen and sometimes beating out of my chest.*

SARAH: *Then we're just going to start with some empathy for your heart to help us understand which vow might be nice to work with. So, first of all, Emma's* *heart, would you like a little acknowledgment that the loneliness of this life-time has been a little terrifying?*

EMMA: *Yes.*

SARAH: *Yes, yes. And that you try to make up for the loneliness by making sure that you stay with the people you love?*

EMMA: *It's by connecting to and understanding and being understood by the people I love. And when that can't happen, it's painful, and almost easier to be away from the people I love.*

SARAH: *So, would you like a little acknowledgment that the terror is so great that it's easier not to be in relationship at all?*

EMMA: *Yes, but then I feel like I am abandoning, giving up, doing harm, plus I lose the reassurance that I get, and need, from being close.*

SARAH: *Yes. Does your heart need acknowledgment that it doesn't know where to rest?*

EMMA: *Yes. That's been a long-time thing of, where is home? What do I call home?*

SARAH: *Yes. And that the home is metaphorical as well as physical. That the heart doesn't have a safe place to rest.*

EMMA: *Yes.*

SARAH: *That people are both immensely challenging and completely needed. What is your heart always trying to do?*

EMMA: *Create harmony. Connect us in ways that heal.*

SARAH: *Is it also always trying to make everything okay for everybody?*

EMMA: *Yes. It's trying to make everything okay for everybody and for me.*

SARAH: *So, let's start there. "I, Emma's heart, solemnly swear to you, Emma, that I will always try to make everything okay for you and everybody."*

EMMA: *Yes. "I, Emma's heart, solemnly swear that I will always try to make everything okay for you and everybody in order to . . . have peace of mind." It's so I can have peace of mind, but it's also more than that. It might have to do with the tribe or the family being okay, and with taking on the role of peacemaker, because the family was not okay growing up. It just felt like it was wrong and broken and I was trying to fix it, or at least understand what was going on."*

SARAH: *So that Emma can have a family where everything is okay?*

EMMA: *And harmony and connection and being able to work through our differences, and that I will make sure that this family is okay, no matter the cost.*

SARAH: *Emma, did you hear the vow that your heart made to you?*

EMMA: *Yes.*

SARAH: *Is that a good vow for Emma's heart? Is that a doable vow for Emma's heart?*

EMMA: *To make sure this family is okay? Right now, it's not so doable. But what will be the cost if she doesn't? If her heart doesn't make sure this family is okay? What will be the cost down the road?*

SARAH: *Emma is a person who has warmth and understanding and care. It's not like once the vow's released, she's going to run screaming for the hills and abandon everybody. I think it's more that, once the vow is released, she'll have more flexibility to make sure that she's taken care of and to make sure that she's responsive to her child and listening. It just seems like there might be more room for everything that Emma wants to have happen if she doesn't have a vow to make sure everybody's okay all the time. Does that make any sense?*

EMMA: *Yes. She can let go a bit and focus on other things. She doesn't have to make sure everything is okay or wait until everything is okay before moving forward. Because things haven't been okay for a long time, and not moving forward is not helping things get better.*

SARAH: *Would you be willing to tell her, "Emma's heart, I release you from this contract"? Just see if it's okay to do it. It may not be okay.*

EMMA: *As long as there's something else that they can lean on.*

SARAH: *Flexibility, adaptability, creativity, energy, stability?*

EMMA: *They can lean on those things?*

SARAH: *Yes. Because this heart, once it's released from its rigid contract, gets to be those things.*

EMMA: *Ah, right. "Emma's heart, I release you from this contract and I revoke this vow, and instead you have my blessing to . . . relax and trust more and worry less."*

SARAH: *Oh, beautiful. How does your heart respond?*

EMMA: *It's calmer. There's stillness in there. There's a lump in here (touches throat), but there is stillness here (in heart).*

SARAH: *In touching on that lump that's there in your throat, is there grief, a grief for this whole life of working so hard and trying so hard?*

EMMA: *Yes.*

SARAH: *Does Emma's body need acknowledgment of the weight and exhaustion of trying to balance an unbalanceable system?*

EMMA: *An unbalanceable system. Wow. Yes.*

SARAH: *I wonder if your body would enjoy a little gratitude from the systems? Like, thank you, Emma, for trying so hard to help us.*

EMMA: *Yes.*

SARAH: *Both of your family systems are bowing to you. Your family of origin and your family of marriage are just saying thank you for trying so hard. How's your throat?*

EMMA: *It's better.*

SARAH: *Thank you, Emma. It's an honor to do this work with you, and to see what the vows are that our hearts have made, because it is indeed our hearts that are so deeply involved in the whole attachment experience.*

One year later, Emma writes:

This work supports me in being able to move forward with less fear and more trust and ease. It helps me separate from the expectations and stories of other people, to become more self-aware and confident, and to breathe more easily. Even though the amount of time I spend with my son is less now than it was at the time this particular piece of work was done, it feels to me that the time we spend together is of a better quality. My relationship with him has not ended. Instead, it is evolving. I sense that, in the long term, my letting go of trying to repair all that appears to me as broken, and instead doing vow work, will continue to positively impact the way I show up in my relationships with significant others in my life.

Some insights that came from this piece of work with my heart:

- *There are a lot of story lines playing out and colliding, and I can only work on mine.*
- *I cannot orchestrate an outcome.*
- *Love includes taking care of myself and making space for others to take care of themselves.*
- *My finding and living from my own center is a contribution to everyone.*
- *Space to live, to integrate, to breathe is very helpful.*
- *People find their own way, in their own time. Letting go (of trying to determine or expedite an outcome) contributes to ease.*
- *Recognizing the promises that our hearts have made to us allows us to realize choice and discover new possibilities we hadn't seen before.*
- *We can't force consciousness to shift or skip ahead of where we are emotionally. What we can do is hold ourselves and one another with warmth, curiosity, and care, and see what vows we might be holding onto that are keeping us stuck.*

CONTRACTS OF ATTACHMENT

In order to continue integrating our learning, please recall what we have discovered about our circuits. You will remember that our SEEKING circuit helps us get things done, and our CARE circuit brings us into relational space with others. Our attachment contracts tend to involve either an emphasis on SEEKING, to the detriment of CARE (avoidant attachment: I will use my SEEKING circuit to take care of myself) or an emphasis on CARE to the detriment of SEEKING (ambivalent attachment: I will try to use my CARE circuit to navigate the world.)

Our contracts around avoidant attachment may sound like this:

- I swear to myself I will trust only myself.
- I will never relax into anyone.
- I will never let anyone close.
- I will take care of myself.
- I will not look closely at other people's faces or into another's eyes.
- I will not notice others' emotions.
- I will not reveal my feelings or even know what they are.

For ambivalent attachment, the vows may sound like this:

- I will never give up reaching for connection.
- I will make that person love me.
- I will track the people around me very carefully.
- I will stay focused on facial expressions.
- I will measure every word to see if I am safe and known and loved.
- There will be no boundaries between me and others.

JOURNALING PROMPT FOR
Finding Your Attachment Contracts

Bringing together everything you have learned about yourself in this chapter, what agreements does your nervous system have with you about relationship? For these contracts, you can even have a contract from your nervous system to your essential self. Take some moments to jot down your own sense of your repeating habits or patterns. How do you sell yourself short, how do you keep yourself isolated, how do you panic when no one else is around?

_____

_____

_____

_____

_____

_____

Attachment Contract Template

Try doing this with each different attachment-related vow that you have identified.

1. I, _____, *solemnly swear to my essential self (or mother, father, sibling, God, universe, etc.) that I will always/never*

   _____

   _____

   in order to _____ *,*
   no matter the cost to myself and those I love.

2. What is the good, historical, lived reason for this contract? When did you first make this contract? How does it make sense within the larger context of your life?

   _____

   _____

   _____

   _____

   _____

3. *Essential self (or mother, father, sibling, God, universe, etc.), did you hear this vow?*

   Yes _____

   No _____

   (If no, then repeat the words of the vow.)

4. *Essential self (or mother, father, sibling, God, universe, etc.), do you want this vow to be kept?*

    Yes _____

    No _____

    (If the answer is "Yes, the vow should stay, no matter the cost," then it's time to use the Time Travel Process to go to the moment in your life in which this unconscious contract makes sense.)

5. The release: *I release you from this vow, and I revoke this contract.*

6. The blessing: *And I give you my blessing to:*

    _____

CHAPTER 9

Moving Toward Trust and Away From Hurt, Disgust, and Contempt

The first and most important thing to understand about disorganized, or traumatic, attachment is that it comes from the impact of collective trauma on family systems. Collective trauma is a difficult event or series of events that impact a whole society. Everyone shares the traumatic loss, grief, and bereavement in response to violent devastation and death. Such an event can be a natural disaster, like a big earthquake. Domestic violence rates can triple after natural disasters. The impacts are even worse when the event is human violence. For example, after the Oklahoma City bombing, alcohol and other drug misuse, suicides, homicides, and violence against women and children increased substantially within the city for a period of about 18 months. And the aftereffects are worse yet when the trauma is a part of systematized genocide of a people. When the Grassy Narrows Reserve in Canada was poisoned by mercury in 1963 by a papermaking company, forcing the indigenous people to move, an epidemic of child neglect, abuse, and abandonment, sexual assault, petrol-sniffing, and death through violence resulted.

QUESTIONNAIRE
If Collective Trauma Has Impacted My Family, When Did It Happen?

Circle the collective traumas that have intersected with your family's history:

Genocide and mass murder

Indigenous peoples all over the world	Cambodia
Holocaust	Russia
Armenia	Bosnia
Rwanda	Ukraine

Nanking   Other: _____

Darfur

War

World War I   War in the Balkan region

World War II   Wars and military conflicts in the Mid-

Korean War   dle East

Vietnam War   Other war: _____

Famines in the past 150 years, many being a direct consequence of colonization practices

Ireland   Iran

Poland   Rwanda

Ukraine   Burundi

Russia   Turkestan

Eastern Europe   Cape Verde

Scandinavia   Morocco

China   Greece

North Korea   Yemen

Cambodia   Holland

Belorussia   Germany

Java /Indonesia   Biafra

Turkey   Central Africa, from East to West

Brazil   Mozambique

Ethiopia   Bangladesh

Cuba   Other: _____

Lebanon

Natural disasters worldwide

e.g., worldwide pandemics, volcanoes with global ash pollution, climate crisis . . .

Other: _____

Do you know anything about how collective trauma brought patterns of violence or addiction into your family?

_____

_____

DISORGANIZED ATTACHMENT AND HOW
ALL VIOLENCE FRACTURES BRAINS

In my 15 years of volunteering in prisons, I have met many women who are incarcerated at least partially as a consequence of domestic violence, violence that they receive and dish out with both men and women. I've watched young, strong women return to prison five years later with broken bones in their faces, bodies thickened and bent from being on the receiving end of violence. This is one end of the spectrum of disorganized attachment. The other end is the loss of self from living with people who have contempt for us or to whom we are invisible—the scars from this may be invisible, but they harm our brains and bodies. Thus,

================THE MAIN QUESTIONS FOR THIS CHAPTER================

Why do people start and continue relationships in which they get hurt? What is happening, whether people are giving or receiving the violence?

The answers to these two questions lie in the aftereffects of trauma. When children are abused or neglected, their brains are fragmented. When a right hemisphere has been wired for alarm and then collapses into dissociation, rather than being held with resonance so that it can grow the fibers of self-regulation, it then responds to every sign of relational danger with alarm and/or dissociation. This combination easily turns into physical and emotional violence.

One of the ways to address these patterns of alarm, dissociation, and violence is to work with unconscious contracts, especially with contracts "not to take it" ever again. When we have contracts "not to take it," then we may meet all difficulties with verbal or physical violence or with dissociation. Our friends and partners can become enemies who are hurting us and against whom we must defend ourselves. They can also become the source of our self-abandonment as we continually dissociate in the face of intimacy.

Our brains can be fragmented by the experience of being on the receiving end of any type of aggression, particularly entangled rage or predatory aggression, unless or until we have had the opportunity for healing work. It's well worth stating, in no uncertain terms, that emotional, verbal, and sexual abuse are also violent and that all violence fragments brains. Verbal abuse by caregivers, for example (being told that you are stupid, or a burden, or you weren't wanted, or that you are too fat, or too skinny, or that no one will love you), leaves traces in the brain and creates even more dissociation than any other form of abuse except sexual abuse by a parent.[1]

The contracts connected with predatory aggression can include, among other possibilities, "I will never lose control," "No one will ever leave me again," "I will make others feel what I felt when I had no protection and was totally alone," "I will tease others as I was teased," "I will be the strong one," "I will never be weak again," or "I will win."

QUESTIONNAIRE
What Are My Places of Disorganization?

What follows is a partial list of symptoms of a brain fragmented by trauma. These statements may be upsetting, as they touch on traumatic experiences. You may become overwhelmed, distressed, or dissociated as you begin to read. If this happens, simply stop and skip this section for now. You may have been the person who did these actions, or you may have received these actions from others. Either way, they are signs of unresolved trauma, and it is important to meet them with radical self-compassion. Circle each experience you have been on the sending or receiving end of.

Starting out a sentence with warmth and ending with a knife in your conversational partner's ribs, such as "I've set up everything to be nice for you, with all the crap that you say you like." Or "That small mark on your tooth looks okay, unless you've been doing methamphetamines!"

Telling people you'll do something or be somewhere, and not following through.

Making excuses for a partner and staying with that person after they have hurt you physically, have told you that you are stupid, ugly, or worthless, or have not spoken to you or looked at you for a day or more.

Telling someone else that they are stupid, ugly, worthless, a burden, or that they shouldn't have been born.

Telling ourselves that we are stupid, ugly, worthless, a burden, or that we shouldn't have been born.

Deliberately not looking at or speaking to an adult you live with for more than a few hours. Deliberately not looking at or speaking to a child. Not noticing that you haven't looked at or spoken to the people you live with and are in the same room with for more than an hour.

Loving and staying in relationship with an addict.

Being addicted to a substance or behavior (experiencing negative consequences from using a substance or carrying out a behavior and still repeating the behavior or the use of the substance).

Leaving a child or a partner behind (driving away deliberately or in a dissociative state) after a stop on a trip, or threatening to do so.

Hurting an animal or person, talking about hurting an animal or person, or threatening to hurt an animal or a person.

Making a child or partner write you a letter of apology before you will speak to them again.

Ignoring power differences in sexual relationships.

Not getting a verbal "yes" before becoming more sexual in relationships, unless you have a prior agreement that your partner doesn't want to be asked.

Nonconsensual infidelity.

Dissociating.

Losing time, not knowing what has been happening for the last moments, hours, or days.

Playing with a child or a partner and realizing you've been scaring them without noticing it.

Scaring or startling another person deliberately and without consent.

Persistent feelings of helplessness or depression.

Immobilization or emotional paralysis.

You may be saddened by what you have circled on this list, and it may be necessary to mourn the ways that trauma has impacted you and the people you love. It is also possible to be angry, or to be bewildered, and to wonder, "Why is this a sign of trauma?" (If you are angry, acknowledge the anger, let yourself feel it in your body, and let it harmlessly roll out of your arms and hands.) What is threatened by this list? What are you longing for? If you are bewildered and disoriented, be gentle with yourself. The discovery and dawning understanding that signs of disconnection are signs of trauma comes to each of us slowly. This is a lifelong journey of healing. Each point that you have circled here can be a starting point for healing work, for time travel or unconscious contract processes.

It is also possible that beginning this learning can lead to disgust and self-disgust. Radical self-compassion for everything, including for the disgust, is the most supportive way forward. Let's look at disgust's purpose and the ways in which it can be used unhealthily or be wrongfully diminished.

DISGUST

Disgust moves us away from contagion, infection, and rottenness that could make us sick. Humans take physical disgust and use it in the moral realm to decide whom it's okay to be close to and who should be excluded. It is a tool for the policing of the access to resources within human societies and is used as a basis for curtailing that access, including economic and professional opportunities, social inclusion, and general civility.

Targets of social disgust include:

- Skin color/hue
- Perceived gender
- Body size/shape/weight
- Other aspects of appearance, including tattoos, piercings, and clothing
- Class
- Behavior/language (accents, grammar)
- Intelligence/education
- Physical and emotional health
- Disabilities
- Nationalities
- Perceived sexuality
- Religious beliefs
- Marital status
- Age/aging
- Occupation/income
- Criminal convictions
- Etc.

JOURNALING PROMPT FOR
Tracking the Social Use of Disgust and
the Impact It Has Had on You

EXAMPLE:

My family was disgusted by: ___fat people, divorced people___

People who had this characteristic were not considered deserving of:

___friendship, time, respect___

This kept my family "safe" from: ___contagion, their pasts, sliding downward in___
___social class___

The impact this has had on me is: ___self-disgust, self-abandonment___

YOUR TURN:

My family was disgusted by: _____

People who had this characteristic were not considered deserving of:

_____

This kept my family "safe" from: _____

_____

The impact this has had on me is: _____

_____

My religious group was disgusted by: _____

_____

People who had this characteristic were not considered deserving of:

_____

This kept group members "safe" from: _____

_____

_____

The impact this has had on me is: _____

_____

People in my school were disgusted by: _____

_____

People who had this characteristic were not considered deserving of:

_____

_____

This kept people at school "safe" from: _____

_____

_____

The impact this has had on me is: _____

_____

The larger society I lived/live in is disgusted by: _____

_____

People who have these characteristics are not considered deserving of:

_____

_____

This keeps my larger society "safe" from: _____

_____

_____

The impact this has had on me is: _____

_____

Now that we have begun to differentiate social disgust from self-disgust and to find some of the roots of self-disgust in the attitudes of the groups that we have belonged to, let's turn our attention directly on self-disgust and self-hate.

SELF-DISGUST AND SELF-HATE

There are four foundations for self-disgust, and none of them are founded in any actual truth that we are disgusting. The first foundation is that we shame ourselves in order to make ourselves smaller so that we can belong to people who don't find it easy to welcome us. We originally learned to do this to become small enough not to be a burden on our families of origin and to find a place where they're actually able to be relational with us. And as we grow older, we can continue to do this with present-day groups and partners.

The second foundation is as nervous system leverage, a tragic cascade of self-hate, shame, and the critical default mode network (also known as the critical or lacerating self-witness), where we're mean to ourselves and so we become small, and in our smallness we may be small enough to belong, but we're also immobilized so we can't move. So then we use self-hate again to try to berate ourselves into movement, and then we try to move, but the critical self-witness has an agreement with us to keep us small, so it blocks any movement. In this double bind there is no good place to be. There's no good energy level to be at, and whatever we do, nothing is right. We never have the right level of expression, contribution, aliveness. Every time we contribute there's a backlash. We speak publicly and then we say to ourselves, "I shouldn't have said that." We speak in a small group and we say to ourselves, "I said it wrong, I failed to express myself with grace and elegance, I wasn't as careful as I wanted to be, I wasn't as generous as I wanted to be, I wasn't as warm as I wanted to be, I'm not as intelligent as I want to be." We're trying to balance between self-hate and shame, but there is only the toxic seesaw between the two. We're trying to hate ourselves enough to stay small enough to belong, but not so much that we become immobilized by the shame-load that comes with it.

The third foundation for self-disgust is that we split from the self in order to bring ourselves out of paralysis and exclusion. We leave the "disgusting self" behind. We, as humans, have the capacity to disown parts of our own brain. We have the capacity to objectify the self that is unable to cope with life and to turn our own predatory aggression against ourselves. We can become identified with the people who disown us in our weakness or grief or pain or aloneness, with the people who are seeing us with contempt. Then we step into the part of our brain that holds a representation of these scornful others and we look at ourselves with scorn. When we work with self-hatred, we're really touching the live wire of unbearable reality. We are touching the ways in which we, as little ones, had an experience that was too lonely to be absorbed, or too frightening or too terrifying to be integrated. (Saying this, I have this quite strong beating heart, almost an alarm in my body. It feels like a combination of alarm and an intense desire to focus, so that I can say this as clearly as possible.) Even after we grow older and have an integrated sense of self, we retain the capacity, when things get too hard, too big, or too painful, to say, "I am not that Sarah. I will hate that weak Sarah. I will turn away from her. She is the cause of all of our problems, and I will not care for her, and she sucks."

Fourth, self-hatred lives inside us as internalized predatory aggression. "Sarah, you are so stupid. It would be better if you had never been born." This kind of communication has masqueraded as truth because it was all our families knew. Now we use it against ourselves as a mutated kind of self-care. This is hardly surprising when it's the only example we have of self-care.

SAMPLE CONTRACTS OF SELF-DISGUST OR SELF-HATE

Each of these different roots of disorganization can show up as self-disgust or self-hate. Some of the vows about not loving the self or not having self-compassion can be very explicit. Here are some examples:

- I will be disgusted with myself in order to have belonging with my family, since they see me with disgust.
- I swear that I will treat myself harshly in order to protect myself from the excruciating disappointment of dashed hopes for love.
- I will believe I am less than others in order to explain the shame residue left on me from trauma and abuse.
- I will hate myself in order to atone for the burden of my birth or life on my father.

Or the connections they make can be more personal and obscure:

- I will experience self-loathing in order to punish myself for breathing and so save all the oxygen in the world for my mother.
- I will not love myself as an act of integrity to protest all of the people in this world who are not loved.
- I swear to not love myself in order to protect my mother from her loneliness.
- I will hate myself in order to never have to experience my pain.
- I will turn away from myself in order to keep from destroying myself with contempt.

One woman doing the work of healing self-hate had been born less than a year after an older sibling had died, as a "replacement baby." She had the sense that her mother had always looked at her with a murderous gaze and that even though her mother had died 10 years ago, she was carrying on the tradition of looking at herself with a relentless, merciless, murderous gaze. When we looked at the unconscious contract, "I will look at myself with a murderous gaze, in order to . . ." she completed the sentence, "kill myself, because my mother only loves dead babies." These are the kinds of agreements we make with ourselves in the absence of warmth and love.

In our relationships, disorganized attachment contracts can be made about another person, which makes them very undoable, and they might sound like this:

- I swear to myself that this person will not leave me.
- This person will love me forever.
- I will not let my partner tell me what to do.
- The people around me will fear and obey me.
- I will control the world.
- My family will treat me with respect.
- I will never let anyone say I am a liar.
- I won't take it.

A WORD ABOUT DISGUST AND SEXUALITY

We often have the sense that disgust is a bad thing, unpleasant to feel, that we should avoid it, that it is shameful to experience it, and that we shouldn't talk about it. But being able to recognize and speak about our disgust is of huge importance to knowing our own internal boundaries and capacities.

Disgust is protective of sexuality coming too early for a child. Think of the first time you heard about French kissing, or about the mechanics of sexuality. Did you experience a "Yuck!" response? If so, that was the initial protective action of disgust, letting you know that you were too young to be sexual. As you came into puberty, your responses might have changed, and things that you found disgusting as a child might have become more interesting. There is a dance of maturation between disgust and sexuality, which helps explain such things as sexual fetishes.

Our disgust tells us when something is a violation. Child sexual abuse and domestic violence perpetrators carry out a series of steps—known as *grooming*—that diminish the disgust response in the recipients of the process. This type of grooming is also a part of disorganized attachment, as the child or partner of the perpetrator becomes fragmented and confused about what love is and about what kinds of behaviors are okay. And this is why healing from sexual abuse, domestic violence, and disorganized attachment includes a restoration of natural, healthy disgust.

STAGES OF *GROOMING* (THE DIMINISHMENT OF DISGUST)

Stage 1:   Choosing a victim.
Who is vulnerable? Who has a need for attachment that will be greater than their need for inviolability?

Stage 2:   Gaining trust.
Kindness, focused attention, fostering bonding.

Stage 3:   Filling a need.
Intimacy, fostering a sense of mattering or being special.

Stage 4:   Testing small intrusions, interweaving them with intimacy to diminish disgust.

Stage 5:   Isolating the victim.
Control, desperation, cutting off contact with others, threats.

Stage 6:   Sexual contact or domestic violence.
Increasing intrusions, replacing disgust with helplessness.

Stage 7:   Maintaining control.
Alternating intrusions with repentance/apologies/isolation.

If you are experiencing nausea as you read this list, greet your disgust with warmth and welcome. Say thank you to your disgust and embrace it as a healthy response. We are not meant to be harmed or violated. Our boundaries are present for a reason. They support our well-being. It would be a dream come true if everyone in this world got to live without being harmed or violated. It is our birthright.

Diminishment of our disgust also happens systemically. Do you remember when you were little and you first saw a homeless person, or a person who was begging for food? A child's natural response to such things is to want to help. And most of us are taught that social problems are too big to be solved and that we have to let go of our desire to help and to let go of our disgust at unfairness. This is also a kind of grooming.

JOURNALING PROMPT FOR
Noticing Your DISGUST Circuit

My own experiences with my DISGUST circuit are:

Self-disgust: _____

_____

_____

Sexual disgust: _____

_____

_____

Someone grooming me out of my disgust: _____

_____

_____

Being systemically groomed out of disgust: _____

_____

_____

Reclaiming my disgust: _____

_____

_____

RECOGNIZING CONTEMPT

If a person is raised in a family where energy is regulated with contempt, a relationship without it may taste like food without salt. It may even be hard to recognize contempt for what it is, because it's the water your family has been swimming in since before you were born. Here are some of the markers of contempt:

- Eye rolling
- Sarcasm
- Criticism
- Interrupting

- Dismissing
- Condescending
- The silent treatment
- Taking over tasks and redoing what the other has done
- Denigrating energy, intelligence, humor, physical skills, artistic or creative capacity, appearance
- Hard falls in tone at the end of sentences
- Having the sense that one partner is ashamed of the other
- Pulling back the corner of one side of the mouth

Laid out in a list like this, these behaviors don't seem very effective, but what makes them compelling is the unspoken "if only" promise. The idea that "If only I were better, I would win my partner's approval," puts people into the position of the lab rats who receive a pellet at random times, so they stay at the lever forever, exhausting themselves pushing it.

Instead of remaining trapped in a cycle of random reward and contempt, the healing journey invites movement into enjoyment of the nuanced flavors of support and warmth and ordinary connection and disconnection. This is very different from the jet-fueled trips into shame that living with a contemptuous partner or friend brings us. In order to escape the disorganization of contempt, it is often necessary to find and resolve our own self-contempt. If we have a lot of self-contempt, we may give it to our partner to hold for us, along with whatever originates in them. Our self-contempt may have come from being groomed into it by our partner and may not have been ours to begin with. Seeing the pattern can give us power. Once we stop our own inner cycle of self-contempt, our partner's behaviors become far less compelling.

WORKSHEET
Contempt Worksheet

In the past week with your partner, best friend, parent, or child, how many times have you received or enacted the following actions of contempt?

My other did these	I did these	# of times each day (spent together) Other/Self
Eye rolling	Eye rolling	_____ / _____
Sarcasm	Sarcasm	_____ / _____
Criticism	Criticism	_____ / _____
Interrupting	Interrupting	_____ / _____
Dismissing	Dismissing	_____ / _____
Condescending	Condescending	_____ / _____
Silent treatment	Silent treatment	_____ / _____
Taking over and redoing	Taking over and redoing	_____ / _____
Denigrating energy, intelligence, humor, physical skills, artistic or creative capacity, appearance	Denigrating energy, intelligence, humor, physical skills, artistic or creative capacity, appearance	_____ / _____
Hard endings to sentences	Hard endings to sentences	_____ / _____
Being ashamed of other	Being ashamed of other	_____ / _____
Asymmetrical mouth quirk	Asymmetrical mouth quirk	_____ / _____
TOTAL	(add up for each party separately)	_____ / _____

SCORING:

1–5 times per day—A person receiving this score is working on their patterns of contempt or comes from a noncontemptuous family.

6–12 times per day—Contempt is sneaking into your relationship. This is a call to heal and change.

13–40 times per day—Whoever is receiving the contempt is also receiving impacts to their health, their brain, and their immune system. Healing work on trauma and contempt and healing for moments of aloneness and abandonment could be very beneficial for the relationship.

More than 40 times per day—Consider whether this relationship is worth the cost to your health and well-being.

RESONANT LANGUAGE PRACTICE
Revisiting Acknowledging What Is

We first practiced this resonance skill in Chapter 7. You will remember that there is something very settling for bodies when words are provided for what is actually happening. The same is true for self-hate. It can be very interesting to ask our self-hating parts if we have any need to acknowledge that we really have heard these words used against us. People are not particularly good at referencing context for themselves.

If we are in a state of suspended fear, and we have been in this state for some years, and someone says "Would you like a little acknowledgment that your fear makes good historical sense, given that you lost property and people in the earthquake in 2018?" If this is true for us, we will often take a deep breath, and something will shift or settle into place. We have been given a context for our fear, rather than just experiencing it as a free-floating state, and we have been invited to bring our sense of time to the fear-party, to help put things into perspective.

Acknowledgment can also just be about the experience of having an emotion and how much energy and attention it takes from you. Another way of asking whether there is a need for acknowledgment is, "Would it be sweet if someone else understood . . . how tired you are . . . how frightened you are . . . how worried you are about your child . . . how much time you are spending being concerned about the vulnerability of an aging parent . . .?"

Both ways of holding something with another person create a sense of being accompanied, which is the most calming thing for our bodies.

Here is a chance for you to practice Acknowledging What Is.

RESONANT LANGUAGE PRACTICE
Acknowledging What Is

Sometimes, no matter how bad things are, all people really need is accompaniment. See if you can fill in the following blanks with acknowledgment of what is rather than by trying to imagine how to fix the situations being presented.

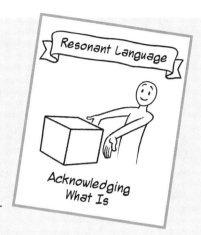

Resonant Language

Acknowledging What Is

Your best friend has just been fired, is behind on their mortgage, has a child with measles, and just discovered that their partner has been unfaithful.

You ask, "Would it be sweet if someone else understood _____
_____
_____

Your adult child must choose between an international position and a relationship with a partner. You ask, "Would you like a little acknowledgment _____
_____
_____

Your partner lost a big contract at work. You ask, "Would you love it if someone else actually understood _____
_____
_____

You suddenly realize that your child has been low in spirits since their best friend moved away. You ask, "Would you like some acknowledgment that it makes sense that _____
_____
_____

Your mother has a cancer diagnosis and doesn't want treatment. You ask yourself, "Would you like acknowledgment that _____
_____
_____

GUIDED MEDITATION
Enjoying Our Own Boundaries and Edges

Some of the possible effects of disorganized attachment are that we may end up not knowing that we exist or that we have edges, or we may have the sense that we have impenetrable boundaries and that we are completely barricaded away from everyone else in the world. Disorganized attachment pushes us out of balance with autonomy and with interdependence. The following meditation will address these possibilities. Part of what we are addressing is that in our areas of disorganized attachment, we are unpredictable even to our own selves.

Begin by noticing your breathing . . . Where does the inhale travel? . . . If you follow your breath into your chest and your belly, where does it reach? . . . What shape does it make inside your body? . . . As you invite your attention to notice your breath, create an even more expansive layer of attention that lets you notice what your attention is doing. And if it wanders away from your breath, acknowledge its good intentions with kindness and resonance . . .

Now allow yourself to notice your own being . . . You are completely and utterly yourself . . . Feel the inside of your body . . . your heart . . . your lungs . . . the inner workings of your intestines . . . This is you . . . You are distinct from everyone else . . . and you are the master of who you let in to your attention . . . and how you let them in . . . First, imagine a neighbor that you don't know well . . . Imagine this person sitting beside you . . . and let yourself feel that this person's presence doesn't affect you at all . . . Now, open the shutters of perception, and allow yourself to be affected by them . . . not overrun, simply changed a bit by warm curiosity and acknowledgment . . . Now close off your attention to the other person . . . and become completely and solely yourself again . . .

Next, allow yourself to imagine someone with whom your relationship is more complicated . . . a parent, a child, a partner . . . Let this person enter your imaginal space . . . and notice how the interior of your body responds to their presence . . . Do they have your consent to affect you? . . . If not, move them as far away as necessary for your body to become your own again . . . This may be as far away as the moon . . . and there may be unconscious contract work to do . . . Do you have your own permission to exist as your own being? . . . Do you get to be the master of your own body? . . . This is a meditation you can return to and practice with until you get to be you, your own person, with your own being . . . and until you can keep other people out of your body except when you consent to their presence . . . The surprise of this practice is that you really do belong to your-

self . . . and you get to choose who you let in . . . and how you let those people in . . . and you get to close yourself to them when you need to . . . for restoration and regeneration of your own energy . . .

Come back to your breath and to its movement within you . . . What do you notice? . . . What are the shapes your breath makes? . . . How does it feel to breathe? . . . Let your attention focus on your breath . . . and notice where it wanders, bringing your warmth to your attention . . .

Now, allow yourself to find the part of you that is completely apart from others . . . Rest in this protected place for a moment . . . Notice that you can bring anyone into your imaginal presence and still remain unchanged . . . This is your insulation . . . Now bring the person you have felt the most warmth for in your life to your imagination . . . How does this affect your body? . . . Do you feel any change in your belly, or in your chest? . . . Allow yourself to imagine the space between you and the other person melting away and becoming a conduit of connection . . . If this feels very peculiar, allow yourself to acknowledge the strangeness of the request . . . If it helps, make the conduit very, very small, so that just one tiny bubble of sensation comes through at a time . . . and notice if you might have unconscious contracts that prevent you from letting others in . . . or from having the hope that connection is possible . . . This is a meditation you can return to and practice with until you feel comfortable letting others in . . . and until you can feel the presence of others with your body . . . with your heart . . . with your guts . . . The surprise of this practice is that you really do get to be connected with others . . . and that it will support the restoration and regeneration of your own energy . . .

Now, take a moment to reconnect with your breathing . . . Allow yourself once again to notice that you are a breathing being . . . that you are here . . . that you exist . . . and that you can bring your attention back to your external life . . . to this book . . . to the dishes . . . to your work . . . to whatever distractions or outer relationships support you . . .

ONE-ON-ONE WORK
Working With Self-Hate

JESS: *What I've been noticing, which has produced a bit of shame in recognizing, is how I still don't necessarily have a sense that I'm worthy of other people's love. Probably three years ago, I would've said it felt impossible to be worthy of my own love. Now that's a lot better, but I'm shaky about being loved by others.*

And in terms of self-hate, there's part of me that actually detests that I need other people. My open-heartedness is both my most favorite part of who I am and I also think, "Gosh, if you weren't so open-hearted you wouldn't have been in an abusive relationship, you wouldn't have gotten so hurt—you wouldn't get hurt."

SARAH: *So, is this what we were talking about earlier, when there is too much pain connected with the self and then we turn away from the self?*

JESS: *Yes, and it is really confusing, to both really like that part of myself and also to feel a sense that this is what led to my PTSD. I'm crying already and we haven't even started. And then, it feels like I'm spinning in a circle because I'm not willing to give that part up, I'm not willing to become distrusting of others. And yet, everything in me says, "This is not a good idea and it gets you hurt. You should know better."*

SARAH: *Let's start with the self-hate for the open heartedness. The first thing I'd like to ask is, if there are two parts of Jess and one turns away from the open-hearted Jess, can we ask the one who has turned away if there is a need to acknowledge worry? If we were to say to that finger-shaking part, "Are you so worried about Jess's well-being? And are you worried about her reserves? Do you really want sustainability?"*

JESS: *Yes, that feels really true.*

SARAH: *Yes. And is there a contract that would be something like, "I, Jess's protector, solemnly swear to my essential self that I will never stop advocating for Jess to take herself into account?"*

JESS: *That's interesting. It's the advocate that wants me to love me? It's a really new voice in the last four years or so. When you say it that way, it feels true that it's the part that wants me to hold on to that self-love that I've cultivated—and can't quite figure out how to be in relationship with other people and still hold on.*

SARAH: *That may be because there may be a false bodhisattva vow that's huge and powerful that the protector is trying to find a way to have some effec-*

tiveness against. Let's look at that and then see how the protector's doing.
The vow would be something like, "I, Jess, solemnly swear to my essential
self to give everything in order to . . ."

JESS: *I will give everything in order to be loved . . . and to contribute . . .*

SARAH: *"and to take a stand to create the world that my integrity is screaming*
for"?

JESS: *Yes, definitely. That feels exactly true. I think that's why I can't get rid of it. I*
really need to live in that world.

SARAH: *Yes, absolutely. This seems even bigger than a vow to the essential self.*
Try saying, "I swear to you, the universe . . ."

JESS: *I, Jess, solemnly swear to you, the universe, that I will give everything in*
order to advocate for the world in which I want to live, no matter the cost.

SARAH: *Now, are you willing to be the universe or creation for me?*

JESS: *Okay.*

SARAH: *Universe, did you hear the vow that Jess made to you?*

JESS: *Mmhmm.*

SARAH: *How do you like that vow?*

JESS: *I don't think it's necessary.*

SARAH: *Thank you. Kind of a big vow for a little person?*

JESS: *And actually, interestingly enough, I feel very full of abundance and love.*
There's something about it being in the natural flow to give love.

SARAH: *That makes total sense. Thank you. Would you please tell Jess, "Jess, I*
release you from this vow . . ."?

JESS: *Jess, I release you from this vow and I revoke this contract. And you have*
my blessing to give to yourself and to others and to actually refill with
resources as well. There's a resourcing and a giving.

SARAH: *That makes a very gentle flow open in my chest. So let's leave the voice*
of the universe and come back and check in with Jess. How are you doing?

JESS: *Yes, let me come back. I feel a little shaky. A little lightheaded.*

SARAH: *Does your body need acknowledgment of unfamiliarity? And of reorien-*
tation?

JESS: *Yes. I've been looking for this balance and it's been hard to find.*

SARAH: *When we have the contracts in place it's very hard to find the balance.*
Now think about what's happening with the critical voice.

JESS: *Mmm. It's a little softer.*

SARAH: *It doesn't have to work so hard against the incredible force of the vow.*

JESS: *Yes, there's almost less fear. It's interesting, because part of the resistance*
was a fear that I'll give up the kindness. There's less worry that the kindness

will suddenly drain from my being if I succumb to this grief. I feel like I'm constantly kind of dealing with a panic that I'll lose my essence. But now it doesn't have to be an either/or. I can still keep that part of myself and flow love toward myself at the same time.

SARAH: *Beautiful. Now, I'd like you to check in with that sense of not being worthy of others' love.*

JESS: *That's still there, unfortunately. Yes.*

SARAH: *Yes. What happens in your body? Is it okay to work with it?*

JESS: *Yes, I would like to find ways to feel more willing to be vulnerable with men, to be more open and to believe them. It's less that I'm not worthy, it's more that I'm not open to their love. There's a little bit of, almost like a recoil. I kind of pull into myself a little bit.*

SARAH: *If this were a vow, would it feel more like "I will retract and make myself smaller in relationship with men" or "I swear to myself that I will believe that I am less than men" or "I swear to myself that I will believe that men cannot love me"?*

JESS: *I really don't feel less than men, even though sometimes it's safer to pretend to be. There's an adamant voice that says, "uh-uh." I think there's something like, "I will protect myself." That feels true. I've experienced receiving the most predatory aggression from men, so it feels like a protective recoil. Of course, it's hard to be open-hearted and vulnerable if you're worried that someone's going to attack you in any second.*

SARAH: *First of all, would you like a little acknowledgment that there's some historical basis for this protectiveness?*

JESS: *It feels like the layer is building over my heart as we talk about it.*

SARAH: *Like one of those animations where all the armor, like, locks into place?*

JESS: *Yes, exactly.*

SARAH: *Just check with the armor. Ask it if we have its consent to work with this today.*

JESS: *Yes, I'm so wanting to take this armor off. It's not serving me.*

SARAH: *Okay. So is it, "I, Jess, solemnly swear that I will retract into myself and protect my heart"? Did we do okay?*

JESS: *Yes, it's interesting. It's not quite what I thought, but of course this is in front of it. It makes sense. "I, Jess, solemnly swear to my essential self that I will retract into myself and protect my heart in order to protect my very essence."*

SARAH: *Ah, beautiful.*

JESS: *It actually plays into the other piece we just worked with, to not harm that very soft core anymore. It gets locked away so it doesn't come out to play. Because it's too dangerous.*

SARAH: *And historically, it has been dangerous. And because of the false bodhi-sattva vow, there wasn't a different way to protect this little one. The grown-up Jess now has skills and abilities that are far beyond the point that this body was at when it created the armor. Is the vow, "I will retract into my body and protect my heart, protect myself, in order to become invisible and still enough or small enough to not be seen so that I can save my softness from obliteration, no matter the cost to myself or others"?*

JESS: *My breath is a little shallow. It feels true. I feel that armor clenching, and I also have that other part that knows I need to take the armor off.*

SARAH: *So, then we'll say, "Jess's essential self, did you hear the vow that this body and spirit made to you to protect the softness?"*

JESS: *Yes, I hear the vow. It was a great vow, it was a really great vow.*

SARAH: *Yes, and not so good anymore?*

JESS: *No. And there's this little voice that's saying, "We can put the armor back on if we need to, but we'll try this for a little while."*

SARAH: *Would the essential self like to say, "Jess, I slowly release you from this vow in the spirit of exploration . . ."?*

JESS: *Jess, I release you from this contract and I revoke this vow and you have my blessing to move as slowly as you need to, to shed the layers and explore, in the spirit of exploration, as an experiment, as you have already been doing. But you get to more wholeheartedly experiment. And lean into the other strengths that you have developed. And you get to walk away when it's not safe, rather than just endure. Yes, I feel more breath.*

SARAH: *How is it if you imagine bringing a male presence into the space?*

JESS: *Hmm. There's more willingness to keep the armor off. I feel like I've been laying it to the side for minutes at a time and then putting it back on. Now it feels a little easier to take off. Yes.*

SARAH: *It will be very interesting to see what happens next with the old patterns of being cruel or unkind or dismissive of the self.*

JESS: *Yes. I'll be curious to check in with the sense of worthiness.*

SARAH: *Thank you so much, Jess. What the work we're doing today beautifully illustrates is that the work with self-hate isn't necessarily a direct path. We're really following the body and its unwinding. I really see this vow work as a disentangling of the nervous system knots that prevent us from full presence in this present moment and just getting to enjoy the heck out of who we are and what we bring.*

One year later, Jess writes:

This vow created quite a shift for me. I had been feeling a lot of sadness and self-blame about not being able to protect a friend from harm (she got into a car accident leaving my house). The self-blame I was feeling largely resolved after this vow work. I was able to have more acceptance that I was helping a friend and had no way of knowing how it would turn out—that she would leave and end up in this accident. I moved from self-blame and guilt to a clear understanding of her responsibility rather than taking it all on myself and thinking I should have seen the future and could have prevented it. I think the process also deepened my understanding of self-love and created sweet space for me to mourn, which I really needed after my friend got hurt, and I needed it for myself to connect more deeply to myself and my experience of love.

I think I am still struggling with some parts of myself in terms of inner conflict about needing other people, but this vow work created a huge shift and allowed me to grieve and accept myself more. The struggle, now, is less about my capacity to love and more about how I need others—it has evolved.

I also notice that this piece of work shifted my sense of agency. Rather than trying to endure harm in order to be loving, the second part of the process allowed me to set better boundaries and begin to see how loving boundaries can be (toward myself and even the other person, too). I was able to connect more deeply with my partner afterward, and it kept us moving toward healing together—we started therapy together and I was willing to trust the process and cultivate patience and flexibility instead of being afraid. I spoke up and advocated for myself more, too, while also being open to whatever the outcome of our time in therapy was.

JOURNALING PROMPT FOR
Finding Your Contracts of Disorganized Attachment

List some of the moments when you have very little choice about how you respond, whether your response is increased activation or reactivity or a temper tantrum or disappearing into dissociation.

_____
_____
_____
_____

For each of the things you have listed, were there models for this behavior that were demonstrated in your childhood?

_____
_____
_____
_____

For the things that have no precedent in your childhood, did any of these behaviors begin after a period of trauma in your adulthood?

_____
_____
_____

For each of the behaviors you have listed, what, or who, might you be protecting with your automatic responses?

_____
_____
_____
_____

What contracts can you guess may lie behind these automatic responses?

_____
_____
_____
_____

Disorganized Attachment Contract Template

Try doing the following process for each of the different disorganized attachment behaviors that you circled in the list earlier in this chapter or determined from the journaling exercise above.

1.   *I,* _____, *solemnly swear to my essential self (or mother, father, sibling, God, universe, etc.) that I will always/never*

     _____

     _____

     in order to _____ ,

     no matter the cost to myself and those I love.

2.   What is the good, historical, lived reason for this contract? When did you first make this contract? How does it make sense within the larger context of your life?

     _____

     _____

     _____

     _____

3.   *Essential self (or mother, father, sibling, God, universe, etc.), did you hear this vow?*

     Yes _____

     No _____

     (If no, then repeat the words of the vow.)

4.   *Essential self (or mother, father, sibling, God, universe, etc.), do you want this vow to be kept?*

     Yes _____

     No _____

     (If the answer is "Yes, the vow should stay, no matter the cost," then it's time to use the Time Travel Process to go to the moment in your life in which this unconscious contract makes sense.)

5.   The release: *I release you from this vow, and I revoke this contract.*

6.   The blessing: *And instead, I give you my blessing to*

     _____

CHAPTER 10

Finding the Path Out of Depression

TWO FLAVORS OF DEPRESSION

There are two main flavors of depression. The first is a constant, inescapable, hostile, or shaming inner voice. The voice goes on relentlessly in a running commentary on all the faults of the self. The second emotional tone of depression can be a deep fall into an aloneness that never ends. There can be a terrible sense of loneliness, a frozen state of alarmed aloneness. Common to both flavors is the blockage of the SEEKING circuit. This understanding comes from Jaak Panksepp's research, which reveals that when we're in the seeking circuit and we hit frustration, we can either move directly to helplessness or we can take a side road into rage. Then if rage doesn't change things, we will go back to helplessness. In either case, after helplessness comes despair and then depression.[1]

Luckily, we can mobilize the range of skills and abilities that we've been learning and the neurons that we've been growing to help us with depression. As we do the work of developing our resonant selves, we subtract self-hate and self-blame from the picture and so relieve the burden these states have on the brain and body. When we clear away the self-hate and self-blame, we start to feel what lies underneath and what it is that we really need help with. There may be loneliness or chronic fatigue or other health issues underneath. As we move toward self-warmth, any underlying condition or inflammation becomes clearer, and our efforts can then be focused on healing and support instead of having to fight the lacerating default mode network. We can do time travel for both trauma experiences and for aloneness. We can do resonant language dialogues with the seeking circuit, and we can try to find out what other circuits SEEKING might be entangled with which are stopping SEEK-ING from being able to work. We can do processes to bring the CARE and PLAY circuits online to balance our endocannabinoid system and help SEEKING from that angle. We can begin to learn to hold ourselves, wherever we are, with warmth and resonance, which can only help. We can discover exactly what kind of self-accompaniment feels best.

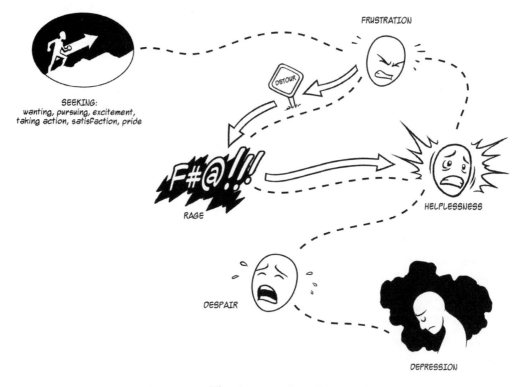

FRUSTRATION

SEEKING:
wanting, pursuing, excitement,
taking action, satisfaction, pride

DETOUR

F#@!!

RAGE

HELPLESSNESS

DESPAIR

DEPRESSION

FIGURE 10.1 The Journey Into Depression

━━━━━━━━━━ THE MAIN QUESTION FOR THIS CHAPTER ━━━━━━━━━━

What is the path out of depression?

When I first started doing this work, the kind of self-accompaniment that I could do was to just sit and look at this mostly dead little girl who was curled up in the fetal position and didn't really want me to come close. And over the years of connection and work, I've watched the shift in what self-accompaniment looks like. After the little girl woke up and became more willing, I could feel a warm presence beside myself, and just in the last month or two, I've had this sense of being able to touch myself and kiss myself on my forehead. It brings me to tears to say this, but it feels like after all these years of work with self-warmth, my body is now willing to begin to receive this level of tangible self-warmth from myself.

One of the things about depression that can be so difficult is that it's an energy-less state, as if the car has run out of gas—and so you can't drive the car to go get gas from a gas station. So then, how do we get gas delivered to the car? One way is to do the self-warmth meditations that go with my first book, *Your Resonant Self*, and are available for free on the www.yourresonantself.com website. They are very healing

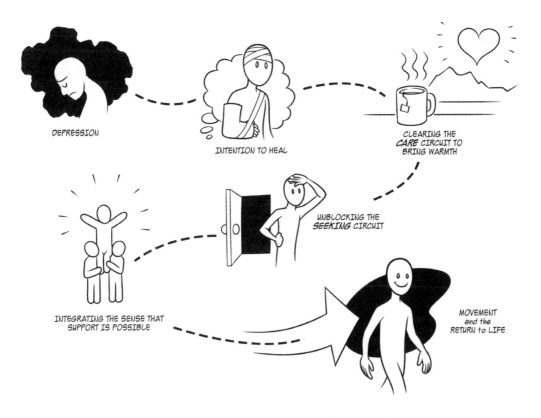

FIGURE 10.2: The Journey Out of Depression

for brains and they start the process of growing the neurons that we need to be able to get some "gas" into our system.

When working with depression, there's so little energy available that we need to find steps that are small enough to be accessible to us. This may be just one breath, one breath of warmth for the self. One breath of saying to ourselves, "Of course you have a sense of helplessness. Of course, there's no energy." Even just that much warmth once a day starts to grow the neurons that we need. Another option may be through a practice of gratitude.

I-YOU LANGUAGE

If the instrumental part of your brain really has a sense only of "I" rather than also knowing who "others" are, then it will take a movement into the relational, resonant brain to realize that other people exist. Or even to realize that your own emotional self exists.

I–You dialogues have three rules:

1. Some form of *I* and *You* must appear in every sentence: I, me, my, or mine and you, your, or yours. (Using *We* or *Us* does not have the same effect, so those words don't count.)
2. Do not repeat yourself or repeat the other person.
3. Each party gets to say only one sentence at a time.

Here is an illustration of some common forms of positive I–You language:

"I love you"

"When I remember you ... it touches me"

"You hurt me"

"How does what I did impact you?"

"What is important to you from what I said?"

FIGURE 10.3 Relational Language (I–You Language)

When we are in a depressed state, we are in a very peculiar I–You relationship with ourselves. It largely consists of blame, accusations, and reproach: *I hate you, I can't believe you did that, I think you are useless/worthless/bad/irredeemable,* and *I wish you were dead.* The sentences often leave off either the second *I* or the *You*, as in, *I am stupid, I should be dead, You are an idiot, You never learn, You are an asshole,* etc.

RESONANT LANGUAGE PRACTICE
I–You Language

It can be interesting to begin to catch these constant messages that take us toward depression and intentionally turn them into an I–You dialogue that goes further than a single shaming sentence. Here is an example of an I–You depression dialogue that goes further into some interesting areas. Each sentence has an "I" and a "you" in it. "A" is the depressed inner voice, and the "B" voice is another, more fluid and responsive part of the self, sometimes angry, sometimes sad, sometimes hopeful.

> **A:** *I'm so overwhelmed I can't function to take care of you.*
> **B:** *I know you are, and I hate that about you.*
> **A:** *Do you wish I were dead?*
> **B:** *Today I wish you were functional, and creative, and whole.*
> **A:** *I am so depressed, and I know it impacts you.*
> **B:** *I think it's because the stress is so great that it stops you from moving purposefully.*
> **A:** *I agree with you—the energy goes into loops of agitation instead of letting itself be focused for movement.*

There is a change in the tone of the conversation when we don't repeat ourselves and we do tell the truth as fully as we can. The tone of the conversation will most often *move from blame and hopelessness toward compassion and the discovery of deeper truths that reveal the depth of grief and worry that are at the root of blame.* Once we begin to track our critical inner voice, we find that it is remarkably repetitive, and this type of dialogue offers something different. Now it's your turn to try. Begin with a sentence that you often hear on repeat in the depressed part of your brain, and start the I–You dialogue after that sentence. Continue for at least five exchanges. "A" is for your depressed voice, and "B" responds in any way you would like, but tells the truth and follows the rules.

A: _____

B: _____

A: _____

B: _____
A: _____
B: _____
A: _____
B: _____
A: _____
B: _____

This kind of dialogue is a beginning point for the journey out of depression—the awakening of the intention to heal. The guided meditation that comes next is a first step to begin to clear the CARE circuit and bring warmth to the self. After the guided meditation, we will focus on the contracts that block both CARE and SEEKING, and finally, we will explore an invitation to our ancestors to give us support.

Here is a meditation that can begin to clear blocks to our CARE circuit in relationship to the self.

GUIDED MEDITATION
The Gentle Path Out of Depression

Invite your attention to come to your breath . . . Find the place where your breath is most alive . . . and see if your attention is willing to settle there . . . It may not be willing . . . or it may not have enough energy to be able to focus . . . Whatever your attention does, bring an exquisite and understanding gentleness to it . . .

As you bring this great gentleness to your attention . . . and to what it's doing . . . allow yourself to let an intention for healing arise . . . This may be the smallest of hints of a longing for something better . . . This may be a tiny willingness to let your ancestors support you . . . This may be a sliver of a memory of what it was like before the depression . . . and a scrap of hope that you will have your life energy back again . . . and let yourself notice and remember any arising of intention that comes . . .

Now allow yourself to begin to notice the messages of your depression and their terrible impact . . . the words you say to yourself that you wouldn't allow another person to say to someone you care about . . . For each message that you hear, see what happens if you ask that voice, "Are you really worried about my survival?" . . .

Sometimes the answer is yes . . . When it is, simply acknowledge the voice and let yourself continue to breathe, without imagining that the voice's evaluation of you is actually true . . . Let the scope of your vision see the family and cultural pressures on the voice . . . see that it wants you to survive in a repressive, oxygen-thin world . . . see that many of us had childhoods that were difficult to survive . . . and that of course this voice only knows how to take care of us by being critical . . .

If the voice is brutal, rather than agreeing that it has your best interests at heart, there are trauma knots and contracts in place preventing real connection with the voice, so gently close the voice away from you so that it does less harm to you . . . and know that the cruelty is not true, it's trauma . . .

And bring an affection to yourself . . . behind walls of your brain . . . as the receiver of these voices . . . under siege . . . with warmth . . . and compassion . . . and so much care . . . and tenderness . . . and sweetness . . . Even if it feels unreachable . . . reach for a hint . . . a clue . . . a small moment . . . of gentleness for your own self . . .

Now, begin the return to the self that exists in the outer world, bringing back with you any tiny sense of warmth for self, or any shred of hope for warmth some-day . . . These shreds of sensation are the feeling of tiny neurons in our brains reaching for each other . . .

And come back to your breath . . . and your attention . . . and any bodily sensations of breathing that you can find . . . if you can find any . . . and invite yourself fully back into your connection with the outer world . . . Open your eyes and look around . . . See where you are . . . and return completely to this moment.

Our next exploration allows us to look at a visual image of any depression that we are in relationship with to help us discover which order to follow when clearing our contracts.

QUESTIONNAIRE
A Picture of the Blocked SEEKING Circuit

Give yourself one point for each line that is true for you. At the end of the questionnaire, you'll be using your totals to create a picture of the way that your own SEEKING circuit may be blocked.

VIEW OF SELF	
Unworthy	
Failure	
Bad	
Wrong	
Guilty	
Shameful	
Sinful	
	Total for VIEW OF SELF _____
ENERGY	
Fatigue, weariness, tiredness	
No energy to wash, dress, clean, make food	
Everything has to be done slowly	
Can't take action	
Feeling trapped	
Lifelessness	
Disturbed sleep	
	Total for ENERGY _____
FOCUS/ATTENTION	
Indecisive	
Unable to read	
Unable to track conversations	

Unable to do arithmetic	
Unable to write	
Unable to work	
Agitated and can't settle	
	Total for FOCUS/ATTENTION _____

VIEW OF THE FUTURE/MEANING/CONTRIBUTION	
Hopelessness	
No interest in life	
Sense of futility	
Everything is boring	
No sense of the future	
No curiosity	
Suicidal thoughts	
	Total for VIEW OF THE FUTURE _____

PLEASURE/JOY	
Everything is gray	
No flavor	
No texture	
No pleasure	
No happiness	
Feeling sad, blue	
Feeling blah	
	Total for PLEASURE/JOY _____

For each section of the pie chart below, use your score from the questionnaire above to darken your number of rows, starting from the middle, showing the score you gave yourself for each section. This pie chart will give you a picture of your particular style of depression.

The most important element in the Wheel of Depression is always your negative

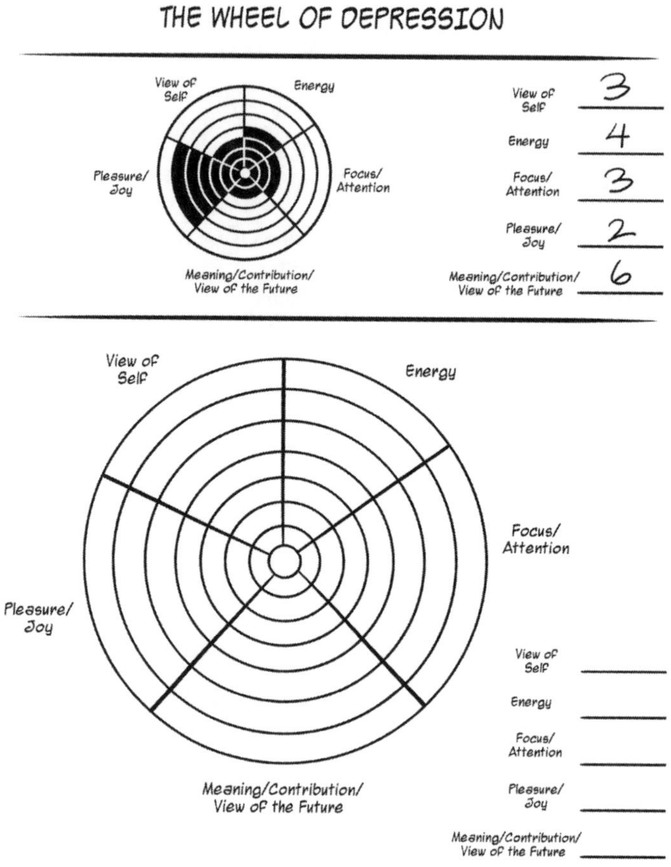

THE WHEEL OF DEPRESSION

FIGURE 10.4 The Wheel of Depression

self-image, so the first step is to begin dissolving unconscious contracts that make you believe bad things about yourself.

For example: *I solemnly swear to my essential self that I will believe that I am a failure and that I am not enough in order to . . . (let my family be right about me so that I will have a place . . . not leave my mother alone . . . make sense of the way I was treated as a child . . . , etc.), no matter the cost to myself.*

The next most important element is energy and whether or not you have your own permission to fully inhabit yourself, so that is the next type of contract to focus on.

For example: *I solemnly swear to my essential self that I will not try in order to . . . (never fail . . . , not have to leave myself . . . , stay with my father . . . , etc.)*

The next area to review for possible contracts is the area of focus and attention. Here you will want to look for contracts that keep you in a state of hypervigilant awareness or agitation, as these nervous system states hinder focused attention on one thing.

> **For example:** *I solemnly swear to my essential self that I will continually stay watchful and vigilant for danger in order to survive, no matter the cost to myself.* (This type of contract can be exhausting as well as keeping us from being able to focus.)

Now we want to bring our attention to contracts that prevent us from looking at the future or finding meaning.

> **For example:** *I promise myself that I will not depend on there being a future in order to prevent heartbreak and disappointment . . . or I will not fully invest in this life in order to be in integrity with my sense of choicelessness about being born, no matter the cost.*

Our blocks to joy and pleasure are often cleared by the work that we have done with the other blocks, but it's also good to make sure that we aren't making agreements with ourselves not to enjoy the world.

> **For example:** *I promise myself that I will not experience joy in order to stay with my family and belong, etc., no matter the cost to myself.*

There is one other type of contract that we need to address that can be so heavy that it will leave those who carry it in a deep hole of depression: unconscious contracts to take on the pain of the world. These contracts also need to be released to let our bodies lighten and move out of the depressive states.

> **For example:** *I solemnly swear to you, the universe, that I will take on all the pain of this world in order that no one carry their pain alone, no matter the cost to myself.*

In this case, we become the universe and look at ourselves through its eyes. We ask the universe, "Do you like this vow?" Most often, the universe looks at us and says, "Oh, this is a very big vow for such a little person. I release you from this vow and I revoke this contract." When we carry such contracts unconsciously, even if we don't have a sense of the contracts being released immediately, the naming of them and their movement into consciousness can lighten our burdens.

Let's take a look at an example of the way that contract work can lift us up.

ONE-ON-ONE WORK
Lifting Helplessness and Depression

SARAH: *Hello, Marie. What's coming up for you in response to the question, "Do you like yourself?"?*

MARIE: *What's coming up for me is the connection with my younger self and a sense of paralysis. I just notice tears. It feels really vulnerable, feeling the part that would never love myself, wouldn't believe I was worthy of anything, or thought that it was always my fault.*

SARAH: *Do you have a sense of how this might be a burden that you still carry in present time?*

MARIE: *Yes, it shows up in relationship, when something happens and I withdraw instead of reaching out. There's a hopelessness.*

SARAH: *Does your body need acknowledgment that when you were little, no matter how hard you tried, it didn't make any difference?*

MARIE: *Yes. That brings up a memory, or a sense that if I can't make a difference, then I need to get really good at guessing what's going to happen next.*

SARAH: *When you say there was a memory, do you have a sense of how old your younger self is in the memory?*

MARIE: *I think I am about six.*

SARAH: *Is it okay with your six-year-old if we go to her?*

MARIE: *Yes.*

SARAH: *Okay. So you and me, funny old ladies, stepping through time and space, coming to be with this six-year-old, freezing everybody and everything else that's in the environment. What's our first guess for what this little one needs acknowledged?*

MARIE: *I'm so helpless.*

SARAH: *Does this little one need acknowledgment that she's living in a world where helplessness and difficulty are everywhere? That it's like living in constant floods and avalanches and forest fires? And that there's a level of emotional overwhelm from other people's upset that is huge?*

MARIE: *Yes. My throat's not being cut off anymore and I can breathe. Like a really huge piece of ice melted. The enormity of it. And acknowledging a sense there was nowhere to turn. I felt like I just came back.*

SARAH: *That takes me toward a contract. Let me just check with the little one and with you and I'll propose a contract. "I, Marie, solemnly swear to my essential self that I will not spend any life energy trying to change what happens in order to stay safe, no matter the cost to myself." Is it something like that?*

MARIE: —to survive—

SARAH: "... in order to survive."

MARIE (AFTER A PAUSE FOR GRIEF): *There were just lots of waves running through my body, in my belly and chest. It's like I never thought it would be held, like I was never allowed to be held. So, there's some surprise and relief to actually be connecting with the experience of this younger self.*

SARAH: *Do you need acknowledgment of how hard it's been, hanging on?*

MARIE: *It was good to breathe. Yes, it felt like I was just holding my breath.*

SARAH: *Sometimes when we hold our breath, we can diminish sensation, which makes it easier to survive overwhelm and horror.*

MARIE: *As I release the breath, it feels like there's a settling and calming relaxation, actually, in my belly.*

SARAH: *Then we'll say to the essential self of Marie, "Essential self of Marie, did you hear the vow that the little one made to you, to accept giving up? Yes? Is that a vow that you'd like for her? (Marie is shaking her head.) No? No. You understand why she made it. But it's not what you'd like for her now, am I understanding?"*

MARIE: *"I release you from this vow and I revoke this contract." Yes. It's like sunshine came in.*

SARAH: *Very nice. Would you like to invite that little one to come back to the present with us?*

MARIE: *Yes. I'm experiencing us on either side of her. We can move out of that kitchen, then out of that world, and into this one where there is love and compassion and it's safe to be seen. It feels good.*

One year later, Marie writes:

The sustained change I am noticing is my willingness to speak up, to have a voice and an opinion rather than withdraw into silence. I'm able to stay engaged in conversation with curiosity, resiliency, and inner confidence, recognizing that my voice truly does matter.

UNCONSCIOUS CONTRACTS THAT LEAD TO DEPRESSION

The kinds of vows that lead to depression create a downward spiral, a never-ending cycle that leaves us in immobilization and can be very hard to come out of—once depression begins, we can be like turtles stuck on their backs—we don't want to be in that position, but it seems impossible to get back on our feet. It can be much easier to find our way out of depression if we release some of these vows. Here is a table of possible intertwined contracts and root causes that can lead to immobilization of our SEEKING circuits, otherwise known as depression. Any of the self-sabotaging actions on the left could match up with any from the column on the right.

TABLE 10.1 Depression Contracts	
I will kill myself with my mother's murderous gaze	in order to be dead, since my mother only loves dead babies
I will never again have hope	in order to save myself from heartbreak and disappointment
I will never try for anything I really want	in order to protect myself from my own lacerating self-hate
I won't start anything new	in order to keep from making mistakes and abandoning myself because of them
I will not move	in order to say fuck you to the people who pushed me
I will never believe I have any worth	in order to keep from seeing my mother's disappointment
I won't reach for a better life	in order not to leave my family by doing better than they did
I will believe I am worthless and should never have been born	in order to make up to my mother for my life being a burden on her
I will not believe that life has meaning	in order to keep from being fully incarnated
I will not invest in the future	in order to keep from wasting my life energy on futility
I will figure this out myself and not let anyone help me	in order to keep from being abandoned

What are the contracts you have about hope, meaning, effort, the future, and how you see yourself that might be blocking your SEEKING circuit?

I will . . .	in order to . . .

Unconscious Contract Template for Working With Depression

1. I, _____, solemnly swear to my essential self (or mother, father, sibling, God, universe, etc.) that I will always/never

   _____

   _____

   in order to _____ ,
   no matter the cost to myself and those I love.

2. What is the good, historical, lived reason for this contract? When did you first make this contract? How does it make sense within the larger context of your life?

   _____

   _____

   _____

   _____

3. Essential self (or mother, father, sibling, God, universe, etc.), did you hear this vow?

   Yes _____

   No _____

   (If no, then repeat the words of the vow.)

4. *Essential self (or mother, father, sibling, God, universe, etc.), do you want this vow to be kept?*

    Yes _____

    No _____

    (If the answer is "Yes, the vow should stay, no matter the cost," then it's time to use the Time Travel Process to go to the moment in your life in which this unconscious contract makes sense.)

5. The release: *I release you from this vow, and I revoke this contract.*

6. The blessing: *And instead I give you my blessing to:*

    _____

    _____

Whenever we think we have to do it all alone, we are essentially depleting ourselves. Our bodies need to belong and be a part of things. Depression can rob us of any belief in transformation or any motivation to do anything that could help, and this is where our ancestors can be important. We can explore saying, "I can't do it. I can't take action to help myself. I can't get out of bed. I can't shower. I can't brush my teeth. Ancestors, I can't do it. If you help me, I might be able to do it." In some moments, calling upon our ancestors can be the most important thing that we do to begin to come out of states of depression.

JOURNALING PROMPT FOR
Calling On Your Ancestors

1. First of all, make sure that you feel that calling on your ancestors might be a good thing. Sometimes it doesn't feel possible or good, in which case simply skip this journaling prompt.

2. Next, and before you bring your attention back in time, allow yourself to imagine your great, great, great grandchild or great, great, great niece or great nephew. Imagine that you can look forward through time and see this child in the future. How do you feel about this little one?

    _____

    _____

3. Do you know any of your grandparents' names? If you do, list them here:

    _____

    _____

4. Do you know any of your great grandparents' names? If you do, list them here:

    _____

    _____

5. Now, take the point of view of one of your great, great grandparents, long dead, traumas long-healed, feuds and resentments long disappeared, looking at you through time. As your own great, great, great grandparent, how is it to see you? Is there affection, warmth, a desire to support, a longing for your well-being? Does your ancestor wish that you could lean back into them and that they could support you? Notice what comes to you:

    _____

    _____

    _____

    _____

    _____

    _____

6. Sometimes there is a sense of neutrality or blankness, in which case there may be traumas or unconscious contracts in the way. If your ancestors are not a resource in this moment, they may well become a strong and vital well of support as you continue along this path.

    _____

    _____

    _____

    _____

    _____

    _____

CHAPTER 11

Working With the Layers of Addiction

DEFINITION OF ADDICTION

A short definition for addiction can be "continued use or continued action despite harm." If we're gambling and it's harming us or the family finances, then that's an addiction. If we're eating food in ways that are harming us, that's an addiction. If we're using heroin or methamphetamines in ways that are compromising our lives or taking well-being from others, it's an addiction. As soon as the compromise and the harm begin, we've entered into a choiceless relationship with a substance or a behavior. That's an addiction.

In looking for our own addictions, the questions we ask ourselves are, "What do we use or do, even though it harms us? And where do we not have choice?" At times, this harm can be hard to acknowledge because the brain can be compromised by different substances in such a way that we can't even see clearly anymore. Sometimes we can find out if we are causing harm by asking our close people what the impact of our substance use or our addictive behavior is on them. And sometimes our close people will stage interventions in which they will tell us, "This is harming you."

JOURNALING PROMPT FOR
Entering a Dialogue with Your Addictions

What do you continue to use or do despite harm to yourself or others?

_____

_____

_____

_____

NEUROSCIENCE OF ADDICTIONS

Addictions happen when we discover a substance or a behavior that balances our brain in ways that we didn't even know were out of balance. This can happen when we're very young. For example, I was at a two-year-old's birthday party recently. No one touched or picked up the two-year-old for the first hour we were there. And then the cakes came out. One was a whole two-layer frosted cake that was meant just for this child to dig into, no fork, just hands. And everyone cheered and clapped, and it was as if I could see the child's nucleus accumbens making the connection—sugar, fat, endogenous opioids, oxytocin—this is what will make me feel good, since there isn't much human touch or warmth.[1]

The nucleus accumbens is the brain area that registers these discoveries about what feels good and solves brain problems and then gives these brain-balancing substances and behaviors high points as desirable and wanted[2] and makes it so that we remember these things as the solution to all our problems. Subsequent encounters rarely equal the balancing power of the first experience, but the brain keeps trying because the nucleus accumbens' initial memory is so powerful. Sad? Have some alcohol. Happy? Have some alcohol. Tired? Have some alcohol.

Each person's brain is a little different, so each nucleus accumbens will find its own addictive cocktail of substances and behaviors to come as close as possible to balancing its brain's circuits and compensating for whatever its brain is missing. And remember, the more difficult events (adverse childhood experiences) that happen to a person, the more the circuits are impacted, the more the brain is out of balance, and the more likely that person is to struggle with addiction (and depression, anxiety, mental health issues, and physical health issues).[3]

QUESTIONNAIRE
What Do Your Addictions Do for You?

Take this questionnaire separately for each separate addictive substance/behavior that impacts your life.

1. My addictive substance/behavior calms me down.

    Yes   No

2. My addictive substance/behavior helps me when I'm sad.

    Yes   No

3. My addictive substance/behavior is how I celebrate.

Yes   No

4. My addictive substance/behavior helps me get through the day.

Yes   No

5. My addictive substance/behavior takes care of my boredom.

Yes   No

6. My addictive substance/behavior keeps me from feeling my shame.

Yes   No

7. My addictive substance/behavior engages me with life.

Yes   No

8. My addictive substance/behavior sharpens my attention.

Yes   No

9. My addictive substance/behavior helps me get things done.

Yes   No

10. My addictive substance/behavior makes me feel safe.

Yes   No

11. My addictive substance/behavior helps me feel social/relaxed.

Yes   No

12. My addictive substance/behavior stops my self-criticism.

Yes   No

13. My addictive substance/behavior stops me from thinking.

Yes   No

14. My addictive substance/behavior helps me feel playful.

Yes   No

15. My addictive substance/behavior helps me feel sexual.

    Yes   No

16. My addictive substance/behavior helps me feel spiritual.

    Yes   No

17. My addictive substance/behavior helps me feel warm and connected.

    Yes   No

18. My addictive substance/behavior keeps depression at bay.

    Yes   No

19. My addictive substance/behavior makes the world less scary.

    Yes   No

20. My addictive substance/behavior helps my anxiety.

    Yes   No

21. My addictive substance/behavior manages my PTSD flashbacks.

    Yes   No

Score yourself by circling your "yeses" under the circuit names below. Those "yeses" will show you which circuits you are managing with your addictive substances and behaviors.

SEEKING

| 1 | 3 | 4 | 5 | 7 | 8 | 9 | 12 | 13 | 18 |

CARE

| 1 | 2 | 4 | 6 | 11 | 12 | 13 | 17 | 20 |

PANIC/GRIEF

| 1 | 2 | 4 | 6 | 11 | 12 | 13 | 17 | 20 | 21 |

FEAR

| 1 | 10 | 19 | 20 | 21 |

RAGE

17

PLAY

3   11   14   16   21

SEXUALITY

6   15

Here is a table that puts your addictive substances and behaviors into the context of the Circuits of Emotion and Motivation and the needs and longings that may be important for you, based on which circuits you gave *yes*es to.

TABLE 11.1 Addiction and the Circuits of Emotion and Motivation			
Circuit	Main Neurotransmitters	Addictions	Longings
SEEKING*	Dopamine Glutamate	Cocaine Methamphetamines Nicotine Gambling Shopping Alcohol** Web and video game use Ketamine	Focus Pride Satisfaction Accomplishment Activity Energy Movement Pleasure
CARE	Oxytocin Endogenous Opioids	Opiates Sugar/Fat/Salt Alcohol	Love Warmth Comfort Relaxation Belonging

* Any addiction is a result of the SEEKING circuit trying to take care of us by using substances and behaviors to compensate for problems with circuits and with the default mode network. A major site on the SEEKING circuit is the nucleus accumbens, the brain organ that assigns values to possible addictive substances and behaviors.[4]

** One of the reasons for alcohol's popularity with humans is its ability to compensate for problems with most of the circuits, but more than anything else, alcohol has the capacity to temporarily reduce shame,[5] which occurs on the PANIC/GRIEF circuit.

PANIC/ GRIEF	Oxytocin Endogenous Opioids	Opiates Sugar/Fat/Salt Alcohol	Love Warmth Comfort Relaxation Belonging
FEAR	Endogenous benzodiazepines Glutamate	Benzodiazepine Alcohol Ketamine	Safety Relaxation Cessation of stress and danger
RAGE	Substance P Glutamate	Opiates Sugar/Fat/Salt Alcohol Ketamine	Survival To know we and others matter Success
PLAY	Endocannabinoids	Cannabis Alcohol	Play Delight Connection to spirituality Healing trauma
SEXUALITY	Steroids Vasopressin Oxytocin	Sex Pornography Strip clubs Alcohol	Sexuality Sensual pleasure Belonging Loss of self Communion
DISGUST	(Panksepp didn't classify DISGUST as a circuit, so I don't have solid research to support a guess at its relationship to addiction)		

GUIDED MEDITATION
Leaning Into New Self-Compassion
About Our Addictions

Let yourself take a breath . . . and then settle into feeling your breathing . . . inviting your attention to travel with your breath . . . in and out of your body . . . Your attention may wander, as attention does when it's trying to take care of us . . . Hold your attention lightly and gently . . . with warmth, no matter what it does . . . and keep inviting it back to your breath.

Now bring your attention to your body . . . How is it to be here, in this body, at this time? . . . What has your relationship been over time to your body? . . . And to this brain of yours? . . . Do you need any acknowledgment of a history of resentment . . . of helplessness . . . of any sense of choicelessness? . . . Have you turned away from yourself . . . because you couldn't do what you wanted to do? . . . Because you couldn't stop what you wanted to stop? . . .

Notice the part of you that you have turned away from . . . the part that has pursued the addiction . . . the part that you have judged for so long as not having enough resolve or enough strength . . . See if it's possible to gently surround this part of yourself with appreciation . . . and warmth . . . and an unaccustomed gentleness . . . See how it feels to thank this part of yourself for its best efforts to take care of you . . .

As you receive this unfamiliar invitation, notice how your body responds . . . Do you stiffen? . . . Or is there any sense of dissociation? . . . Whatever you experience, meet it with warmth . . . with an "Of course you feel this way," . . . Acknowledge any resistance, helplessness, or frustration with this whole process . . . and bring another layer of warmth for any difficult feelings that arise . . . How does your body receive this unaccustomed care and tenderness? . . .

And now, allow yourself to return to your breathing . . . and just for a moment, let yourself follow your breathing in . . . and out . . . bringing your attention to the sensations of breath . . . and coming all the way back to the present moment.

That may have been an unusual or unfamiliar journey into the body. Now that we have your body reawakened, let's return to our resonant language skill of tuning into and naming body sensations.

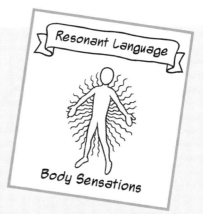

RESONANT LANGUAGE PRACTICE
Naming Body Sensations

To work with our addictions, we need to reference what's happening in our bodies when we make resonant guesses for ourselves.

Imagine that you will never get to do your addictive behavior again, and put check marks beside the body sensations that arise for you.

- Pain in the head
- A band around the head
- Dissociation, spaciness
- Agitation in the arms
- Weakness in the limbs
- Empty heart
- Pain in the heart
- A sense that the heart stops beating
- Agitation in the chest
- Jangling in the chest
- Buzzing in the chest

- Deadness in the chest
- Electrical feelings in the chest
- Constriction in the chest
- A sense that you stop breathing
- Discomfort in the stomach
- Pain in the abdomen
- Constriction in the abdomen
- Deadness in the abdomen
- Loss of all energy

JOURNALING PROMPT FOR
Your SEEKING Circuit and Your Addictions

How is your SEEKING circuit trying to take care of you? We can begin to guess at which circuits SEEKING is trying to take care of for us by imagining stopping our addictive behavior or substance. What happens in your body when you do this? What are the longings you might have that you haven't even known about?

Body sensations when you imagine stopping:

_____

_____

_____

_____

The feelings that these body sensations might be linked with:

_____

_____

_____

_____

_____

_____

Possible longings you might have:

_____

_____

_____

_____

_____

_____

UNDERSTANDING THE HARM OUR ADDICTIONS INFLICT ON OUR FAMILIES

You may remember that addiction is very highly correlated with adverse childhood experiences. We might think that what children really need is adequate food and housing and for their families to have some level of physical wellbeing; and all this is true, but little brains also need to be nourished and fed by connection, and if they grow up without relationship, they'll turn to addictions to fill the gap.

The quality of numbness and insulation that most addictions bring, where they place a bit of screen between addict and other or addict and the world, is devastating for the children of addicts. Children need their parents to be alive in the relational connection. They need their parents' faces to respond. That's why the use of an addictive substance or behavior by a parent—even something which doesn't seem harmful, like food, cannabis, or shopping—is one of the formally studied childhood traumas, called Adverse Childhood Experiences (ACEs),[6] because the parent's capacity to be in a truly relational space is compromised.

The more traumas and the more different kinds of traumas and alarmed aloneness we experience, the more an effect it has on our brains and the more our brains try to compensate for the effects of the ACEs by using external substances and behaviors.[7] It's not the drugs that are addictive; it's the brain's discovery of a solution for a brain problem that becomes addictive.

Can relational neuroscience help us with the daily grind of living with an addiction?

THE ADDICTION AS PART OF THE SELF

Our brains don't know that they are located inside our skulls and bodies. Our brains think that everything familiar belongs to them. They make our cars and violins into parts of our bodies,[8] and they seem to believe that our chemical and behavioral addictions are a part of our brains, too. Our brains are, after all, in charge of balancing and downshifting our cortisol levels, taking care of our health, well-being, and cognitive function, and they are responsible for physical integration and grace.

Through this work, I have come to think of addictions as our effort to survive without a compassionate and resonating self-witness. The substances and behaviors and experiences almost become an external compassionate and resonating self-witness we use to supplement our own brains.

This means that when we're working with addiction and vows, we need to revoke our vow to use a substance or behavior, and the addiction also needs to release its vow to save us.

Once the brain decides that alcohol (or any other addiction) is a good remedy for whatever's wrong, then the brain stays convinced. No matter how harmful its use has become for us, and no matter how much liver or brain damage we have sustained, the brain continues to give the addictive substance or behavior a very high score as a problem solver. This is why, in 12-step groups, there's the statement, for example, "My name is Sarah, and I'm an alcoholic." What we're basically saying is, "My name is Sarah, and my brain has been forever changed by alcohol (or, in other groups, by marijuana or by the use of a sugar that allows me to cope")." This is different from saying, "I am indistinguishable from my addiction." We may have a reaction to these statements in the 12-step groups, feeling that they reduce or limit our sense of possibility of growth and change. But if we reduce it to the brain science, we see that the potential for change comes through strengthening the other parts of the brain so that we're not defaulting to the nucleus accumbens and what it believes about how we should use behaviors or substances in order to survive. We're always in relationship with the parts of our brains that think the addiction is still going to work, and yet the more we have the right hemisphere working and holding us, the less power the nucleus accumbens has.

While the nucleus accumbens is an essential part of the SEEKING circuit, and is necessary for acquisition of our addiction, the nucleus accumbens becomes less important once the addiction has been established. Once the addiction is established, the dorsolateral striatum plays an even more important role in keeping the addiction going.[9] The dorsolateral striatum is the part of the brain that takes over when we devour a whole carton of ice cream without even realizing we got it out of the freezer. We find ourselves with half a bottle of wine already gone without even realizing we started to drink. When this happens, the dorsolateral striatum is in action. When scientists block the dopamine receptors in the dorsolateral striatum rather than in the nucleus accumbens, well-established, habitual, drug-seeking behavior decreases.[10] This shows us that a different part of the brain is engaged once a behavior is habitual.

The longer the time period that we've been in a relationship with our addictions, the more we've outsourced to them. This means that there are a lot of "I will take care of you" contracts that our addictions have with us. Each piece of work with contracts can lighten the chain of contracts by a link. When the addiction impairs the prefrontal cortex, the brain becomes more compulsive and the impulses become harder to resist.[11] The greater the number of years an addiction has been in effect, the greater the number of epigenetic[12] and neuronal changes[13] that occur, and so the more work we need to do with this link of chains, adding the contract work to whatever else we're doing for sobriety. Many of these brain effects are reversible once the addiction is stopped. (For example, after a year of abstinence, the methamphetamine user's brain is beginning to recover some of its decision-making capacity.)[14]

Let's take a look at the work someone did with addictions and unconscious contracts.

ONE-ON-ONE WORK
Contract Release Work With a Substance

SARAH: *Hello, Anya. What can we do for you this evening?*

ANYA: *Well, I have been sober from alcohol for a long time. I really don't feel cravings for alcohol. I go to a lot of 12-step meetings. One of the things though that I find myself very tempted by and would like to explore is prescription pain medication. I am not in chronic pain, but when pain comes up and I am medically prescribed a round of OxyContin—in the old days it used to be Demerol—and with any of those opioids, I can feel that addictive thing. So, I'd like to explore this idea of what the drug is saying to me.*

SARAH: *What happens in this process is that you get to step into being the pain pills. And you get to name the contract that OxyContin has with Anya. So, you say, "I, OxyContin, solemnly swear to you, Anya, that I will take care of you . . ."*

ANYA: *"I will relieve your pain and allow you to really relax. Every cell of your body. I will take care of the pain you don't even know that you have."*

SARAH: *"I will take care of the pain that runs inside of you in a subterranean river that you're not even aware of"?*

ANYA: *Yes. Yes! And there's this companionship thing, too—it's about doing it without humans. "I will be your lover, your comforter, your companion. You can fall into my arms and rest, truly rest, no matter the cost to you."*

SARAH: *Now we come back to talking with Anya. Anya, did you hear the contract?*

ANYA: *Yes. And, you know, the truth is, it feels good. It feels really good. And yet, I know the cost.*

SARAH: *You don't want the cost?*

ANYA: *I don't want the cost. If it were cost-free, I would hang in with it, but it's not. And I also know, from my experience with alcohol, that there can be a point where it stops working.*

SARAH: *Yes. So, would you like to release OxyContin from this contract with you?*

ANYA: *Yes, I would.*

SARAH: *Would you please tell OxyContin, "OxyContin, I release you from this contract . . ."*

ANYA: *"OxyContin, I release you from this contract and I revoke this vow. And instead I give myself the blessing to use over-the-counter medicines for pain, if I need them, and to keep learning to relax. And to reach out for help from humans."*

SARAH: *From humans. Tell me, how does your body do with this release?*

ANYA: *Yes. I feel more spacious, and I feel a little nervous.*

SARAH: *Do you want to just receive a little support for the nervousness?*

ANYA: *Yes, sure.*

SARAH: *Do you need acknowledgment that humans have not been that great?*

ANYA: *Yes.*

SARAH: *And it's hard to imagine the sweetness with humans. Is there a moment that you've ever experienced when a group of people made you laugh?*

ANYA: *Yes.*

SARAH: *Or when you were with people and you felt tremendous tenderness for someone?*

ANYA: *Yes.*

SARAH: *How is it to be reminded of those?*

ANYA: *It's lovely.*

SARAH: *What happens with the nervousness?*

ANYA: *It just evaporates.*

SARAH: *Wow. And so, as you sink back into checking this out with the OxyContin, what's OxyContin saying to you now?*

ANYA: *You know, I don't have any words. Earlier, when I was being the OxyContin, it was very big. It was the most important thing. But now it seems very small.*

SARAH: *Beautiful. Yes. Thank you for letting us sink into this a little bit, Anya.*

One year later, Anya writes:

During this COVID-19 pandemic period, I have been experiencing a lot of anxiety and not sleeping well. This is exactly when I would be reaching for the narcotics. Instead, I am learning to trust my body to sleep when it needs to sleep and to be awake when it's ready to be awake. I use yoga, meditation, music, and prayer to help me relax. A few times I have felt the pull for a drug, but it's been easy to not follow the impulse to take it. This freedom is a direct result from the session with Sarah.

Reaching out to others for support is still hard for me, though I am better at it. There is more work to be done, [there are] more unconscious contracts to uncover. I suspect there are some contracts that I hold that I haven't been ready to release. But this is an area where I want to grow, and I believe that growth will happen. And that sense of hope in my own capacity to grow and change is one of the beautiful effects of this work.

More generally, my experience of the long-term effect of the unconscious contract work is that I get to feel the flow of feelings. The contracts kept buried deep feelings of rage, sorrow, jealousy, shame, and fear. Releasing the contracts has allowed me and my feelings to flow. For the first time, I experience myself as an organic part of nature, rather than as a machine, programmed to perform on cue.

All of this means that the unconscious contracts around addiction yield less immediately to our process work. We need to nourish the permaculture gardens of resonant right hemisphere neurons that will hold us instead of our addictions, release our contracts with ourselves to use our addictions, and release our addictions from the contracts they have with us. This means there are two areas to work on when we're thinking about addictions and contracts. Here are some of each kind of contract.

SAMPLE CONTRACTS WE HAVE WITH OURSELVES TO USE OUR ADDICTIONS

- I will never allow myself to be bored/hungry/lonely/etc. again.
- I will take care of myself with my substance or behavior.
- I will use this substance or activity to take me away from unlivable contracts to not exist, or to not have needs, or to not matter.
- I will use this substance or behavior to nullify my power/strength/energy/rage so that I'm not too much for others.

WORKSHEET
Addiction Contracts You May Have With Yourself

I, _____ [your name here], solemnly swear to you,

my _____ [essential self, mother, father, siblings, world, universe, God, etc.], that I will use _____ [my substance or behavior of choice] in order to _____ [save, protect, honor, have a parent, keep you from being alone . . .], no matter the cost to myself.

SAMPLE CONTRACTS OUR ADDICTIONS HAVE WITH US TO TAKE CARE OF US

- I will comfort you when you are sad/angry/afraid/lonely/happy.
- I will take care of you. I will fill the hole in your heart.
- I will make you forget the shame.
- I will take away your body.
- I will take away your memories.

- I will take away your nightmares.
- I will make you sleep.
- I will give you energy.

WORKSHEET
Contracts Your Addictions May Have With You

Here's a form for the unconscious contracts vow connected with addiction.

I, _____ [the addiction], solemnly swear to
_____ [your
name] that I will take care of you by _____
_____
[name the gifts your addiction gives you] in order to
_____
[save you, protect you, give you a parent, keep you from being alone], no matter
the cost to you.

Since our addictions are not always to substances, let's take a look at the way
this process works with something else—in this case, food.

ONE-ON-ONE WORK
Addiction to Food

RACHEL: *So, the addiction is to food with me. It's totally food.*

SARAH: *Food is very complex and multilayered. We'll do one link in the chain this evening and you can always keep working. Which food would you like to hear from this evening?*

RACHEL: *Sugar.*

SARAH: *Is it any sugar, or is it sugar in a particular form? Is it a Starbucks drink? Is it a chocolate bar? Is it sugar in your tea? What's the way that the sugar speaks to you?*

RACHEL: *It's various forms of chocolate, cookies, cake. Narrowing it down is really hard for me.*

SARAH: *Okay. Are they always chocolate cookies, or are they any cookies?*

RACHEL: *Chocolate's my favorite, but any cookies will do in a pinch.*

SARAH: *Okay. Do you also eat chocolate bars, or do you mostly eat baked goods?*

RACHEL: *I eat chocolate bars.*

SARAH: *Let's do chocolate. So, you'll get to be chocolate.*

RACHEL: *Okay.*

SARAH: *And you'll say, "I, chocolate, solemnly swear to you, Rachel . . ."*

RACHEL: *"I, chocolate, solemnly swear to you, Rachel . . ."*

SARAH: *"That I will take care of you . . ."*

RACHEL: *"That I will take care of you." I believe it.*

SARAH: *Yes. How does chocolate take care of you? You can start saying, "I will . . ."*

RACHEL: *"I will make you feel loved. I will be your friend. I will take the edge off your anxiety."*

SARAH: *Warmth, accompaniment, comfort, soothing.*

RACHEL: *Yes, yes. "I will make you feel dreamy, instead of all anxious, about life."*

SARAH: *Does chocolate help you get into creative space?*

RACHEL: *No, doesn't work there.*

SARAH: *So, it downshifts you then.*

RACHEL: *Yes, because it makes me all floaty and less able to think.*

SARAH: *"I will stop you from thinking . . ."*

RACHEL: *Yes. "I'll stop you from worrying . . ."*

SARAH: *"I'll take away the voices in your head . . ."*

RACHEL: *Yes. Yes. Those judgmental voices.*

SARAH: *"I will give you peace and safety . . ."*

RACHEL: *Yes. We can't take too much reality.*

SARAH: *"I will take the edge off of reality for you . . ."*

RACHEL: *Yes. So I have to give that up?*

SARAH: *I don't know. You know, it depends on what the cost feels like.*

RACHEL: *Right. Well, I was very alarmed when I saw that picture of the obese person's brain.*

SARAH: *Well, we don't know for sure what the background was of that person's brain. There can be different health issues that contribute. Let's explore the lived cost though. So say, "I, chocolate, will take care of you . . ."*

RACHEL: *"I, chocolate, will take care of you in all the ways we've just described, no matter the cost to you . . ." That's a bit alarming.*

SARAH: *Is there a cost?*

RACHEL: *Oh yes. I don't feel so good. I don't have a lot of energy, and I don't get things done that I ultimately would like to get done. I have a foggy brain. I'd rather not have a foggy brain.*

SARAH: *Rachel, did you hear the vow that chocolate made to you?*

RACHEL: *Yes.*

SARAH: *Yes. Do you want chocolate to continue to have this contract with you?*

RACHEL: *To be honest with you, I do. And that's a little alarming, that I'm so entangled with my chocolate. It's pretty serious with us. 'Til death do us part.*

SARAH: *Do you need acknowledgment that you have not had an experience of humans being able to hold you in this way?*

RACHEL: *I have had a few experiences with humans, but many, many more with chocolate.*

SARAH: *It has reliability.*

RACHEL: *Yes. It's much more available.*

SARAH: *And is predictable and continuously available.*

RACHEL: *Yes. As sad as that is. So, where do we go from here?*

SARAH: *Well, just tell me how your body's doing?*

RACHEL: *It's more relaxed than it was before. I was anxious to speak about this, but now that I'm looking at it, I get why I do this. I understand it. I forgive. But there is a cost, because my weight is not where it should be, and my gut is not as healthy as it could be. There is definitely a cost.*

SARAH: *I want to hold that our bodies are just right. Just as a radical point of view.*

RACHEL: *Can I write that down? My body is just right.*

SARAH: *So now, I'd like to know your intention. Is this good for tonight? Did we get to name something that hadn't been named before and this is just right for tonight? Or is there more that you have as an intention for yourself?*

RACHEL: *Well, can I just bring up that I had a very intense weekend with family. Lots and lots of family staying here, and another sister decided that we should celebrate her birthday in the middle of plans we already made. It was just so, so much, and I'm still not recovered. I don't feel like I'm resting up from this weekend, so I'm just turning to my chocolate because it helps. I'm reading books because it helps.*

SARAH: *Yes. Rachel's cells, do you need acknowledgment that being with your family disorients you and you lose your "North Star of self"? That all the cells get completely turned around and confused and they don't even know how to orient themselves?*

RACHEL: *That's true. Yes. I judge myself because I react, and I don't want people to know that I'm reacting. But I was reactive all weekend, you know? It was hard.*

SARAH: *Do you need acknowledgment of shame?*

RACHEL: *Yes, yes.*

SARAH: *Yes, and when you're with your family, you don't get to be the person you want to be because there's so much reactivity?*

RACHEL: *Yes, yes. I don't feel like I grew at all despite working on myself for 30 years. Oh my God, what was the use! Then again, I know family is like graduate school. And eight of them at the same time in my house. Oh my God, two nights and three days. Oy, oy, oy.*

SARAH: *What is happening with your cells as you're telling us this, and we get to laugh together?*

RACHEL: *There's a little bit of pressure in my head and there's also a little bit of lightness. There's a little bit more acceptance, like "Of course you're freaking out! Of course you are." I guess I'd like to stop "shoulding" on myself. You know, "I should be this, I should be that, I should take everything."*

SARAH: *Okay, let's do that vow instead of the chocolate vow, and you can do the chocolate vow later.*

RACHEL: *Okay. "I, Rachel, solemnly swear to my essential self that I will 'should' on myself continually in order to meet the unmeetable standards of my mother and father, no matter the cost to myself."*

SARAH: *Rachel, did you hear the vow that you made to yourself?*

RACHEL: *I did.*

SARAH: *Is that a good vow?*

RACHEL: *No, no. I hate that vow. "Rachel, I release you from that contract . . . and I revoke that vow . . . and instead you have my blessing to be authentic . . . even when you're reactive . . . and to like Rachel no matter how I act."*

SARAH: *How is that for you?*

RACHEL: *Oh, it's freeing. That sounds great.*

SARAH: *Very nice. And, just check back in to see, how are you doing with chocolate?*

RACHEL: *Well, you know, I'm kind of grateful to chocolate.*

SARAH: *Very sweet. I love us getting to touch this stuff, because as we work with the links in the chain, we start to get to know them and become more clear about what we want, what we're willing to be with, and so on.*

One year later, Rachel writes:

The long-term effects of this work are that I gave up all sugar in February of this year. I've had one slip with sugar since then and it was with some Coconut Bliss whipped cream.

I have also joined a 12-Step group, Food Addicts in Recovery Anonymous. They provide an excellent support network with fellow participants, many of whom have been abstinent from sugar and flour for decades. I attend at least three Zoom meetings each week. I have also released some weight as well.

This is considered a way of life, and I expect to continue with FA, Food Addicts in recovery, for my life.

CHAPTER 12

Reclaiming the SEXUALITY Circuit and the Self

OUR SEXUALITY ALWAYS BELONGS TO US

There is a delight in stepping into exploration of the SEXUALITY circuit, even for those of us who are not now, have never been, or have not been sexually active for a long time. This is because the SEXUALITY circuit is the pathway that each of us has traveled (or is traveling) from childhood to adulthood.[1] This is our neuroscience concept for this chapter. Our SEXUALITY circuit carries our individuality, our maturity, our capacity to form bonds with people outside of our family of origin, and in some ways touches on who we are. It doesn't matter how old we are or whether we've been using this circuit explicitly—it still lies at the root of self. It's still ours.

The idea that we are somehow morally clean before we have sex, that we lose something when we start having sex, or that purity is taken from us in sexual violence or sexual activity is not a truth. There is no neurobiological basis for these beliefs. They seem to arise from systems of thinking in which women are considered property, rather than people, with virginity being something sold to the male buyer in the marriage contract. Perpetrators of sexual violence cannot take our sexual innocence from us. Our sexual innocence, the cleanness of our souls, is ours forever, and it cannot be violated. Perpetrators of violence can and do take from us our innocence about people being kind or our innocence about our needs mattering to others, but they cannot make us dirty. The dirt and the shame belong to them, not to us.

The sexual abuse of children does start the activity of the child's SEXUALITY circuit earlier than it would naturally have started, including making puberty start earlier than if the child had not been harmed,[2] but that is an effect of trauma, not a loss of essential innocence.

═══════════════ THE MAIN QUESTION FOR THIS CHAPTER ═══════════════

How has my journey from being a child to being an adult shaped me?

JOURNALING PROMPT FOR
Reclaiming Your SEXUALITY Circuit

How has my SEXUALITY circuit taken me from childhood to adulthood?

What I remember about what it felt like to be me as a child, before my SEXUAL-ITY circuit had much effect on me:

_____

_____

_____

_____

_____

What I remember about the awakening of my SEXUALITY circuit, either my early sexual experiences, the awakening of a sense of myself as separate from my family, or both:

_____

_____

_____

_____

_____

_____

What I remember or imagine about my felt sense of self in the years when sex-uality was central, if it ever was, or the years when I was clearly creating some-thing different than being in my family of origin or both:

_____

_____

_____

_____

_____

_____

What I know or imagine about my felt sense of self in the years when sexuality was no longer as important, if it ever was, or the years when I was settling into being older:

_____

_____

_____

_____

_____

Now that you have refreshed your memories of your own life journey, let's experience a guided meditation exploring our self-emergence.

GUIDED MEDITATION
Warm Connection With the SEXUALITY Circuit,
the Circuit of Emergence of the Self

Let yourself notice that you are a breathing being . . . Where do you feel the breath moving? . . . If you aren't too ambivalent about being alive, take a moment to enjoy your breath . . . Here it is, a mostly effortless flow of energy to help keep you alive . . . acknowledging folks who have to struggle to breathe, as well . . . leaning in, for a moment, to the miracle of our red blood cells picking up oxygen . . . and feeling your breath . . .

Invite your attention to move with your breath now . . . and notice how far down in your body your breath can reach . . . See if it's okay to let your breath move you slightly as you breathe . . . This is all your body . . . It doesn't belong to anyone else . . . and all your circuits are your own . . . and your breathing is exactly right for you . . .

Now, beginning as far down in your body as you can feel your breath moving you, let yourself imagine, only if it is pleasant to imagine, a plant in your favorite shade of green unfurling and growing within you . . . a plant of the felt sense of self, that started when you were very small . . . and has grown and grown since then . . . There is nothing wrong with this plant . . . If it has grown in a direction that you don't enjoy, notice the trauma that it was trying to live around . . . and bring warm accompaniment . . . wherever possible . . . to this sweet growing sense of self . . . inviting it back toward your heart . . . where it might be able to feel itself loved . . . and appreciated . . . for its unfurling . . .

Notice how this plant is not like anyone else's plant . . . and notice how this plant, this felt sense of self, is the center of its own story . . . There may be supporting characters . . . but they are not as important as this plant is . . . This may be a radically strange idea, the understanding that to this body, there is no other

felt sense of self that is more important . . . but stretch toward this understanding
if you can . . . and say thank you to this body . . . and say thank you to this emerg-
ing, just right sense of self . . . and say thank you to your breath . . .

And now, bring your attention back to your breath . . . to the most alive place
of your breathing . . . and let yourself feel your weight against whatever you are
resting on . . . and come all the way back to the present moment.

This meditation is an invitation to experience the sweetness of affection for self, but it still may not be so easy to feel. The traumas of violation and humiliation can block our self-warmth, especially in relationship to our sexuality. In the following questionnaire, you will be able to look at where you are located in regard to your SEXUALITY circuit. After you score yourself, look at the recommendations for healing and self-connection.

QUESTIONNAIRE
Do You Get to Enjoy Your Emergent Self?

1. Do you like the self that wakes up in the morning? Are you glad to greet this self?

    No   Yes
    1   2   3   4   5   6   7   8   9   10

2. Do you like the self you put clothes on every day? Do you enjoy your own body?

    No   Yes
    1   2   3   4   5   6   7   8   9   10

3. Do you delight in the kind of friend, partner, and/or lover you are?

    No   Yes
    1   2   3   4   5   6   7   8   9   10

4. When you think of the story of who you are, do you enjoy it?

    No   Yes
    1   2   3   4   5   6   7   8   9   10

5. Do you feed yourself with thoughtfulness and care?

    No   Yes
    1   2   3   4   5   6   7   8   9   10

6. Do you like your working self?

    No   Yes
    1   2   3   4   5   6   7   8   9   10

7. Do you give yourself time to play during the day?

    No   Yes
    1   2   3   4   5   6   7   8   9   10

8. Do you give yourself time to rest during the day?

    No   Yes
    1   2   3   4   5   6   7   8   9   10

9. Do you like yourself as you are falling asleep?

    No   Yes
    1   2   3   4   5   6   7   8   9   10

10. Do you enjoy the self you find in your dreams?

    No   Yes
    1   2   3   4   5   6   7   8   9   10

SCORING:

10–25   You are not experiencing much enjoyment of your emergent self. You
         may be struggling with a negative self-image or blankness in relation-
         ship with yourself. This is making life much more difficult than we want
         it to be for you.
         Recommendation: Work with Chapter 1 on Self-Warmth, and release
         as many contracts as you can that keep you from having affection for
         yourself.

26–50   You only get to have a little enjoyment of your emergent self. This lack
         of self-affection may leave you fairly functional, but without much of a
         sense of meaning.
         Recommendation: Work with Chapter 2, and specifically focus on

moments when you were in alarmed aloneness or had traumatic experiences connected with your body, sexuality, and trauma, including being physically punished, hit, choked, or slapped.

51–75   At this level, you get to have moderate enjoyment of your emergent self. Life is a little easier here, but it could be even better. Recommendations: Work with Chapter 3 on Self-Sabotage, particularly in terms of self-care and care for your body.

76–100   You are moving into a lovely enjoyment of your emergent self. Recommendations: Make sure to review Chapter 4 on shame, and celebrate the gains and the resonant stability that you have and are nourishing.

Another way to review your own relationship with sexuality is to look at it in relationship with your other circuits. This relational view of things will hint at what kinds of experiences and emotions could be blocking or impacting your warmth for your body and your emergent self.

WORKSHEET
Make a Relational Map of Your Circuits With Colors and Shapes

Copy the following circuit names onto half sheets of paper. Color them if you would like to, and cut them into shapes with scissors. Then stand and arrange them around yourself to give yourself a sense of the geometry of your interrelated circuits. Copy what you have done onto a separate piece of paper so that you can remember where all your circuits were around you in relation to one another.

SEEKING	**RAGE**
CARE	**SEXUALITY**
PANIC/GRIEF	**DISGUST**
FEAR	**PLAY**

As you look at your map, are any of the circuits blocking your access to others? And what about SEXUALITY? Which circuits seem most in relationship with SEXUALITY? What truths do you need to acknowledge to yourself or what traumas do you need to work with to clear your blocks to connection with this circuit? How could resonant language support your access to and your connection with your life energy?

RESONANT LANGUAGE PRACTICE
Metaphor Guesses for Your Circuits

If you had a conversation with your circuits, using metaphors to inquire about their truths in relationship to your SEXUALITY, what would it sound like? Let's practice. For example:

FEAR circuit, is it like you really have decided that SEXUALITY doesn't exist, that there's just a ghost in the wind behind you there?

RAGE circuit, is it like you want to kill SEXUALITY, so that I'm never hurt again, almost like a feral cat stalking prey?

Now you try:

SEEKING circuit, is it like _____
_____
_____

CARE circuit, is it like _____
_____
_____

PANIC/GRIEF circuit, is it like _____
_____
_____

FEAR circuit, is it like _____
_____
_____

RAGE circuit, is it like _____

_____

_____

SEXUALITY circuit, is it like _____

_____

_____

DISGUST circuit, is it like _____

_____

_____

PLAY circuit, is it like _____

_____

_____

JOURNALING PROMPT FOR
Accessing Your SEXUALITY Circuit

What contracts might your circuits have that limit your access to the SEXUALITY circuit?

_____

_____

_____

_____

_____

_____

_____

_____

_____

Now we will accompany our next reader on her journey to reclaim a healthy, sweet connection with her SEXUALITY circuit.

ONE-ON-ONE WORK
Unconscious Contract Work With a Reader

JANET: *I feel like I've been on and off depressed most of my life. I think some of it is brain chemistry in my case. My brother was autistic, and I think that chemistry is in my family. But beneath it is this feeling of isolation and not being able to trust anyone, including myself. My father committed incest with me at a very young age, preverbal I believe, and after a gazillion years of therapy, I'm still angry at men and not trusting. I trust women a little more, but basically I don't trust anyone, including myself.*

I'd love to explore this because I'm sick of it. I'm 73, and I want to break free. I will just say, on the subject of the ancestors, that I'm Jewish and when I have tried to connect to my ancestors, I've always been very sad. With my ancestors there is also a sense that they were no strangers to sadness. And I never thought of myself as a Holocaust survivor, but my Dad escaped Hitler and lost most of his family in the camps. It was never spoken about, as is common in most Holocaust families, so there was this huge secret, but at a certain point I realized that I was carrying the guilt and sadness of the ancestors who died in the camps. When I did a process with my ancestors earlier this year, and they took back what was theirs and they blessed me, that helped a lot.

SARAH: *I'm going to close my eyes for a minute and just drift into our connection and your voice and the experience that you had as a tiny person of physical violation and betrayal. Is the vow, "I will never forgive my father"?*

JANET: *Yes. And I think probably more to the point is that the only way my father knew how to connect with me was sexually. That's the only way I had a connection with him. He was a trauma survivor. He served in Saipan in the Second World War, and then also escaped Hitler. And his buddy died next to him in the foxhole when he lit a cigarette and took enemy fire. My father wasn't present for any emotional connection, and this was the only way he seemed to be able to connect with me. I don't have a lot of specific memories, just a few. And I'll just say briefly, my emotionally disturbed brother was autistic, schizophrenic, and in and out of institutions. When he was home during my adolescence, he would walk around naked with an erection, and so I just shut down my sexuality to just survive, really. And I guess because of all the shame around it. And my mother didn't safeguard any of my secrets. Just the reverse. So, I felt completely unsafe in my home.*

SARAH: *So then, of course you wouldn't trust. You can follow any of these three* *trails we have open right now: the sexuality, never forgiving men, and never trusting anyone. But, for a moment, just see what it's like to say, "I will never forgive my father," "I will never forgive my brother," and "I will never forgive men." See which one is more powerful.*

JANET: *"I'll never forgive my father or brother in order to keep myself safe." That's not quite it. It's close. Really, it's in order to survive. And to know myself as separate. "To know myself as separate." Yes. "No matter the cost to myself and to any relationship I would ever have with any person on the planet."*

SARAH: *Janet's essential self, did you hear the vow that Janet made to you? Is this a good vow for Janet?*

JANET: *Not anymore. It was. It was then. "Janet, I release you from this contract and I revoke this vow, and instead you have my blessing to open your heart and share your love. And to trust that I'll survive even if I'm not loved back in the way I would like."*

SARAH: *How is it to receive that blessing from your essential self?*

JANET: *I don't feel it. I feel numb about it. I heard it, but I didn't really grok it, so to speak. Yes.*

SARAH: *Mmhmm. Let me just think.*

JANET: *I don't think I trust it. There you go.*

SARAH: *Well then that tells us which one to do next. "I will never trust anyone, including myself."*

JANET: *I will never trust anyone, including myself, in order to survive.*

SARAH: *And feel into the word "survive." Just reach into it, so that we know the flavor of survival that not trusting anyone, including yourself, gives you.*

JANET: *I'm not getting much. The only thing that came to me is breath, something about holding my breath. I have some memories of my father putting a pillow over my face during whatever he did. So, I have entrapment and suffocation issues.*

SARAH: *Yes. It sounds like we should just step through time and space and get the pillow off. Would that be okay with you?*

JANET: *Ah! What a great idea. Actually, I love to laugh and that makes me laugh, the idea of getting the pillow off. Might have a lot of dust mites in it after 73 years.*

SARAH: *Yes, no kidding. So, stepping through time and space and freezing your father, turning him to dust and blowing him away, and then you can turn the pillow to dust, or you can just take it off.*

JANET: *Let's try turning the pillow to dust. I have trouble turning my father to dust. It feels too violent—I don't know if that's me being disempowered, but I* want to say goodbye to him in a more loving way. Yes. I'm putting him into a heart-shaped, pink bubble and sending him off.

SARAH: *Wonderful, wonderful. And the pillow has been turned to dust. How's the little girl doing?*

JANET: *She's smiling and kicking.*

SARAH: *Oh, very nice. She just wants to breathe, huh?*

JANET: *Yes.*

SARAH: *Yes, do you just want to breathe and be alive? Would it be fun to live in a home that's not carrying the burden of history? Would it be sweet to live with people who were not trying to figure out how to survive the unspeakable and unthinkable? Would it be very sweet, just for a moment, to be held by hearts that could really step into joy?*

JANET: *Oh, that would be so lovely.*

SARAH: *You can see if she wants to come home with you, if she just wants to come back to present time and have a sweet space in your heart and in your home, where she can just be exactly as she is.*

JANET: *Yes, she's ready for that.*

SARAH: *Okay, so we're stepping through time and space, bringing her along, letting her be here. And if it's okay to tell me, how is your body feeling?*

JANET: *It feels more relaxed. But there's self-hatred there too, because my mother was very critical that I could never do anything right. Even protecting myself in this way with my vow, which I needed to do to survive. I'm down on myself for being such an isolationist and not trusting.*

SARAH: *"I, Janet, solemnly swear to my essential self that I will hate myself for my own survival strategies"?*

JANET: *Yes. And probably because the ancestors died in the camps. I bet that's part of it. And my brother died in a mental institution, and I'm not allowed to survive. Yes . . . Oh my God, that's amazing. I'm not dead. Yes, that's it, Sarah. I will hate myself for surviving. And feel guilt and shame . . .*

SARAH: *"In order to honor the deaths of those who are gone"?*

JANET: *Yes, I think so. I think I have survivor's guilt. I, Janet, solemnly swear to the ancestors and to my brother that I will hate myself and have guilt and shame because I am alive when you are dead, no matter the cost to myself.*

SARAH: *Thank you. Now I'd like you to step into the shoes of your ancestors.*

JANET: *Okay. The ones who died in the camps?*

SARAH: *Yes.*

JANET: *And then my maternal grandmother ran from the Cossacks, so I got it from both sides.*

SARAH: *Yes, no kidding. Our sweethearts.*

JANET: *I guess I'm strong. So, it's given to me.*

SARAH: *Yes.*

JANET: *Okay, step into their shoes. Ancestors.*

SARAH: *Ancestors of Janet, did you hear the vow that Janet made to you?*

JANET: *"Yes, we heard her."*

SARAH: *Is that a good vow for Janet?*

JANET: *"No. We want her to have the fulfillment and happiness that we couldn't have."*

SARAH: *Oh, please tell her, "Janet, we release you from this vow."*

JANET: *"Janet, we release you from this vow and we revoke this contract . . . and you have our blessing to have happiness and the joy-filled life that we didn't have. Even though we rightfully couldn't trust and our lives were taken from us unjustly, when you trust yourself and remember us, you can tune into us and ask us, because we've had a lot of experience with whom not to trust. There are still Nazis around, but not everyone's a Nazi."*

Yes, that feels good. So, I can trust myself and that they're here to help me. They're here to help me when I'm feeling confused.

SARAH: *Very, very good.*

JANET: *Yes, that created a deeper sense of relaxation in my belly.*

SARAH: *Very good.*

JANET: *They're smiling.*

SARAH: *Ah, that's wonderful. Yes.*

JANET: *My grandmother is hiding in the weeds in the fields where she ran from the Cossacks. She's a little girl and she's poking her head out from the weeds and smiling.*

SARAH: *Oh, very nice. And then, you can see if this is a point where you'd like to check in with your brother as well, because you made the vow to the ancestors and the brother. Would you like to check in with your brother?*

JANET: *Yes. Every time I check in with him, he winks at me. It's been going on for a long time, but I still was carrying it even though he winked at me. He tells me he's much better off where he is.*

SARAH: *Oh, very good. And he doesn't want you to have this contract with him either?*

JANET: *He doesn't. I sort of settled that with him in the past, but it hasn't really sunk in. Hopefully this release will sink in.*

SARAH: *Well, let him say to you, "I release you from this vow . . ."*

JANET: *"I, Phillip, release you from this vow and I revoke this contract. What's mine is mine and what's yours is yours. And you did everything you could to help me. You did everything you could to help me."*

SARAH: *He wants you to know that he knows that?*

JANET: *Right. I was the only one that he really felt understood by because he didn't talk. We had a very deep connection, which is why I'm sure that I'm so intuitive and an empath, for better or for worse, and, his greatest pleasure is for me to have a joy-filled life. You know, in a way to make up for the lousy life he had.*

SARAH: *How is it to be Janet who has trust in herself?*

JANET: *Lovely, lovely. It's been a long time coming. I especially love having the help of the ancestors.*

SARAH: *So now, let's go to the vow to shut down your sexuality. When you think of your sexuality, what happens in your body?*

JANET: *Shame. Blame. It's mostly shame. I feel like damaged goods.*

SARAH: *Yes. "I, Janet, solemnly swear to my essential self, that I will surround my sexual being with shame and self-blame in order to . . ."*

JANET: *I know incest survivors often feel like it's their fault. I think it's something like, I was too much of a siren with my father. In my head I know that's not true, but . . .*

SARAH: *The cells of your body carry the responsibility.*

JANET: *Yes, that if I'm sexually open or warm . . .*

SARAH: *Let me check this. "I, Janet, solemnly swear to my essential self, that I will blame myself for even having a sexuality in order to . . ."*

JANET: *"In order to take responsibility for my father's action, and in order to not be raped, and taken advantage of, and violated, and in order to survive, no matter the cost to myself." Somehow it's the only way to protect myself from men that I know in my cells will inevitably rape me and violate me. I think I see sexuality as a violation.*

SARAH: *Is there an entanglement between the harm that you received and even having a sexuality?*

JANET: *Yes.*

SARAH: *Yes. "I will blame my sexuality because it is the cause of violation."*

JANET: *"I will withhold my sexuality because it is the cause of betrayal and violation . . . no matter the cost to myself." I took on some big ones, didn't I?*

SARAH: *Yes! Janet's essential self, did you hear the vow about sexuality?*

JANET: *"Yes."*

SARAH: *Is that a good vow for Janet?*

JANET: *No, it stinks. "Janet, I release you from this contract, and I revoke this vow, and instead you have my blessing to have fun, in body and mind and spirit."*

SARAH: *How is that for you?*

JANET: *Good. I actually like having fun.*

SARAH: *Yes. Okay, just come back to Janet for me. How is it to be with this?*

JANET: *It's good. I don't trust it entirely, but I'm very curious to see what will unfold.*

One year later, Janet writes:

It was interesting to read the transcript, and I remember asking you when I was taking the course if you sensed that this work changed things in the long term. As a life coach, I benefited from watching you work, your gorgeous empathy and your ability to hold a very safe container.

While I found it useful to recognize the contracts I made clearly, I can't say that the work changed my ability to trust in any noticeable way. The understanding remained in my head but doesn't seem to have affected my behavior. It's possible, however, that the work put me in closer touch with my inner child and the pain she has been experiencing and this is all to the good for self-empathy.

I have recently discovered some somatic work that seems to be helping to rewire my nervous system and so far is giving me more hope for change than any form of talk therapy.

It is important to know that this work can have very different effects for different people and that there are many approaches to healing. If this type of contract work doesn't speak to you, please follow any and all paths to healing, as Janet models for us.

TABLE 12.1 Sample Contracts Connected With SEXUALITY

I will not become my true self	in order not to leave my birth family
I will not enjoy or have affection for my own body	in order to keep my SEXUALITY circuit turned off and prevent humiliation and ridicule
I will sleep with anyone who asks me	in order to take care of my father and make sure he is not alone (even if he is dead)
I will turn off my sexuality	in order to manage murderous rage against the people who harmed me
I will forget I ever had a sexuality	in order to belong to my mother's line, who all forgot they had any sexuality

If any of these resonate for you, or if something is arising for you and you would like to work with contracts that are connected to your SEXUALITY circuit, here is the template to support your work:

Contract Template for the SEXUALITY Circuit

I, _____ [*your name here*], solemnly swear to you, my _____ [*essential self, mother, father, siblings, world, universe, God, etc.*] that I will _____ [*how do you diminish or exaggerate your sexuality?*], in order to _____ _____ [*save, protect, honor, have a parent, keep you from being alone, etc.*], no matter the cost to myself.

CHAPTER 13

Dissolving Contracts That Block Joy

Completely aside from our thoughts and experiences of the past and the future, even with everything else that is going on in the world, we have the potential to experience the present as a joyous moment. And yet, this may feel inaccessible to us because of the contracts we carry that limit life, energy, and joy. An example of this would be a contract that says we should not be joyful because of the state the world is in. Another, very common contract is to not move into joy and full expression in order either to not kill anyone with our joy (this kind of contract arises from having caretakers who dissociate in the presence of their child's joy) or to avoid humiliation, ridicule, and shame. Why on Earth might we have contracts like these?

================ THE MAIN QUESTION FOR THIS CHAPTER ===============

How can I use what I'm learning about contracts to help me step into my joy?

RELATIONAL NEUROSCIENCE CONCEPT: JOY IS RELATIONAL

When you think about babies who are really energized in a positive way, you probably imagine them expressing joy with their chuckles, waving arms, squeals of glee, and cascading laughter. Our vulnerability as human babies, and as adult humans, is that joy and the expression of play and life energy happens most easily in the company of others, and we stop our joy when our others cannot accompany us. Nonaccompaniment may look like a smaller smile than ours, no laugh when we are laughing, or even dismissal, disapproval, or contempt.

You will remember from our earlier chapters that researcher Beatrice Beebe has discovered that we tailor our natural capacity for every facial expression down to just those facial expressions in which our mother can easily join us. If our mothering person cannot bear grief, and turns away from it, babies stop making and recognizing the grief face. If our mother diminishes our joy, rather than expanding it, then our expressions of joy become smaller and more limited.[1]

Joy needs to be accompanied and resonated with, so that we can feel its upper edges and then return to center, otherwise our unaccompanied joy mostly disappears, and then when it breaks through, it makes us bounce all over, without regard for others. As adults, we continue to limit and be limited by windows of joy. Windows of welcome matter so much. By turning away from, dismissing, discounting, ignoring, and scorning one another, people turn away from each other's joy and rob the world of its human life energy. People turn away from each other in part because the joyful expressions are outside their window of welcome for joy. Starting when they were little, they too were turned away from expressions of joy, and so they feel embarrassed about the "overexcitement." Sometimes they also turn away because unaccompanied joy, bursting out into exuberance, isn't relational. The more accompanied and supported we are in our joy, the more connected we are to the other when either of us experience it. PLAY, the circuit that joy lives on, is the most vulnerable of all circuits to relational disconnection and other stressors.

To understand our own capacities to access joy, it's helpful to look at what happens for moms when their babies move into joyful places. Depending on how they were raised and how their joy and life energy were responded to, mothers may dissociate in the presence of joy. They may turn away from their own life energy and diminish their babies' joy.

When the mother dissociates in the presence of joy or life energy, the baby experiences a total loss of their mother. The world basically disintegrates in response to the baby's expression of joy. In essence, it's as if the mother nearly dies. These understandings speak to the sense of great disquiet that many people carry. It is a sense that says, "If I really step into my full life energy, the world will be destroyed. If I step into my full life energy, my mother will die. If I'm as big as I feel like I'm made to be, then the world will come tumbling down." These are all true after-effects of a mother moving into dissociation when their baby has an expression of joy. It may sometimes sound like people are exaggerating when they say that they can't be their full selves or someone will die, but they are telling us the absolute truth that, yes, in fact their world *did* fall apart. Yes, in a way, their mother *did* die (she dissociated) when they moved into their full expression of life energy. It's really good for us to know such a statement is not an exaggeration; instead, it is a real experience of what the window of welcome for joy has been in a person's original relationships.

JOURNALING PROMPT FOR
Inviting Integration

Where (in which relationships) has your joy been able to flow? Who has been joyful with you? Where has your joy ebbed? Are there relationships in which your joy has changed over time?

_____

_____

_____

_____

_____

_____

The capacity for joy to be supported and diminished exists in every relationship, self with self, self with other, self with group, self with society, self with planet.

QUESTIONNAIRE
How Much Room Do You Give Your Joy to Exist?

Circle 0 for "not even within the realm of possibility" and 5 for "very much."

1. I often make time in my intense work schedule to move, rest, and play.

    0   1   2   3   4   5

2. I feel mostly safe and my needs are mostly met, so it's easy for me to play.

    0   1   2   3   4   5

3. Even though I love my family and community deeply, I take care to plan and carry out times for me to rest and relax and laugh. (Or these times happen spontaneously with great regularity.)

    0   1   2   3   4   5

4. Although there are moments when I am grieving my losses, it is easy for my friends and families to make me laugh.

    0   1   2   3   4   5

5. I love to laugh and go out of my way to make sure I do it regularly.

0   1   2   3   4   5

6. Despite the outrage and fury I feel about the world and its systemic injustices, I still have moments of joy, awe, and maybe even transcendence.

0   1   2   3   4   5

7. When I touch into my own uniqueness and sweetness, I can feel at least a few bubbles of joy in my chest.

0   1   2   3   4   5

8. I can use the words "delight," "enjoyment," and "self" in the same sentence without experiencing shame, dismissal, or disgust.

0   1   2   3   4   5

9. I know what brings my body joy and what it considers play.

0   1   2   3   4   5

10. There are flavors, dances, pieces of music, or pieces of art that bring me bubbles of happiness.

0   1   2   3   4   5

Add up your points from the questionnaire.

0–20   If you would like to find a new way of living with your brain, you've made a good start. Your brain may still be a tough or even cruel place to live. As you dive into this material, it will bring joy closer and closer, with more and more openings for laughter and play.

21–30   Glimmers of joy are starting to appear in your life. Congratulations on the work you have done so far, and there is a lot of encouragement here for continuing on the path of self-warmth.

31–40   You have been devoting your resources to nourishing safety both inside and outside yourself. You are just on the edge of being able to lean into joy as a resource. Happiness! Things only get better from here.

41–50   Joy is an ongoing source of nourishment for you. Occasionally it even suffuses you and fills your chest with bubbles of enjoyment and happiness, delight, and awe. Welcome to your brain being a very good place to be.

This questionnaire has many similarities to the Self-Warmth questionnaire in Chapter 1 of this book. You have come full circle and are starting to integrate the possibility that self-warmth leads us to joy.

For our next exercise, let's take a step into territory we have not yet explored—the entire world of nonverbal resonance.

WORKSHEET
Resonant Language Practice:
Moving Into Nonverbals

Observing smiles and how they affect us

With this worksheet, for the first time in this book, I invite you to step beyond the personal relationship with yourself into your relationships with other people.

Choose a friend who smiles easily to do this exercise with you on a video call or in person.

Ask them, "I want to try something out. Are you willing to help me? When I smile at you, please smile back at me, but smile a smaller smile than my smile."

Smile at your friend. What happens to you when their smile is smaller than yours?

_____

_____

_____

_____

Ask your friend, "Now I will smile again. This time when you smile back at me, please make your smile a little bigger than mine."

Smile at your friend again. What happens to you when their smile is bigger than yours?

_____

_____

_____

_____

In secure attachment, when the mothering or fathering person has been really supported in their own joy, the parent is actually looking for opportunities to expand their baby's joy. Their PLAY circuit has to be engaged in order for them to participate in joy, and Panksepp says that the PLAY circuit is the most vulnerable to stress and danger, so parents need a lot of social support. Economic stability is also hugely helpful for us in trying to access PLAY and joy.

You may have just experienced what it feels like to have your joy invited in the last exercise. You can see, from this drawing, a little bit of what is happening.

When the baby starts to smile, the mom will offer a smile to the baby that's a bit bigger. And if the baby follows her and also smiles a little bigger, the mom's smile will get even bigger. And if the baby gets a little bigger with that, then the mom will start laughing, and they'll both start laughing. Joy is dyadic. We are encouraged to be with joy by the nervous systems of the people around us.

In avoidant attachment, the opposite happens and the mother smiles less than the baby. Instead of the baby smiling a little bit and the mom's smile getting a little bigger, the baby smiles and there's a diminishment, a downshifting of and turning away from the joy by the mom, instead of an uplifting and encouragement of joy.[2] If we are not met in our joy, then we experience a crash in our endogenous opioids

Joy

PLAY:
amusement, happiness,
delight, joy

Window of Welcome
for Joy

The securely attached mom expands the baby's capacity
for joy by taking a little more delight in the baby's joy
than the baby is showing. This lets the baby have certainty
that it's good to be happy.

FIGURE 13.1 Joy

and oxytocin and a spike in our cortisol—a shame crash. Shame causes the largest cortisol spike of any emotional experience among humans.[3] Avoidant moms and dads really tend to be in their SEEKING circuit, which doesn't understand PLAY. The SEEKING circuit says, "What are you wasting time on? Why are you laughing? We don't need to waste time on that. We need to finish feeding you so that we can get your brother to school." Whenever humans are fully taken up by their SEEKING circuit, it's as if they don't understand the importance of joy. This skepticism about joy can live on in our body as a contract to really buckle down and get things done and not stop to play.

ADDING IN THE VAGUS NERVE AND SOCIAL ENGAGEMENT

As we start to feel the way the vows work and the way the vow releases feel, we begin to notice what this deep relational joy feels like. There are all kinds of benefits to this sweet nervous system and body sense that we matter and belong. When we are in this state, the fine muscles of the face are engaged for relationship, and the eyes focus on the human face. When the eyes focus on the human face, the muscles of the middle ear tighten to the sound range of the human voice.[4] Knowing this can give us an embodied sense of our relationality, and can reassure us that we are meant to be relational beings. No matter how dangerous humans are, no matter how much they betray our trust, and no matter how much we long for freedom from them if we carry avoidant attachment, we are made for relationship.

When we have the sense that we're safe and we matter, the voice box also opens and relaxes.[5] Humans can tell what emotions others are having from their vocal bursts, sound elements that are even shorter than words. Even if the recording is of a stranger's voice, we can tell if the other person is happy, sad, angry, afraid, amused, contemptuous, or one of 18 other emotions.[6] When we experience being safe and welcomed, the variability of our heart rate increases, allowing our heart to dance in response to our breath and to relationship. The bronchi of the lungs open and expand. The red blood cells carry more oxygen, which helps our whole system. Our diaphragm relaxes and we belly-breathe. And all of our organs and intestines get the go signal, where our stomach can digest, our intestines can digest, and the blood flow supports our organs. And at the level of the immune system, we're creating cells to fight viruses and cancer.[7] When we consider the physiology of the vagus nerve and how belonging and mattering bring us into our highest levels of nuanced responsiveness with each other (social engagement, or high heart rate variability), we see the convergence of PLAY, joy, and social connection. Our joy is most sustainable in safe, warm relationships.

As this dance of the body shows, we are marvelously made for relational connection, and the contracts we keep limit us from our movement into relational connection. Over the course of this book, we've looked at the eight Circuits of Emotion and Motivation. When we enter the realms of relational joy, we're in the PLAY circuit. Sometimes this is combined with the deep self-connection and authentic expression that comes with the SEXUALITY circuit. You will remember that the SEXUALITY circuit is not just for sex, but also carries us from childhood into the full maturity of our adulthood, where we find our full capacity to bring our own individual stamp of life energy and contribution to this world.

Sometimes we will feel awe and joy and love but these emotions may not show on our face. When we've experienced situational trauma, like incarceration and military action, our face can disconnect from our emotions. People who are incarcerated learn very quickly not to show in their faces what they're feeling inside. In families where it isn't okay to show emotion, we may not express joy. This can also happen with some neurodivergence, which affects the vagus nerve and contributes to part of the social awkwardness and the lack of a syncing. It's important to remember that even though facial expression is so interesting and nuanced and tells us so much when someone is alive and fully integrated, we can't always tell from the outside how somebody is feeling. They may feel very differently on the inside. To be truly relational, we do have to have a warm curiosity about what the other person is experiencing.

Of course, people can't always tell how they're feeling, especially if they've shifted into their doing-brain and they can no longer read their emotional body map. In these moments, somebody could be angry or sad or even joyful, without even knowing it. What we need to know about this is that intimacy, dialogue, and the experience of being genuinely and warmly curious can take us toward actual intimate connection. An example of this is that if somebody says to us, "I feel so much love for you," yet their face is not moving, we can say, "Your face is not moving. Tell me what's happening inside." We get to actually bring observation and clarity to those moments and are able to talk about these things that have always been implicit instead of explicit, that have always been unconscious instead of conscious.

When we're talking about joy that is deeply integrated into our bodies and allows us to really see one another, we're talking about something different from happiness. We're talking about something deeper, something a little bit transcendent, where we see others, and our hearts are filled with a warm feeling, a sensation that's kind of spilling over. It's a my-heart-runneth-over kind of sensation, similar to delight, but with more energy, where the eyes are engaged and we're seeing one another with a lot of participation and investment and engagement. It's a different invitation than an invitation into happiness. Let's feel into this with a meditation.

GUIDED MEDITATION
to Explore Joy

Begin this meditation by breathing . . . Notice yourself as a breathing being . . . Invite your attention to rest on the sensation of breath, wherever you feel it . . . See if you can invite your upper belly, around the bottom of your ribs, to move out when you inhale . . . and bring yourself back to breathing however your body breathes on its own, just allowing yourself to notice your breath . . . Where do you feel the sensation of breathing? . . . Is it in the rise and fall of your belly? . . . Is it in the small movements of your ribs and shoulders? . . . Is it the passage of air, a slight coolness, through your nose, sinuses, mouth, or throat? . . . Breathe for a moment, and allow yourself to notice the thoughts and worries that break over you like waves on a shore, taking you away from the sensation of breath . . . and let yourself return to your breath, each time you are carried away . . .

Now, if you are willing, allow yourself to visualize a very small shimmer of joy around your heart . . . Does it get to exist? . . . This may be a foundational gratitude for participating in life itself . . . It may be an uncontainable radiance of expansive joy . . . Or it may be a small paradoxical joy in your capacity to resist life . . . a sense of your own integrity and wholeness . . . It could be a very pure experience of life . . . And it could be a snort of amusement at the idea that you would be grateful to life . . . Whatever you find there, acknowledge how it feels to your body to touch this . . . Is it a lift . . . a lightness . . . a tingle . . . a chime . . . a tickle . . . a radiance?

Now imagine your resonating self-witness is there with you and is able to notice this small joy . . . and that your resonating self-witness may be delighted with you, exactly as you are . . . joyful or grumpy . . . sweet or sour . . . and see how it is for your body if your resonating self-witness smiles back at your joy with a slightly larger joy than yours . . . understanding your joy . . . and happy that you have it . . . Do you allow yourself to enjoy this support?

If you do not allow yourself this enjoyment, then allow your sense of the blocks to your joy to become visible . . . What do they look like? . . . What shape are they? . . . Can you feel them? . . . Do they have a texture? . . . If they are con-

tracts, what might they be? . . . Let yourself wonder gently . . . What is more
important to you than joy? . . . Whose life are you saving by locking yourself away
from it? . . . Whatever you find, say, "Of course!" to yourself with warmth and
affection.

And now, allowing yourself to come back to the area right around your heart,
feel whether your sense of your small or radiant joy has shifted or changed with
this meditation . . . And bring yourself back to your breathing . . . and back to
present time . . . Allow your eyes to open, and look around at your surround-
ings . . . letting yourself find your feet . . . and the ground . . . and your belong-
ing . . . bringing with you a sense of joy as your birthright.

With this meditation, we have begun to think about the contracts that block
joy. Here are some examples of what these contracts may sound like.

CONTRACTS THAT BLOCK JOY

I will . . .	In order to . . .
not express joy	keep from being too big and so keep my mother alive
stay small and not breathe	make room for somebody else to be able to breathe
not exist	keep from being a burden
not be happy	keep my mother from being lonely
not be my true size	keep from threatening my father
not be joyful	accompany my sibling
not reveal my excitement	save myself from humiliation and disappointment
not be joyful	stay in integrity with my mourning for the world

JOURNALING PROMPT FOR
Finding Contracts That Block Joy

Do any of these sample contracts seem similar to any of the contracts that you hold?

_____

_____

_____

_____

What is your sense of the circuits that are more important to you than PLAY?

_____

_____

_____

_____

Do you want to keep living the way you have been living, or would you enjoy it if things were a little different?

_____

_____

_____

_____

Unconscious Contract Template for Joy

I, _____ [*your name here*], solemnly

swear to you, my _____

[*essential self, mother, father, siblings, world, universe, God, etc.*] that I will

_____

[*how do you diminish or exaggerate your PLAY?*] in order to

_____

_____

[*save, protect, honor, have a parent, keep you from being alone, etc.*], no matter the cost to myself.

ONE-ON-ONE WORK
Working With Finding Joy

SARAH: *Hello Juna—what's coming up for you today?*

JUNA: *It's like I'm not enough—what I have is not enough. It's like nobody in the world is interested in what I have. So in this way, I'm also too much.*

SARAH: *Could we begin by making a guess for your body? "Juna's body, have you had to live in a world with people who have been so distracted that they could not even see Juna's existence?"*

JUNA: *Yes.*

SARAH: *What happens for your body as we touch into this, Juna, if it's okay to ask?*

JUNA: *I feel very tense.*

SARAH: *It seems important to me to check for your body's consent. Is your body okay with us moving forward?*

JUNA: *You just saying that helps.*

SARAH: *Very good. Let's look for this sense of not being enough and see if it's okay to start naming the vow with, "I, Juna, solemnly swear to you, my essential self, that I will believe that I am not enough"—are we doing okay so far?*

JUNA: *I need to add something about what I bring to not being enough. I don't feel empty, but full of things that are not recognized or appreciated. They are not seen as a gift.*

SARAH: *As you're touching on this, do you have a sense of a memory that comes?*

JUNA: *I have general memories about when I felt joy and life energy bubbling in me, I was shut down by my father. I was not allowed to feel the life energy. I sensed I was bad for feeling this joy.*

SARAH: *Do you have a moment in mind that we could time travel to? If it's general we can still time travel, but just give me a sense of whether there's something specific or if it's general.*

JUNA: *The memory that comes now is when I was five, I was running around on the pavement near the street. I was running in a joyful state and ran into the street. My father just immediately took me and beat me. I remember—it was a total shock.*

SARAH: *Absolutely, a total shock. So, you and I, we'll step through time and space and just freeze your father. We'll lie him down on the sidewalk and take a cloth and cover up his head, so we don't have to look at him. We'll freeze everybody in area—stop all the cars and buses, just stop everything. What's our first acknowledgment for this little one? What's the first thing we want to acknowledge?*

JUNA: *Starting before it even happened, right?*

SARAH: *Yes.*

JUNA: *I really would like to acknowledge the joy.*

SARAH: *Yes. We could say to this little one, "Wouldn't it be really fun if, when you're joyful, other people would understand and could experience it with you?" What happens for her?*

JUNA: *There is this feeling of relaxation and being more in the body.*

SARAH: *Maybe she'd also like us to say something like, "Do you need acknowledgment that when someone responds in this way, it's so shocking that we leave our bodies?"*

JUNA: *Yes.*

SARAH: *And that it's scary to have somebody respond from that punitive place . . .*

JUNA: *It's still very scary.*

SARAH: *Yes, and maybe it's a little lonely too? And it's such a change, to go from joy to suddenly being hit. What a big change. We might think that joy is dangerous.*

JUNA: *Definitely.*

SARAH: *Yes. So you can check to see if this little one made a promise to herself to never be joyful again, or never to show it.*

JUNA: *It's about the level of joy—to keep it under a safe level.*

SARAH: *So the little one is saying something like, "I, five-year-old Juna, solemnly swear to you, my essential self, that I will keep my joy under a safe level . . ."*

JUNA: *Yes. "I, five-year-old Juna, solemnly swear to my essential self to keep my joy under a safe level, in order to . . . survive."*

SARAH: *In order to survive. Did we get the right word?*

JUNA: *Yes. "No matter the cost to myself."*

SARAH: *And then we'll check with your essential self. Essential self of Juna, did you hear the vow that this little one made to you?*

JUNA: *"Yes."*

SARAH: *Is this a good vow for her?*

JUNA: *"Not anymore."*

SARAH: *You completely understand why she made it and it might even have been lifesaving at the time. But it isn't good anymore. Will you tell her, "Five-year-old Juna, I release you from this vow"?*

JUNA: *"I release you from this vow and I revoke this contract, and you have my blessing to have undiminished joy."*

SARAH: *How does your body do?*

JUNA: *It feels like joy has made progress. There's this urge to laugh.*

SARAH: *Just for a moment, close your eyes and let the sparkles of joy find their way as deeply into your body as they want to go. Yes. And how is your body now?*

JUNA: *It's a bit tense but there is more light inside.*

SARAH: *And now we've come back to your starting point. You started out with the sense of both being too much and of being not enough. When you touch into this now, "I, Juna, solemnly swear to my essential self that I will believe that I am not enough." What happens with that, with your sense of that truth now?*

JUNA: *The contract is still there.*

SARAH: *Will you say it?*

JUNA: *I, Juna, solemnly swear to my essential self that I will believe I am not enough, in order to . . .*

SARAH: *Does anything come?*

JUNA: *"To be loved."*

SARAH: *"In order to be loved." It's almost like, if Juna could believe that she was not enough, then she could also believe that if only she tried harder, she would be loved. Does that feel like we're touching it?*

JUNA: *Yes, it does. "No matter the cost to myself."*

SARAH: *How's this for your body?*

JUNA: *It feels a bit heavy.*

SARAH: *Did we do okay with the words? Do they feel true at this moment?*

JUNA: *Yes.*

SARAH: *Then we'll ask your essential self, "Juna's essential self, did you hear the vow that Juna made to you?"*

JUNA: *"Yes."*

SARAH: *Is this a good vow for Juna?*

JUNA: *No. "Juna, this is not a good vow for you. I release you from this vow and I revoke this contract."*

SARAH: *How does your body do?*

JUNA: *When I say, "I revoke this contract," there is a huge amount of relaxation.*

SARAH: *Do you have a blessing for Juna? Is there something you would like her to have instead of this contract? A belief instead of this contract?*

JUNA: *There is some shyness. Something is keeping me from doing it. There is not enough belief that it is possible.*

SARAH: *Ah, not enough belief that it's possible.*

JUNA: *There is this voice that says there is no meaning.*

SARAH: *I'm going to propose something. You don't have to say it, but I want to know how your body responds. My proposal would be that the blessing would be, "Juna, you have my blessing to know that you are enough. You have my blessing to begin to see that when the people around you can't acknowledge you, it's because they're running into their own contracts and vows that prevent them from being present."*

JUNA: *Yes, I like this second part very much.*

SARAH: *And do you have any trouble with the first part? You have my blessing to know that you are enough.*

JUNA: *I would like to have a blessing that I can show everything which is inside me because it's so much.*

SARAH: *How is it to hear that blessing?*

JUNA: *It feels cold and it's energizing.*

SARAH: *Nice. Yes, so just go ahead and say it. "Juna, you have my blessing . . ."*

JUNA: *"Juna, you have my blessing to show all of your gifts inside." Yes. This makes me smile.*

SARAH: *So now that we've done the release, just check back in to see if there's any truth to that idea that Juna is not enough.*

JUNA: *No.*

SARAH: *Very good. And you had said that you believed both things in the beginning, that you believed you were not enough and you believed you were too much?*

JUNA: *Yes.*

SARAH: *Check and see. We've been working with not enough. We started working with too much, because that was the joy. We've worked with not enough, and now we want to check back in and see if there's any part of you that still believes that Juna is too much.*

JUNA: *There is now this acceptance that for some people I am too much, but not in general.*

SARAH: *Very nice. Very nice. Thank you, Juna.*

JUNA: *Thank you so much.*

One year later, Juna writes:

I have had a lot of bad experiences with my ex-partner (father of my daughter) lately. There is a lot being triggered about not being enough and being too much. Compared to his lover, I feel unworthy of being loved because I was not enough in some areas and too much in others; it causes lots and lots of pain, as the betrayal is on the plate.

Although, beside this, I feel quite rooted and calm inside, with lots of trust in the universe's plan for me. I keep deepening my trust that this divorce is happening as a strange favor for me to enable me to really flourish and deliver my gifts to those who can enjoy them. I have been together with this guy for 22 years and I chose him following my earliest contracts. He suited my pattern perfectly.

FALSE BODHISATTVA VOWS

Before we come to the end of this book, there is one more type of contract that I would like to mention. It is one that keeps us working and worrying so hard that we don't get to relax into play, laughter, and joy very often. We can call this type of contract the "false Bodhisattva vow" because we make it when we are about nine years old, when our brain development lets us begin to notice the trouble the world is in, but we are still too little to do anything about it. The contract is essentially "Universe, I swear to you that I will love the world so much that I will help all this pain, because there's nothing else I can do, no matter the cost to myself." The child commits to making a better world, or to saving the world, no matter the cost.

Commitment and contribution are very important and life serving when they do not cost us everything. The adult carrying this vow is driven by a sense of mission so great that everything else is sacrificed to it—health, family, creativity, and especially joy. There is no reason to release a contract if there isn't a cost, but if the cost is too great, you might want to consider asking, "Universe, do you like this vow?" And as you step into the role of the universe and look back at yourself, the universe most often replies, "That's a very big vow for such a little person. I release this vow and I revoke this contract. Live your own life, and do what you can to make the world a better place, but not at the cost of your joy. The universe needs your joy, too."

A FINAL WORD

We use unconscious contracts to help us function in a world where we have not really been accompanied, and to make up for our brains not getting to grow the way that they were supposed to. We create a web out of these contracts that keeps us from having to actually touch and mourn the way the world really is. What we can't see, we can't change. The contracts keep us in trance states that stop us from being able to fathom the global climate crisis, from being able to see and take action to stop systemic racism, from being able to perceive and change world-destroying and people-destroying patterns of all kinds. Surprisingly, with this small piece of work, you have begun a world-changing journey, and the sweetness of a new capacity for relationality will give you accompaniment as you travel.

More than for any other reason, I teach about language's ability to heal trauma and our enormous need for accompaniment and resonance in order to see people's faces lift and their smiles come more easily as they release their contracts and step into the expansiveness that is the birthright of us all. We need everyone's joy in order to be able to transform our world into a relational place, where we notice and act swiftly, both personally and systemically, to right wrongs, to change systems, and to save and restore our beautiful planet and ecosystems.

APPENDIX

DAILY LOG

Here is a daily log for you to fill out and track your activities. Daily participation is best for your brain and nourishes the most neuronal growth.

DATE			

GLOSSARY

Accompaniment: the real or imagined presence of a person who we feel cares about us. One of the forms of self-regulation.

ACE(S): Adverse Childhood Experiences Study: a huge study (17,000 participants) that correlated experiences of trauma with ill health, addiction, and early death.

Adult attachment styles: the categories that attachment researchers use when they are talking about patterns of adult attachment. They include secure, fearful avoidant, dismissive avoidant and anxious/preoccupied.

Adverse Childhood Experiences (ACE) Study: a huge study (17,000 participants) that correlated experiences of trauma with ill health, addiction, and early death.

Ambivalent attachment (also Anxious/Ambivalent): a style of bonding in which people move directly into fight/flight/alarmed aloneness under stress. Everyone in the ambivalent attachment pattern is continually trying to get resourced and people move to sending behavioral signals of distress. No one is easily soothed.

Amygdala: an organ in the limbic system that is responsible for emotional and non-conscious (implicit) memory, and filters everything that comes in, automatically sorting present day experience to see if there are any similarities to difficult or dangerous situations from our past, and sounding the alarm when it finds matches.

Anxiety: an emotion that the body interprets as a warning sign that something is wrong. A persistent feeling state of dread and anticipation. 50% of the time it is accompanied by depression.

Anxious/Ambivalent Attachment: a style of bonding in which people move directly into fight/flight/alarmed aloneness under stress. Everyone in the ambivalent attachment pattern is continually trying to get resourced and people move to sending behavioral signals of distress. No one is easily soothed.

Attachment: patterns of learning about how to bond and what to expect from relationship.

Avoidant Attachment: a pattern of bonding in which people have learned to take care of themselves, as they don't have the sense that the other's body is a resource for them.

Brain: the entire nervous system running throughout the body, including the brain in the skull.

CARE circuit: one of Panksepp's Circuits of Emotion, this one supporting warmth and affection and nurturing others and the self.

Circuits of Emotion and Motivation: the basic emotional networks that carry our different life energies as mammals, as defined by neuroscientist Jaak Panksepp. They include: CARE, SEEKING, PANIC/GRIEF, RAGE, LUST, FEAR and PLAY. This book adds DISGUST to that list.

Cortisol: a chemical that the brain and body work together to produce to mobilize resources when there is stress, and to turn off the stress response when safety has returned.

Default mode network (DMN): an automatic network of thought which brings together memory and creative thinking and integrates both of these with the sense of self.

Depression: a persistent feeling-state of sadness, loss of a sense of pleasure, and loss of interest in life. Can be accompanied by fatigue and constant overwhelm. 50% of the time it is accompanied by anxiety.

DISGUST Circuit: one of the Circuits of Emotion and Motivation, this one devoted to getting toxins out of the system and preventing contagion.

Disorganized/traumatic attachment: a pattern of bonding characterized by depression, overriding anxiety, addiction, mental illness, violence, abuse, neglect, outbursts of temper, and shame. Children with terrifying or terrified parents will often need intimacy desperately, but find it alarming and respond to it unpredictably. Their bodies will react strangely and unpredictably to relationship and to intimacy.

Dissociation: a disconnection between the felt sense of being in the body, and the conscious awareness of the sense of self.

Dopamine: one of the brain's main neurotransmitters. Very supportive of the SEEKING circuit, provides energy and pleasure.

Dorsolateral striatum: a cluster of neurons deep in the brain which contribute to habitual behaviors.

Earned secure attachment: movement out of insecure attachment into more balance and an anticipation of warmth from others and for ourselves as a result of healing work or supportive relationships.

Endocannabinoids: the brain's own THC (the active compound in marijuana.) One of the brain's primary chemical responses to support the healing of trauma.

Endogenous benzodiazepines: a set of brain chemicals that have antianxiety, muscle relaxing, sedative and hypnotic effects, like valium.

Endogenous opioids: (also called endorphins) The brain's own morphine and heroin. They blunt pain and support a feeling of well-being.

Epigenetics: the study of the modification of gene expression, rather than alteration of the genetic code itself.

Explicit memory: memory we are conscious of. What we know that we know.

FEAR circuit: one of Panksepp's seven, this one supporting running away, withdrawing and hiding Circuits of Emotion and Motivation in the face of danger.

Fight/Flight/Alarmed Aloneness: sympathetic activation of the body's response to stress with increased heart rate and the need to either take action to protect/defend, to get away from the source of danger, or to find a missing important person.

Heart rate variability: the varying tempo at which our heart beats.

Hemispheres: the two halves of the vertebrate brain.

Hippocampus: an organ in the limbic system involved in forming, storing, and processing memory, especially explicit memory.

Immobilization: the body's response if Fight/Flight/Alarmed aloneness is not effective: a shutdown into helplessness during stress. This state includes shock, hopelessness, frozen immobility, and dissociation.

Implicit memory: memory we are not conscious of. What we don't know that we know.

Insecure Attachment: any of the three forms of attachment that are not secure attachment, including avoidant, anxious/ambivalent and disorganized attachment.

Left hemisphere: the half of the vertebrate brain that is on the left side of the body.

Limbic system: a different kind of brain tissue from the cortex, tucked deep inside the skull-brain, linking body and skull-brain, that helps us with emotions, memory, bonding and watching for danger. It includes the amygdala and the hippocampus, among other organs and tissue.

Neuron: a basic cell in the brain.

Neurotransmitter: one of a number of chemicals that the brain uses to communicate between neurons.

Oxytocin: the bonding hormone.

PANIC/GRIEF circuit: one of Panksepp's seven Circuits of Emotion and Motivation, this one responding to abandonment, loneliness, loss and mourning.

PFC (Prefrontal cortex): the front of the frontal lobe, the location of the intentional part of the Resonating Self-Witness, as this is the area that helps the brain with self-regulation, planning and carrying out the actions that make up our lives.

PLAY circuit: one of Panksepp's seven Circuits of Emotion and Motivation, this one supporting active and mutual interaction that is fun and brings people and animals laughter.

Post-Traumatic Stress Disorder (PTSD): a brain state of continuing injury and disruption from trauma experiences, which can include intrusive memories of trauma and dissociation.

Prefrontal cortex (PFC): the front of the frontal lobe, the location of the intentional part of the Resonating Self-Witness, as this is the area that helps the brain with self-regulation, planning and carrying out the actions that make up our lives.

RAGE circuit: one of Panksepp's seven Circuits of Emotion, this one responding to frustration of needs for safety, respect, well-being and effectiveness.

Resonance: the experience of sensing that another being understands us and sees us with emotional warmth and generosity. It is the sense that *we know* that they could try on our skin, and that our feelings and longings would make sense to them.

Resonant language: shifts us into relational space and includes wondering about and naming: emotion; the naming of dreams, longings and needs; body sensations; what is happening in relationship; and fresh metaphor, visual imagery, and poetry.

Resonant/Resonating Self-Witness: a personification of the parts of the brain that are capable of self-warmth and self-regulation.

Right hemisphere: the half of the skull-brain that is on the right side of the body.

Secure attachment: the embodied anticipation that the other can be depended upon for predictable warmth, responsiveness and resonance.

SEEKING circuit: one of Panksepp's seven Circuits of Emotion and Motivation, this one supporting taking action to get what is needed and to explore and discover.

Self-management: externalized strategies that we use to respond to stress, including addictions, compulsions, controlling others and the environment, as well as standing outside ourselves to judge and criticize ourselves.

Self-regulation: having the ability to control bodily functions, come back to balance after experiencing powerful emotions, and maintain focus and attention.

SEXUALITY circuit: one of Panksepp's seven Circuits of Emotion and Motivation, this one supporting sexuality and the maturation of self from child to adult.

Social engagement: the nervous system state in which people feel safe, they start to run on oxygen as their main fuel, and their brain and body shift into the capacity for nuanced reading and expression of social cues.

Sympathetic activation: the nervous system shift into elevated heart rate and respiration.

Transgenerational trauma: when the effects of difficult historical and personal events show up in the neurobiology of the survivors' children and grandchildren.

Trauma: the moments during or after events when what is happening is too difficult, terrifying or painful for the brain-body to bear, we are unaccompanied by resonance, and the ability to integrate experience becomes impossible.

Traumatic dissociation: the disconnected state of being where connection between the inner world and the outer world and the sense of self and the sense of body become fractured.

Unconscious contract: a behavioral agreement we make with ourselves without being fully aware that we made it. These agreements force us into rigid patterns that look like self-sabotage.

Vagus nerve: a nerve bundle that runs up from the inside of the body to the skull-brain, mostly carrying information from all of the organs and digestive system, heart and lungs. (About 80% of the fibers of the vagus nerve run up to the brain, and about 20% run down to the body.)

Warmth (Emotional warmth): the experience of being met or meeting others with affection and welcome. On the body level, when we are close enough to feel one another's body heat, there is warmth, so this concept also encompasses closeness and the possibility of comfort with physical contact.

Window of Welcome: the emotional expression and intensity that can actually be met with warmth and understanding, and is easily reflected and resonated with in a relationship.

REFERENCES

INTRODUCTION

1. Neff, K. D., & Bluth, K. (2018). New frontiers in understanding the benefits of self-compassion. *Self and Identity, 17,*(6), 605–608. Retrieved from https://www.tandfonline.com/doi/abs/10.1080/15298868.2018.1508494

2. Rauch, S. L., Shin, L. M., & Phelps, E. A. (2006). Neurocircuitry models of posttraumatic stress disorder and extinction: Human neuroimaging research—Past, present, and future. *Biological Psychiatry, 60*(4), 376–382. https://doi.org/10.1016/j.biopsych.2006.06.004

CHAPTER 1

1. Raichle, M. E. (2015). The Brain's Default Mode Network. *Annual Review of Neuroscience, 38,* 433–447. Retrieved from https://www.annualreviews.org/doi/abs/10.1146/annurev-neuro-071013-014030

2. Bartzokis, G., Beckson, M., Lu, P. H., Nuechterlein, K. H., Edwards, N., & Mintz, J. (2001). Age-related changes in frontal and temporal lobe volumes in men. *Archives of General Psychiatry, 58*(5), 461. https://doi.org/10.1001/archpsyc.58.5.461

3. Szyf, M. (2013, July). *Epigenetics.* [Paper presentation]. Brain Development and Learning Conference, Vancouver, British Columbia, Canada.

4. Williams, R. H. (2010). *Adult Attachment Styles as Predictors of Posttraumatic Stress Severity and PTSD Among U.S. Army Soldiers.* Texas Woman's University, ProQuest Dissertations Publishing.

5. Hiraoka, R., Meyer, E. C., Kimbrel, N. A., Debeer, B. B., Gulliver, S. B., & Morissette, S. B. (2015). Self-compassion as a prospective predictor of PTSD symptom severity among trauma-exposed U.S., Iraq, and Afghanistan War veterans. *Journal of Traumatic Stress, 28*(2), 127–133. https://doi.org/10.1002/jts.21995

6. Thome, J., Terpou, B. A., Mckinnon, M. C., & Lanius, R. A. (2019). The neural correlates of trauma-related autobiographical memory in posttraumatic stress disorder: A meta-analysis. *Depression and Anxiety, 37*(4), 321–345. https://doi.org/10.1002/da.22977

CHAPTER 2

1. Ranganath, C., & Hsieh, L.-T. (2016). The hippocampus: A special place for time. *Annals of the New York Academy of Sciences, 1369*(1), 93–110. https://doi.org/10.1111/nyas.13043

CHAPTER 3

1. Baron-Cohen, S. (2013). *Cerebral lateralization and theory of mind. Understanding other minds: perspectives from developmental cognitive neuroscience.* Oxford University Press.
2. Daianu, M., Jahanshad, N., Dennis, E. L., Toga, A. W., Mcmahon, K. L., Zubicaray, G. I., . . . Thompson, P. M. (2012). Left versus right hemisphere differences in brain connectivity: 4-Tesla HARDI tractography in 569 twins. *2012 9th IEEE International Symposium on Biomedical Imaging (ISBI).* doi:10.1109/isbi.2012.6235601
3. Gapp, K., Bohacek, J., Grossmann, J., Brunner, A.M., Manuella, F., Nanni, P., Mansuy, I.M. (2016). Potential of environmental wnrichment to prevent transgenerational effects of paternal trauma. *Neuropsychopharmacology.* doi: 10.1038/npp.2016.87.

CHAPTER 4

1. Beebe, B., & Steele, M. (2013). How does microanalysis of mother–infant communication inform maternal sensitivity and infant attachment? *Attachment & Human Development, 15*(5–6), 583–602. https://doi.org/10.1080/14616734.2013.841050
2. Dickerson, S. S., & Kemeny, M. E. (2004). Acute stressors and cortisol responses: A theoretical integration and synthesis of laboratory research. *Psychological Bulletin, 130,* 355–391.
3. Schore, A. N. (1998). Early shame experiences and infant brain development. In P. Gilbert & B. Andrews (Eds.), *Series in affective science. Shame: Interpersonal behavior, psychopathology, and culture* (pp. 57–77). Oxford University Press.
4. Panksepp, J., & Biven, L. (2012). *The archaeology of mind: Neuroevolutionary origins of human emotions.* W. W. Norton & Company.
5. Schmidt, G. L., Debuse, C. J., & Seger, C. A. (2007). Right hemisphere metaphor processing? Characterizing the lateralization of semantic processes. *Brain and Language, 100*(2), 127–141. https://doi.org/10.1016/j.bandl.2005.03.002

CHAPTER 5

1. Panksepp, J., & Biven, L. (2012). *The archaeology of mind: Neuroevolutionary origins of human emotions.* W. W. Norton & Company.
2. Ibid.
3. Brooks, J. A., Shablack, H., Gendron, M., Satpute, A. B., Parrish, M. H., & Lindquist, K. A. (2017). The role of language in the experience and perception of emotion: A neuroimaging meta-analysis. *Social Cognitive and Affective Neuroscience, 12*(2), 169–183. https://doi.org/10.1093/scan/nsw121
4. Panksepp, J., & Biven, L. (2012). *The archaeology of mind: Neuroevolutionary origins of human emotions.* W. W. Norton & Company.
5. Hoehn-Saric, R. (1982). Neurotransmitters in anxiety. *Archives of General Psychiatry, 39*(6), 735. https://doi.org/10.1001/archpsyc.1982.04290060075015
6. Bonfiglio, J. J., Inda, C., Refojo, D., Holsboer, F., Arzt, E., & Silberstein, S. (2011). The corticotropin-releasing hormone network and the hypothalamic-pituitary-adrenal axis: Molecular and cellular mechanisms involved. *Neuroendocrinology, 94*(1), 12–20. https://doi.org/10.1159/000328226

CHAPTER 6

1. Panksepp, J., & Biven, L. (2012). *The archaeology of mind: Neuroevolutionary origins of human emotions*. W. W. Norton & Company.
2. Ebner K, Singewald N. (2006). "The role of substance P in stress and anxiety responses". *Amino Acids*. *31*(3), 251–72. doi:10.1007/s00726-006-0335-9. PMID 16820980. S2CID 23380355.
3. Panksepp, J., & Biven, L. (2012). *The archaeology of mind: Neuroevolutionary origins of human emotions*. W. W. Norton & Company.

CHAPTER 7

1. Porges, S. (2017). *The polyvagal theory*. W. W. Norton Company.
2. Xu, K., & Terakawa, S. (2013). *Myelinated fibers and saltatory conduction in the shrimp: The fastest impulse conduction in the animal kingdom*. Springer.
3. Mussa, B. M., Sartor, D. M., & Verberne, A. J. (2010). Dorsal vagal preganglionic neurons: Differential responses to CCK1 and 5-HT3 receptor stimulation. *Autonomic Neuroscience*, *156*(1–2), 36–43. https://doi.org/10.1016/j.autneu.2010.03.001
4. Siegel, D. J. (2020). *The developing mind: How relationships and the brain interact to shape who we are*. New York: Guilford Press.

CHAPTER 8

1. Beebe, B., & Lachmann, F. (2020). Infant research and adult treatment revisited: Cocreating self- and interactive regulation. *Psychoanalytic Psychology*. Advance online publication. https://doi.org/10.1037/pap0000305
2. Kotler, T., Buzwell, S., Romeo, Y., & Bowland, J. (1994). Avoidant attachment as a risk factor for health. *British Journal of Medical Psychology*, *67*(3), 237–245. https://doi.org/10.1111/j.2044-8341.1994.tb01793.x

CHAPTER 9

1. Lanius, R. (2019, June 13–14) *Traumatic Dissociation, Emotion Dysregulation and Loss of Self: Toward a Pathway of Recovery* [Paper presentation/Conference session]. Traumatic Dissociation, Emotion Dysregulation and Loss of Self: Toward a Pathway of Recovery, Calgary, Canada.

CHAPTER 10

1. Panksepp, J., & Biven, L. (2012). *The archaeology of mind: Neuroevolutionary origins of human emotions*. W. W. Norton & Company.

CHAPTER 11

1. Bond, C. W., Trinko, R., Foscue, E., Furman, K., Groman, S. M., Taylor, J. R., & Dileone, R. J. (2020). Medial nucleus accumbens projections to the ventral tegmental area control food consumption. *The Journal of Neuroscience*, *40*(24), 4727–4738. https://doi.org/10.1523/jneurosci.3054-18.2020
2. Quintero, G. (2013). Role of nucleus accumbens glutamatergic plasticity in drug addiction.

Neuropsychiatric Disease and Treatment, 2013(9), 1499–1512. https://doi.org/10.2147/ndt
.s45963

3. Ross, N., Gilbert, R., Torres, S., Dugas, K., Jefferies, P., Mcdonald, S., Savage, S., Ungar, M. (2020). Adverse childhood experiences: Assessing the impact on physical and psychosocial health in adulthood and the mitigating role of resilience. *Child Abuse & Neglect, 103,* 104440. https://doi.org/10.1016/j.chiabu.2020.104440

4. Panksepp, J., & Biven, L. (2012). *The archaeology of mind: Neuroevolutionary origins of human emotions.* W. W. Norton & Company.

5. Luoma, J. B., Guinther, P. M., Desjardins, N. M. L., & Vilardaga, R. (2018). Is shame a proximal trigger for drinking? A daily process study with a community sample. *Experimental and Clinical Psychopharmacology, 26*(3), 290–301. https://doi.org/10.1037/pha0000189

6. U.S. Department of Health and Human Services. (2020, April 3). *Preventing adverse childhood experiences (ACEs): Leveraging the best available evidence.* Retrieved from https://www .cdc.gov/violenceprevention/pdf/preventingACES.pdf

7. Ibid.

8. Miller, L. E., Montroni, L., Koun, E., Salemme, R., Hayward, V., & Farnè, A. (2018). Sensing with tools extends somatosensory processing beyond the body. *Nature, 561,* 239–242. Retrieved from https://www.nature.com/articles/s41586-018-0460-0

9. Smeets, J. A. S., Ramakers, G. M. J., Lesscher, H. M. B., Adan, R. A. H., & Vanderschuren, L. J. M. J. (2018). Functional changes in the dorsolateral striatum in loss of control over reward seeking. *European Neuropsychopharmacology, 28*(1), S34–S35. Retrieved from https://www.sciencedirect.com/science/article/pii/S0924977X17320904

10. Zhang, T., Zhang, L., Liang, Y., Siapas, A. G., Zhou, F.-M., & Dani, J. A. (2009). Dopamine signaling differences in the nucleus accumbens and dorsal striatum exploited by nicotine. *The Journal of Neuroscience, 29*(13), 4035–4043. Retrieved from https://www.ncbi.nlm.nih .gov/pmc/articles/PMC2743099/

11. Goldstein, R. Z., & Volkow, N. D. (2011). Dysfunction of the prefrontal cortex in addiction: neuroimaging findings and clinical implications. *Nature Reviews Neuroscience, 12,* 652–669. Retrieved from https://www.ncbi.nlm.nih.gov/pmc/articles/PMC3462342/

12. Godino, A., Jayanthi, S., & Cadet, J. L. (2015). Epigenetic landscape of amphetamine and methamphetamine addiction in rodents. *Epigenetics, 10*(7), 574–580. Retrieved from https:// www.ncbi.nlm.nih.gov/pmc/articles/PMC4622560/

13. Koob, G. F. (2009). Dynamics of Neuronal Circuits in Addiction: Reward, Antireward, and Emotional Memory. *Pharmacopsychiatry, 42*(S 01). doi:10.1055/s-0029-1216356

14. Wang, G., Shi, J., Chen, N., Xu, L., Li, J., Li, P., Sun, Y., & Lu, L. (2013). Effects of length of abstinence on decision-making and craving in methamphetamine abusers. *PLoS One, 8*(7), e68791. Retrieved from https://www.ncbi.nlm.nih.gov/pmc/articles/PMC3722210/

CHAPTER 12

1. Panksepp, J., & Biven, L. (2012). *The archaeology of mind: Neuroevolutionary origins of human emotions.* W. W. Norton & Company.

2. Noll, J. G., Trickett, P. K., Long, J. D., Negriff, S., Susman, E. J., Shalev, I., Li, J. C., &

Putnam, F. W. (2017). Childhood Sexual Abuse and Early Timing of Puberty. *Journal of Adolescent Health*, 60(1), 65–71. Retrieved from https://www.ncbi.nlm.nih.gov/pubmed/27836531

CHAPTER 13

1. Beebe, B., & Lachmann, F. (2020). Infant research and adult treatment revisited: Cocreating self- and interactive regulation. *Psychoanalytic Psychology*. Advance online publication. https://doi.org/10.1037/pap0000305
2. Ibid.
3. Lupis, S. B., Sabik, N. J., & Wolf, J. M. (2016). Role of shame and body esteem in cortisol stress responses. *Journal of Behavioral Medicine*, 39(2), 206–275. Retrieved from https://www.ncbi.nlm.nih.gov/pmc/articles/PMC5125296/
4. Porges, S. (2017). *The polyvagal theory*. W. W. Norton & Company.
5. Ibid.
6. Cowen, A., Anger Elfenbein, H., Laukka, P., & Keltner, D. (2018). Mapping 24 emotions conveyed by brief human vocalization. *American Psychologist*. Retrieved from https://www.researchgate.net/publication/329824563_Mapping_24_Emotions_Conveyed_by_Brief_Human_Vocalization
7. Porges, S. (2017). *The polyvagal theory*. W. W. Norton Company.

INDEX

Note: Italicized page locators refer to figures; tables are noted with a t.

internalized, self-hate and, 192
predictability, secure attachment and, 161
prefrontal cortex (PFC), 7, *7*, 9, 161
   addiction and, 236
   mother inside every cell of, 8, 51
PTSD. *see* post-traumatic stress disorder
   (PTSD)
puberty, child sexual abuse and start of, 245

racism, 1
rage, depression and, 209, *210*
RAGE circuit, 71, 72, *72*, 113
   addiction and, 231*t*
   autobiography of, 116–17
   being with personal rage, 127–28
   being with rage about systems, 128–30
   broken contracts and, 124
   color of dissociation and, 144
   contract template, 136–37
   disentangling FEAR circuit from, 101
   disentangling PANIC/GRIEF circuit from, 105
   dissociation and, 142
   entangled with other circuits, 120–22
   feelings list, 17*t*
   making relational map of, with colors and shapes, 250
   metaphor guesses for, 84, 252
   other types of contracts connected with, 124
   threats to resources and, 114, 118–20
   time travel and working with rage, 130–35
   tuning into healthy rage, 115
   unconscious contracts connected with, 135–36
   what your addictions do for you and, 230
   window of welcome contracts guided meditation, 76
   window of welcome scale worksheet, 74
   see also anger
random reward and contempt, cycle of, 196
reassurance, resonance *vs.*, 32–33, *33*
relational brain, 211

dissociation and, 139
   instrumental brain *vs.*, 52–53
   self-regulation and, 59
relationality, embodied sense of, 266–67
relational neuroscience, xii, xv
resonance, 4, 276
   contract work and, 85
   joy and, 261
   reassurance *vs.*, 32–33, *33*
resonant language, xii
   Circuits of Emotion and Motivation and, 89, 90
   types of, 8–9, *9*
resonant language practice
   Acknowledging What Is, 147–48, 198–99
   Body Sensations, 53–55
   Feelings and Needs, 14–16, 16–17*t*, 18*t*
   Fresh Metaphor, 82–85
   Impossible Dream Guesses, 96
   I-You Language (Relational Language), 213–14
   metaphor guesses for your circuits, 251–52
   moving into nonverbals, 264
   naming body sensations, 233
   Poetry and the Poetic Visual, 125–26
   reassurance *vs.* resonance, 33–35
   Swearing, 175
resonating self-witness, 160, 163
   addictions and surviving without, 235
   birth of, 7, 8
   connecting with, 41
   contracts stopping us from having, 85
respiratory system, sense of safety and, 266
right hemisphere of brain, 52
   fresh metaphors and, 83
   secure attachment and, 161
   violence and, 185
road rage, 120
Rosenberg, M., 14

salt, addiction to, 230*t*, 231*t*
secure attachment, 163, 164
   description of, 160

ABOUT THE AUTHOR

Sarah Peyton is a neuroscience educator, Certified Trainer of Nonviolent Communication, and constellation facilitator. She integrates brain science and the use of resonant language to heal emotional trauma, increase resilience, and nourish self-warmth with exquisite gentleness. She also teaches internationally, and is the author of Resonance series: *Your Resonant Self, Your Resonant Self Workbook*, and *Affirmations for Turbulent Times*. She lives with two cats and a dog in a multigenerational family household in Vancouver, Washington. Find her ongoing work online at www.sarahpeyton.com.